N SEAS ENTERTAINMENT PRESENTS

If It's For My Daughter I'd Even Defeat a Demon Lord
vol.4

story by CHIROLU   art by Hota.   character design by KEI·TRUFFLE

TRANSLATION
Angela Liu

ADAPTATION
Julia Kinsman

LETTERING
Ochie Caraan

COVER DESIGN
KC Fabellon

PROOFREADER
Kurestin Armada
Janet Houck

EDITOR
Shanti Whitesides

PRODUCTION MANAGER
Lissa Pattillo

MANAGING EDITOR
Julie Davis

EDITOR-IN-CHIEF
Adam Arnold

PUBLISHER
Jason DeAngelis

...ASHITARA MAOU MO

...RPORATION, Tokyo.
... CORPORATION, Tokyo.

Seven Seas press and purchase enquiries can be sent to Marketing Manager
Lianne Sentar at press@gomanga.com. Information regarding the distribution
and purchase of digital editions is available from Digital Manager CK Russell
at digital@gomanga.com.

Seven Seas and the Seven Seas logo are trademarks of
Seven Seas Entertainment. All rights reserved.

ISBN: 978-1-64275-713-2

Printed in Canada

First Printing: October 2019

10 9 8 7 6 5 4 3 2 1

FOLLOW US ONLINE: www.

READING DIRECTIONS

This book reads from *right to left*, Japanese style.
If this is your first time reading manga, you start
reading from the top right panel on each page and
take it from there. If you get lost, just follow the
numbered diagram here. It may seem backwards at
first, but you'll get the hang of it! Have fun!!

STORY

Latina, a young demon girl, was adopted by Dale, a talented adventurer, and they now live together at the Dancing Mackerel Tabby, an inn that serves as a refuge for adventurers.

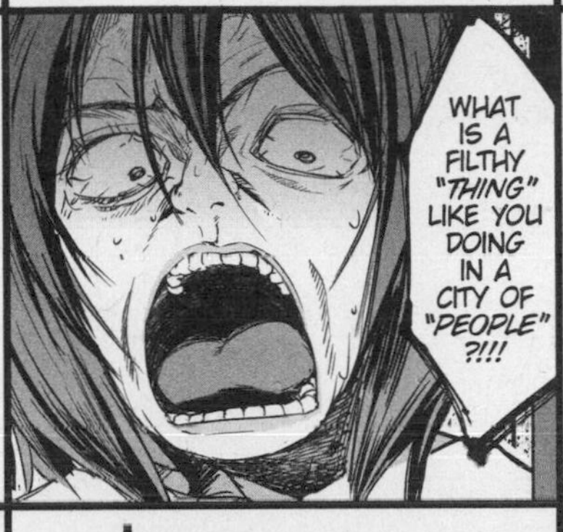
WHAT IS A FILTHY "THING" LIKE YOU DOING IN A CITY OF "PEOPLE" ?!!!

Latina gets accustomed to her new surroundings and goes to school, but a new teacher lambastes her when she discovers Latina is a demon girl.

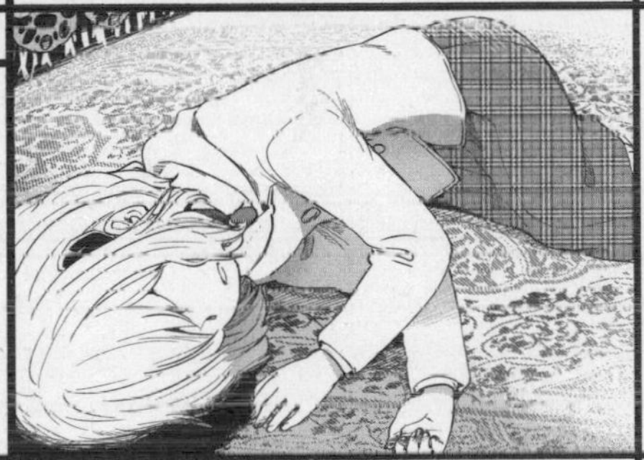

Latina is surprised to learn of the differences between the human race and the demon race, and as a result, she hurts herself.

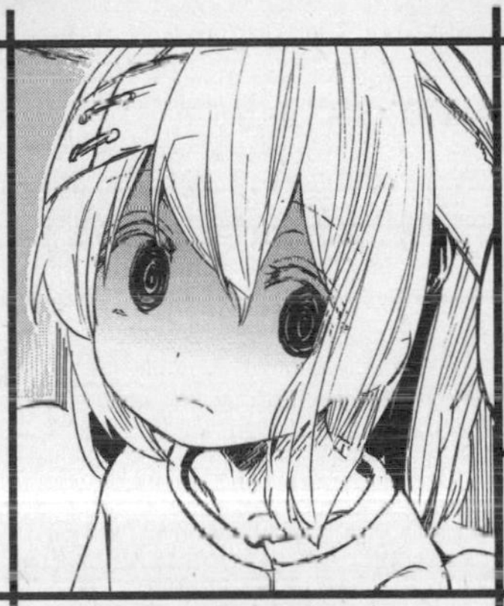

In her despair, she shuts herself away.

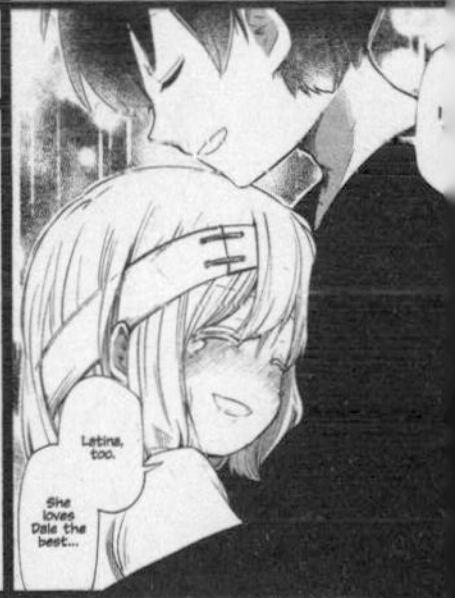
Latina, too.
She loves Dale the best...

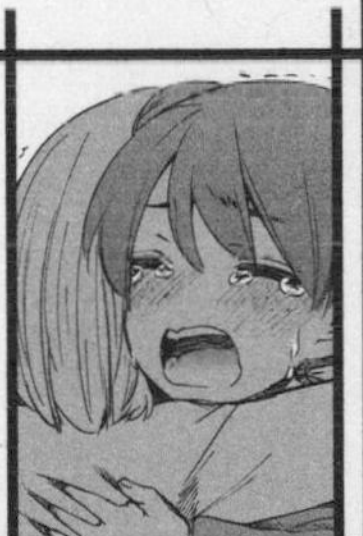

Over-coming hardship after hardship, Latina grows cuter by the day.

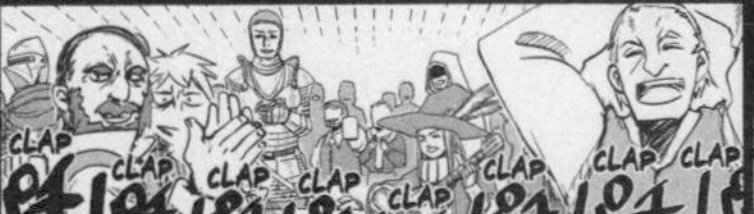
CLAP CLAP CLAP CLAP CLAP CLAP CLAP CLAP

But the ones who love her--her friend Dale, and the people of the Dancing Mackerel Tabby--are able to open the closed door to her heart.

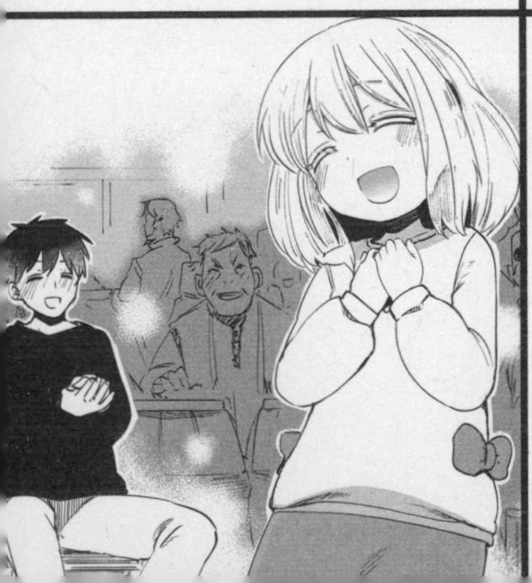

If It's For My Daughter, I'd Even Defeat a Demon Lord.

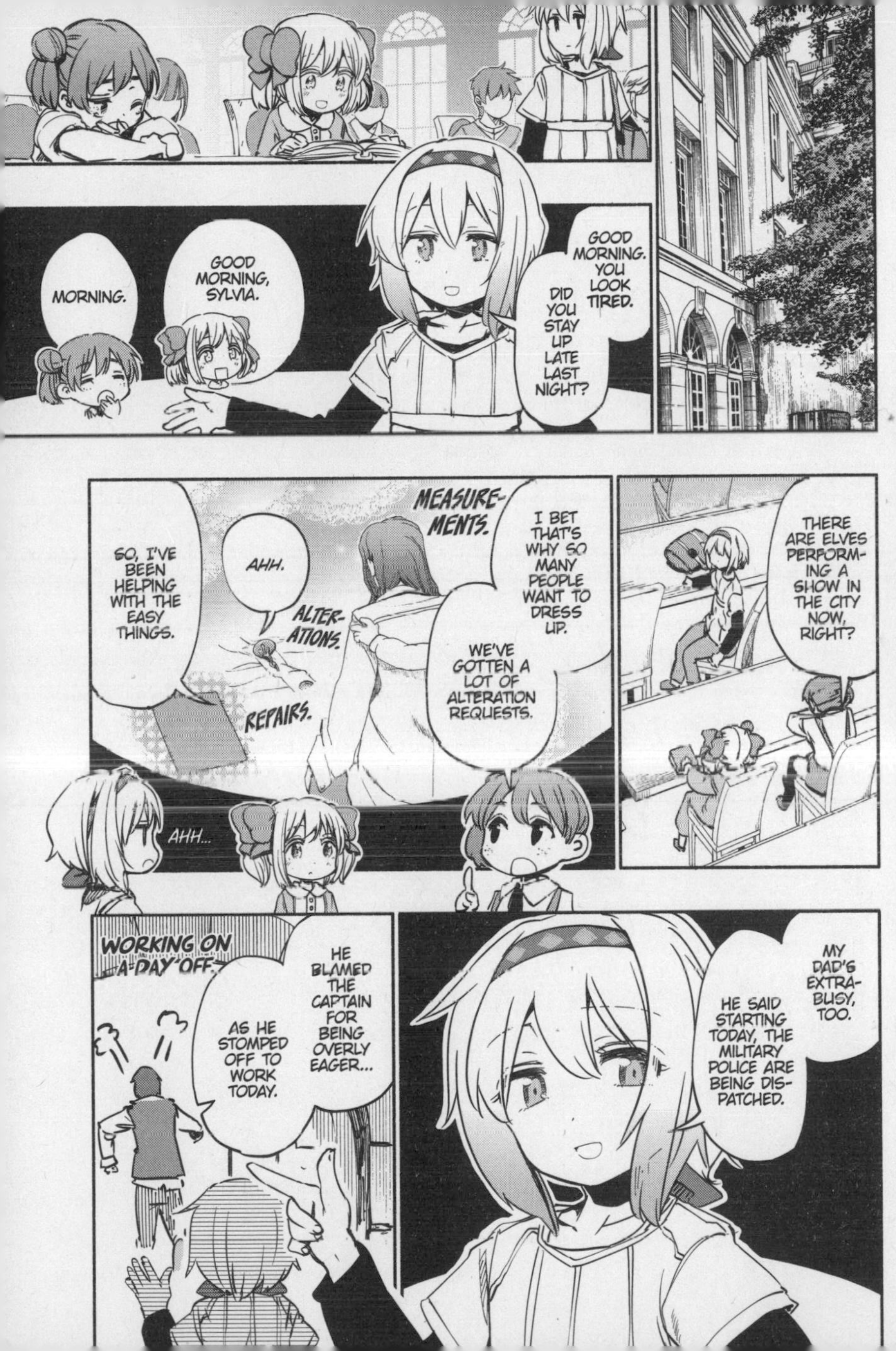
GOOD MORNING. YOU LOOK TIRED.
DID YOU STAY UP LATE LAST NIGHT?
GOOD MORNING, SYLVIA.
MORNING.
THERE ARE ELVES PERFORMING A SHOW IN THE CITY NOW, RIGHT?
I BET THAT'S WHY SO MANY PEOPLE WANT TO DRESS UP.
WE'VE GOTTEN A LOT OF ALTERATION REQUESTS.
MEASUREMENTS.
ALTERATIONS.
REPAIRS.
AHH.
SO, I'VE BEEN HELPING WITH THE EASY THINGS.
AHH...
MY DAD'S EXTRA-BUSY, TOO.
HE SAID STARTING TODAY, THE MILITARY POLICE ARE BEING DISPATCHED.
HE BLAMED THE CAPTAIN FOR BEING OVERLY EAGER...
AS HE STOMPED OFF TO WORK TODAY.
WORKING ON A DAY OFF

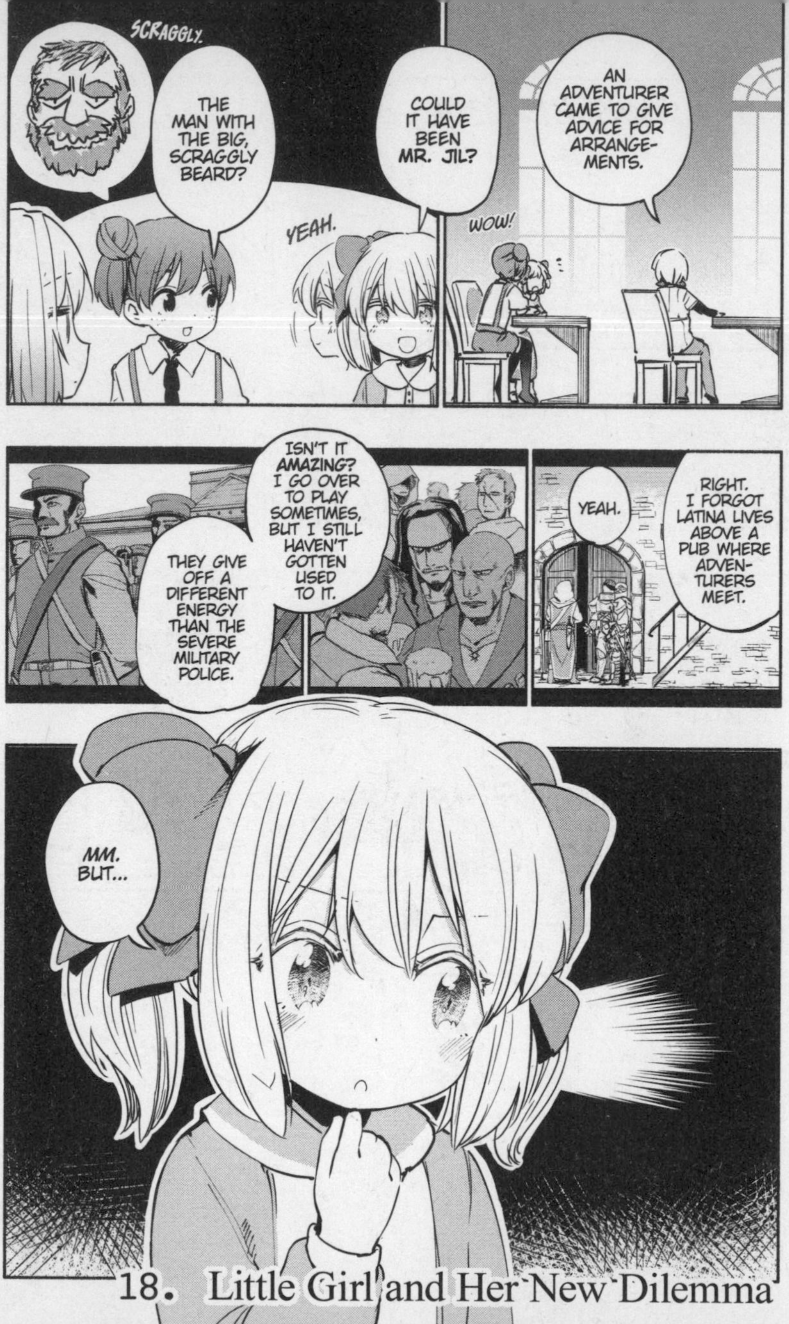
AN ADVENTURER CAME TO GIVE ADVICE FOR ARRANGE-MENTS.
WOW!
COULD IT HAVE BEEN MR. JIL?
YEAH.
THE MAN WITH THE BIG, SCRAGGLY BEARD?
SCRAGGLY.
RIGHT. I FORGOT LATINA LIVES ABOVE A PUB WHERE ADVEN-TURERS MEET.
YEAH.
ISN'T IT AMAZING? I GO OVER TO PLAY SOMETIMES, BUT I STILL HAVEN'T GOTTEN USED TO IT.
THEY GIVE OFF A DIFFERENT ENERGY THAN THE SEVERE MILITARY POLICE.
MM. BUT...

18. Little Girl and Her New Dilemma

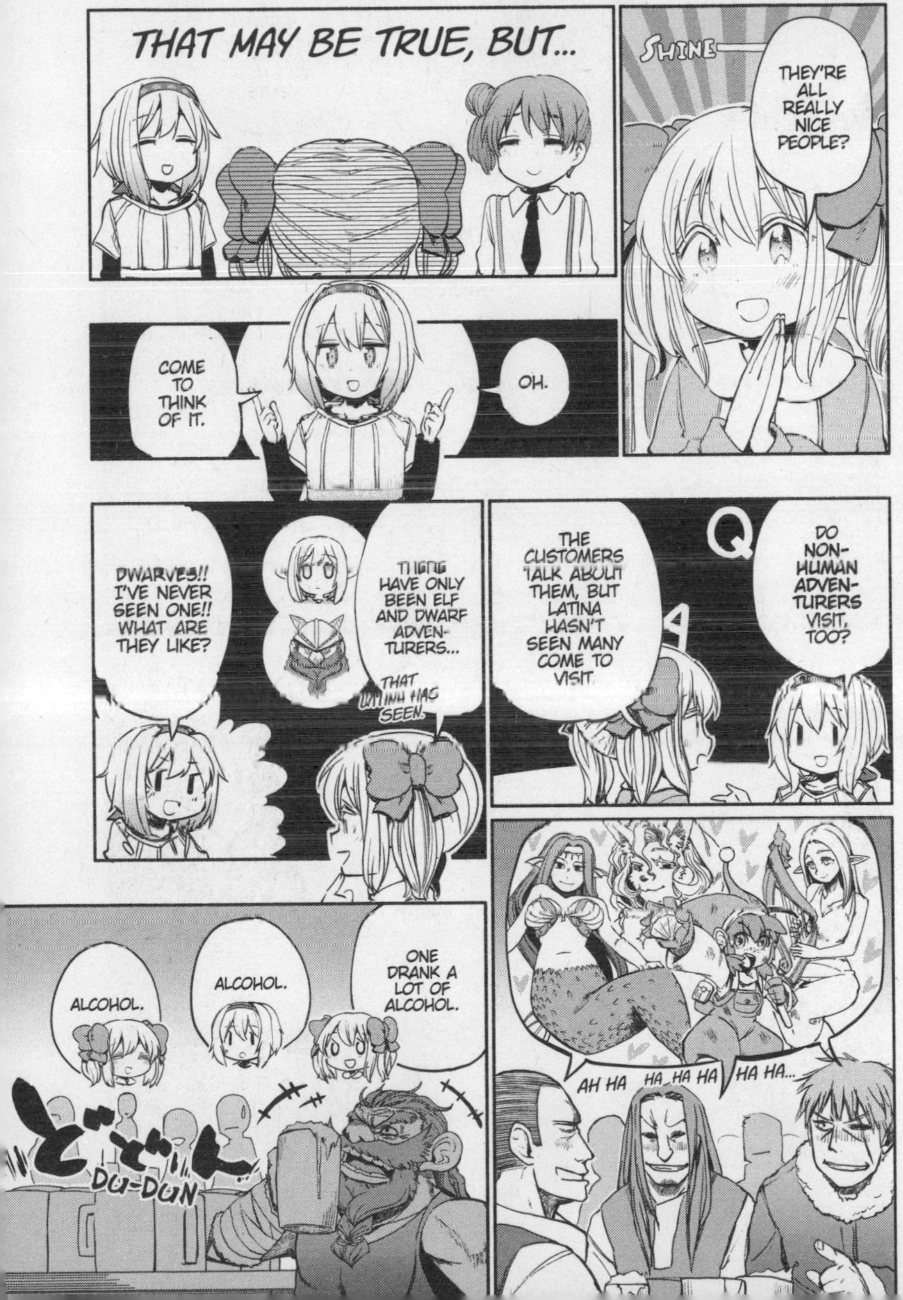
SHINE
THEY'RE ALL REALLY NICE PEOPLE?
THAT MAY BE TRUE, BUT...
OH.
COME TO THINK OF IT.
DO NON-HUMAN ADVENTURERS VISIT, TOO?
Q
A
THE CUSTOMERS TALK ABOUT THEM, BUT LATINA HASN'T SEEN MANY COME TO VISIT.
THERE HAVE ONLY BEEN ELF AND DWARF ADVENTURERS...
THAT LATINA HAS SEEN.
DWARVES!! I'VE NEVER SEEN ONE!! WHAT ARE THEY LIKE?
AH HA HA HA HA HA HA...
ONE DRANK A LOT OF ALCOHOL.
ALCOHOL.
ALCOHOL.
DU-DUN

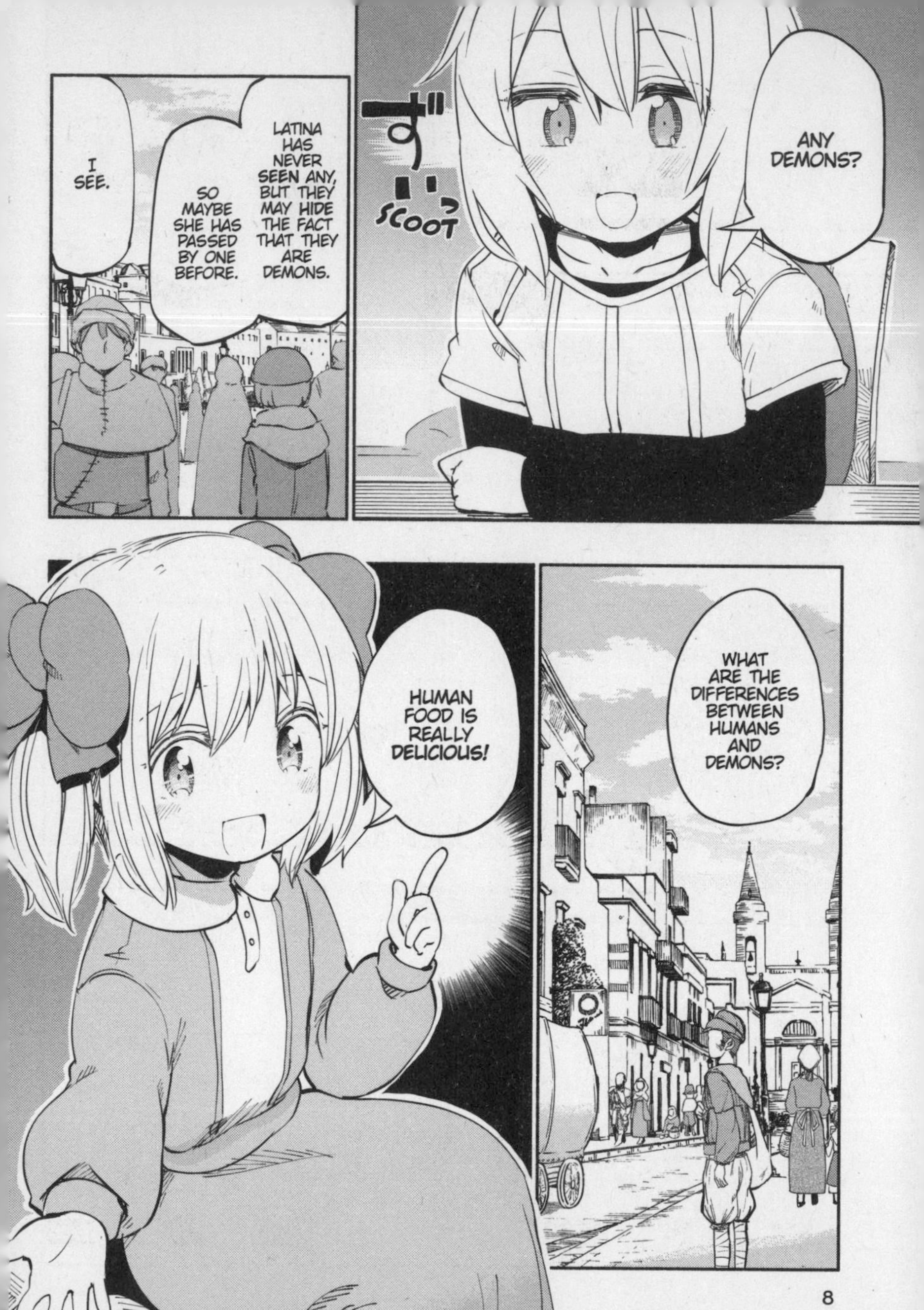
ANY DEMONS?
ずいっ
SCOOT
LATINA HAS NEVER SEEN ANY, BUT THEY MAY HIDE THE FACT THAT THEY ARE DEMONS.
SO MAYBE SHE HAS PASSED BY ONE BEFORE.
I SEE.
WHAT ARE THE DIFFERENCES BETWEEN HUMANS AND DEMONS?
HUMAN FOOD IS REALLY DELICIOUS!

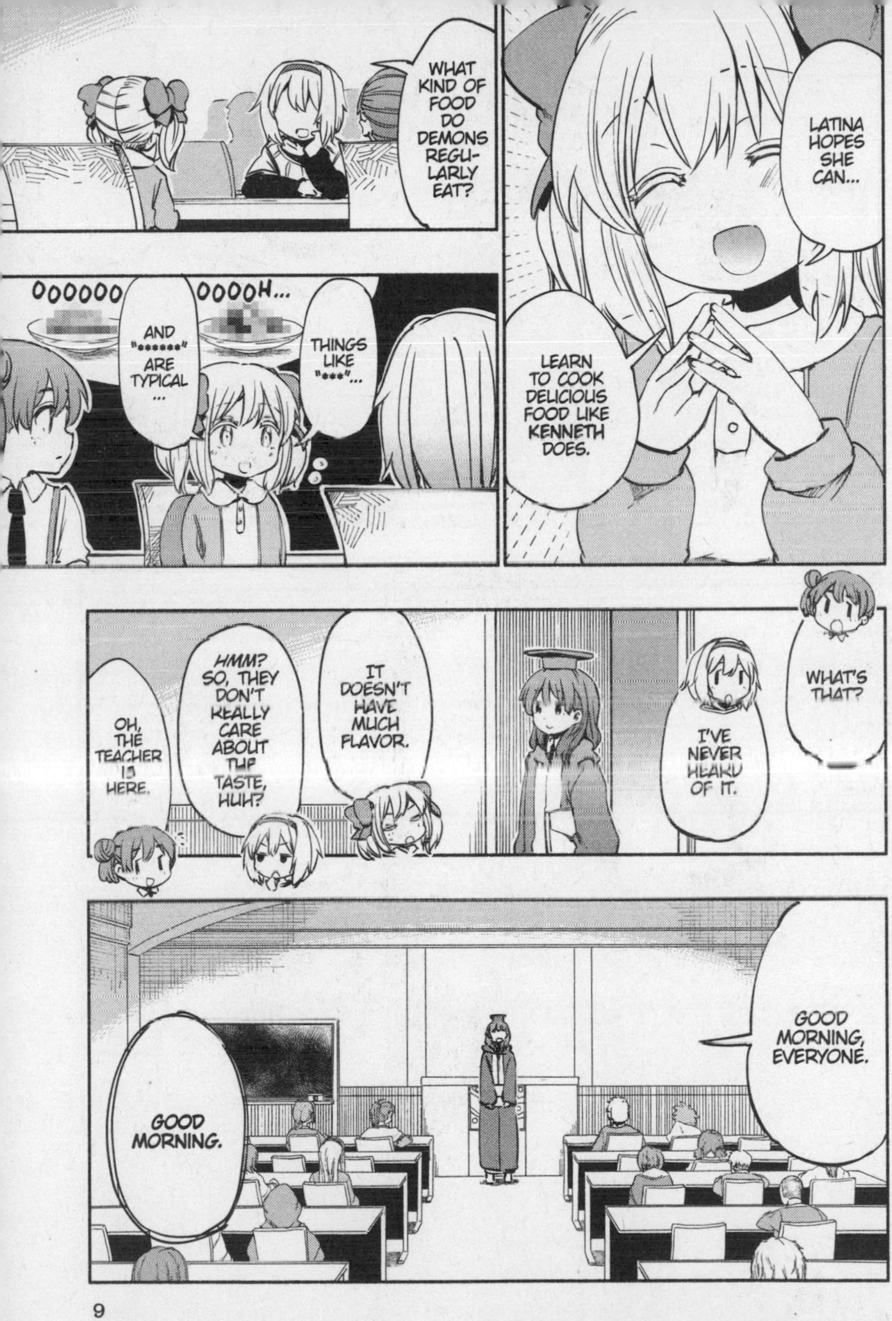
LATINA HOPES SHE CAN...
LEARN TO COOK DELICIOUS FOOD LIKE KENNETH DOES.
WHAT KIND OF FOOD DO DEMONS REGULARLY EAT?
THINGS LIKE "***"...
OOOOH...
AND "******" ARE TYPICAL ...
OOOOOO
WHAT'S THAT?
I'VE NEVER HEARD OF IT.
IT DOESN'T HAVE MUCH FLAVOR.
HMM? SO, THEY DON'T REALLY CARE ABOUT THE TASTE, HUH?
OH, THE TEACHER IS HERE.
GOOD MORNING, EVERYONE.
GOOD MORNING.

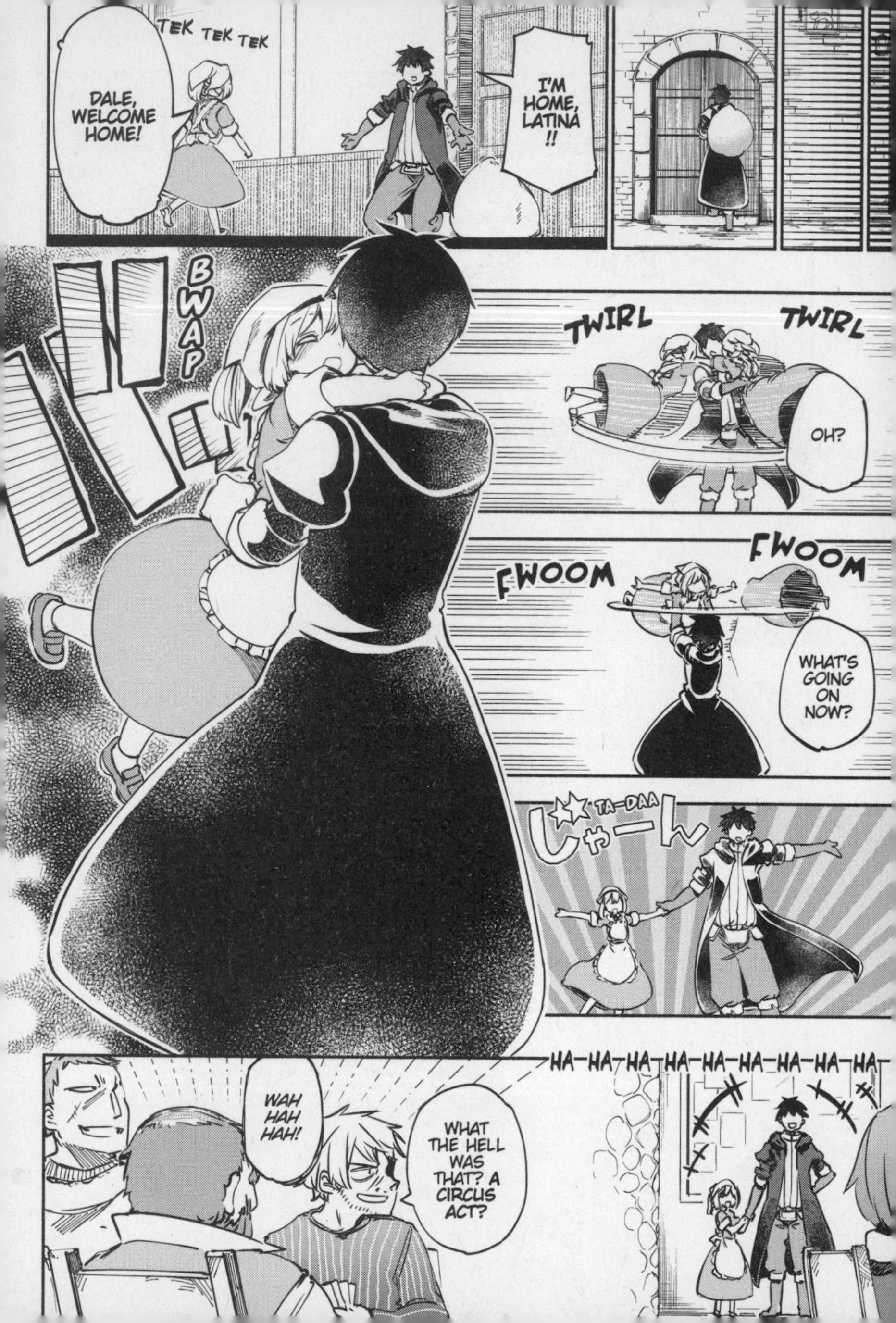
I'M HOME, LATINA !!
TEK TEK TEK
DALE, WELCOME HOME!
TWIRL TWIRL
OH?
FWOOM FWOOM
WHAT'S GOING ON NOW?
TA-DAA
じゃーん
BWAP
HA-HA-HA-HA-HA-HA-HA-HA-HA-
WHAT THE HELL WAS THAT? A CIRCUS ACT?
WAH HAH HAH!

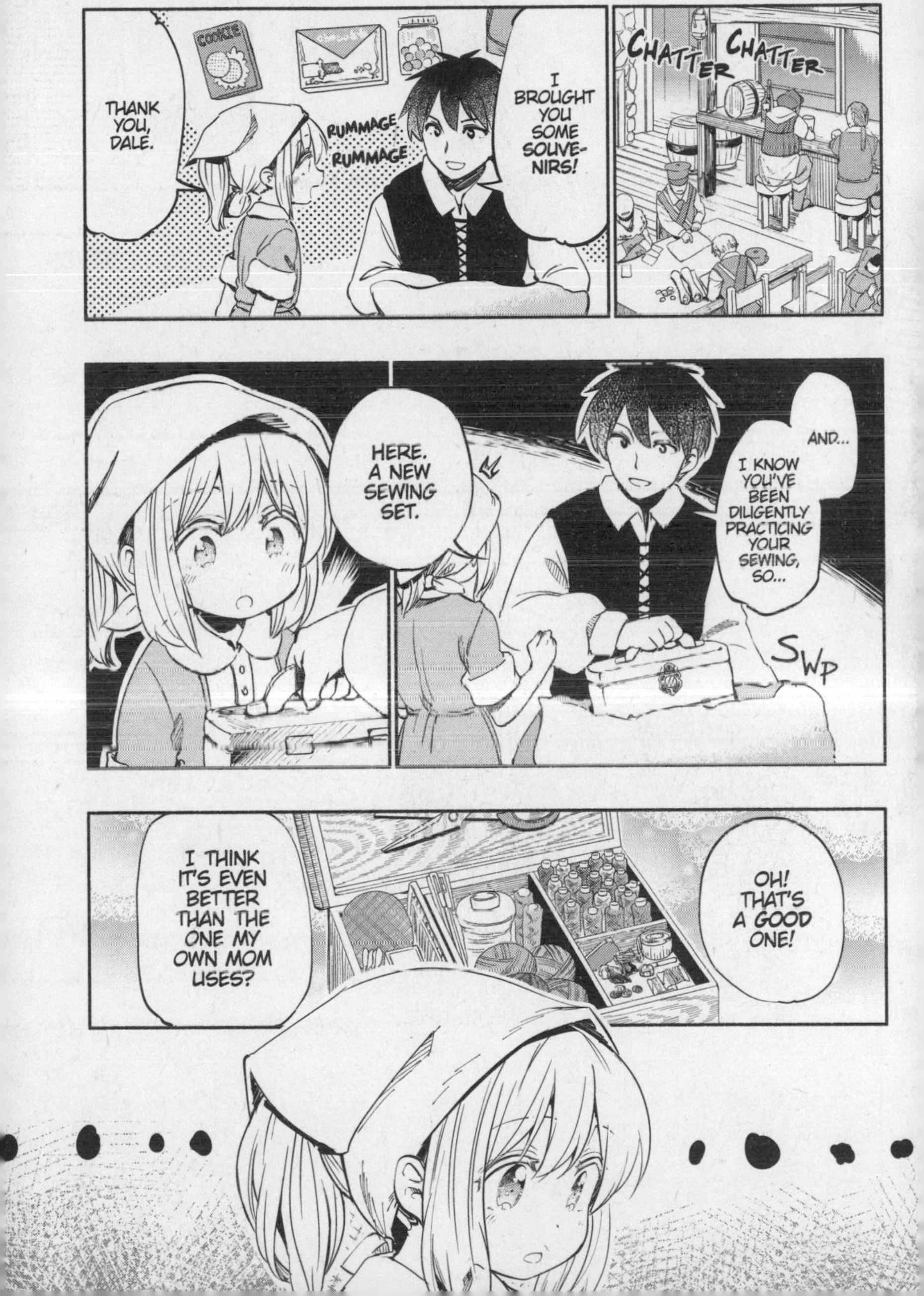
CHATTER CHATTER
I BROUGHT YOU SOME SOUVENIRS!
RUMMAGE RUMMAGE
COOKIE
THANK YOU, DALE.
AND...
I KNOW YOU'VE BEEN DILIGENTLY PRACTICING YOUR SEWING, SO...
SWP
HERE. A NEW SEWING SET.
OH! THAT'S A GOOD ONE!
I THINK IT'S EVEN BETTER THAN THE ONE MY OWN MOM USES?

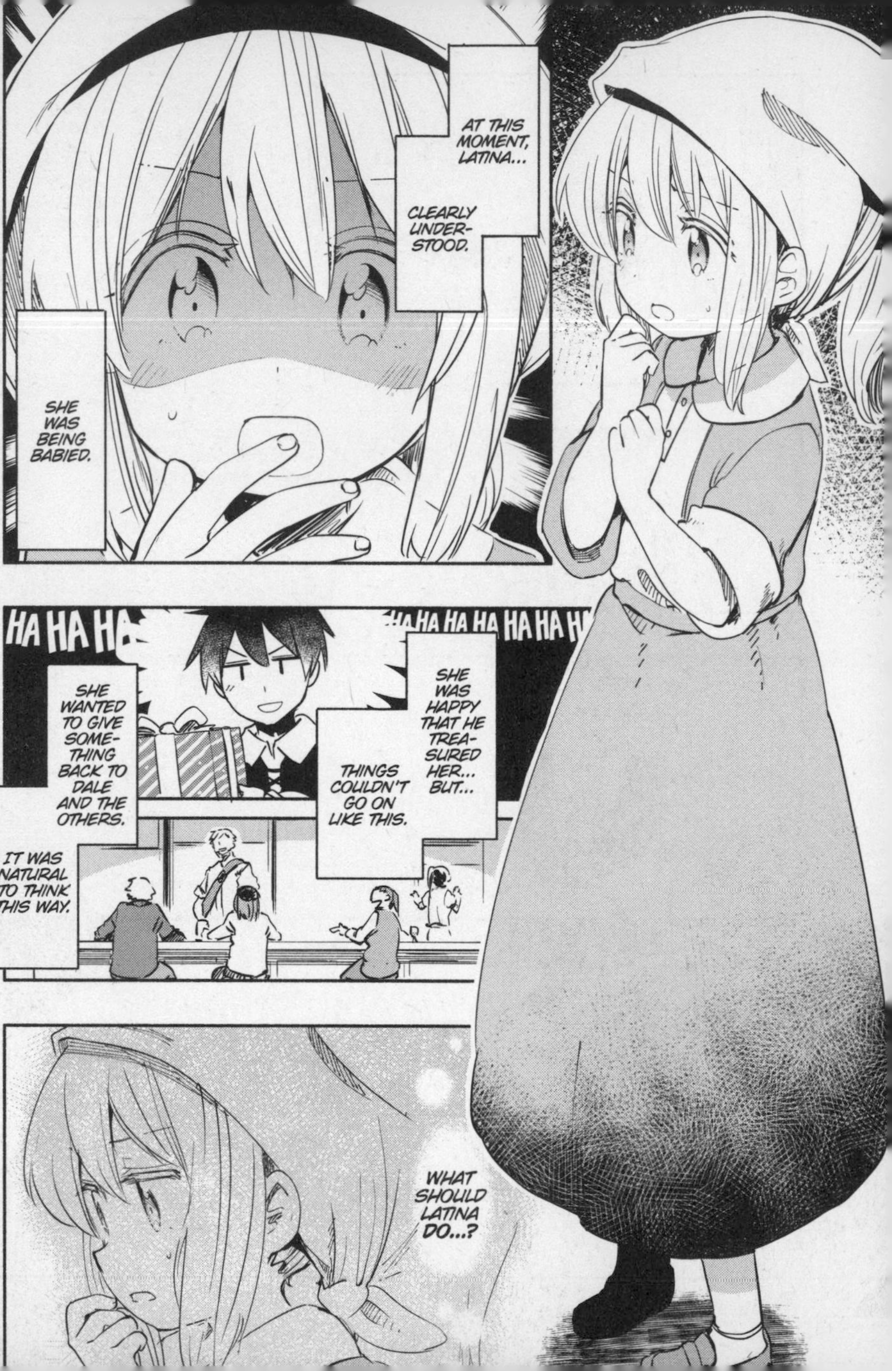
AT THIS MOMENT, LATINA...
CLEARLY UNDERSTOOD.
SHE WAS BEING BABIED.
HA HA HA HA HA HA
HA HA HA
SHE WAS HAPPY THAT HE TREASURED HER... BUT...
THINGS COULDN'T GO ON LIKE THIS.
SHE WANTED TO GIVE SOMETHING BACK TO DALE AND THE OTHERS.
IT WAS NATURAL TO THINK THIS WAY.
WHAT SHOULD LATINA DO...?

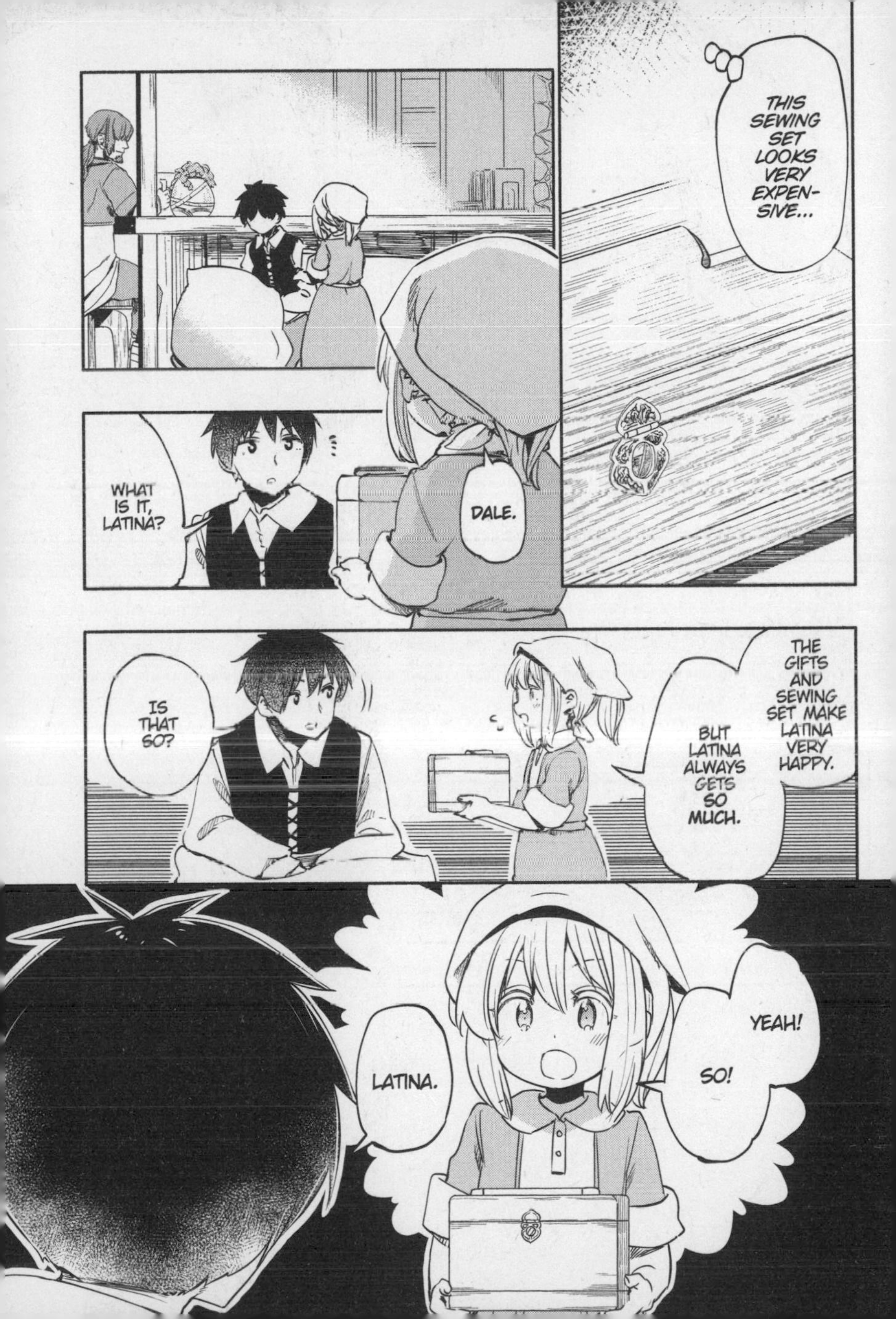
THIS SEWING SET LOOKS VERY EXPENSIVE...
DALE.
WHAT IS IT, LATINA?
THE GIFTS AND SEWING SET MAKE LATINA VERY HAPPY.
BUT LATINA ALWAYS GETS SO MUCH.
IS THAT SO?
YEAH!
SO!
LATINA.

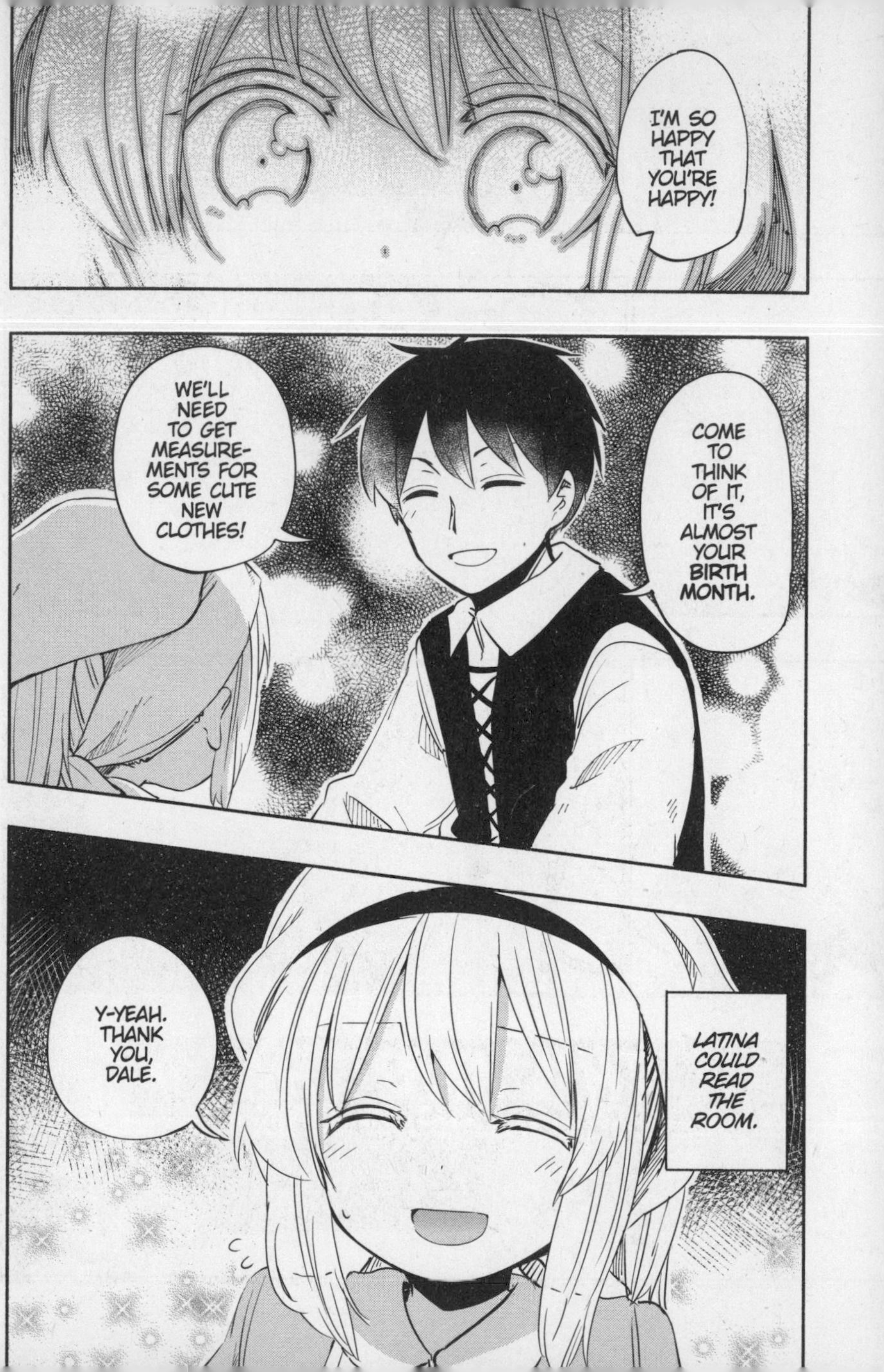
I'M SO HAPPY THAT YOU'RE HAPPY!
COME TO THINK OF IT, IT'S ALMOST YOUR BIRTH MONTH.
WE'LL NEED TO GET MEASURE-MENTS FOR SOME CUTE NEW CLOTHES!
LATINA COULD READ THE ROOM.
Y-YEAH. THANK YOU, DALE.

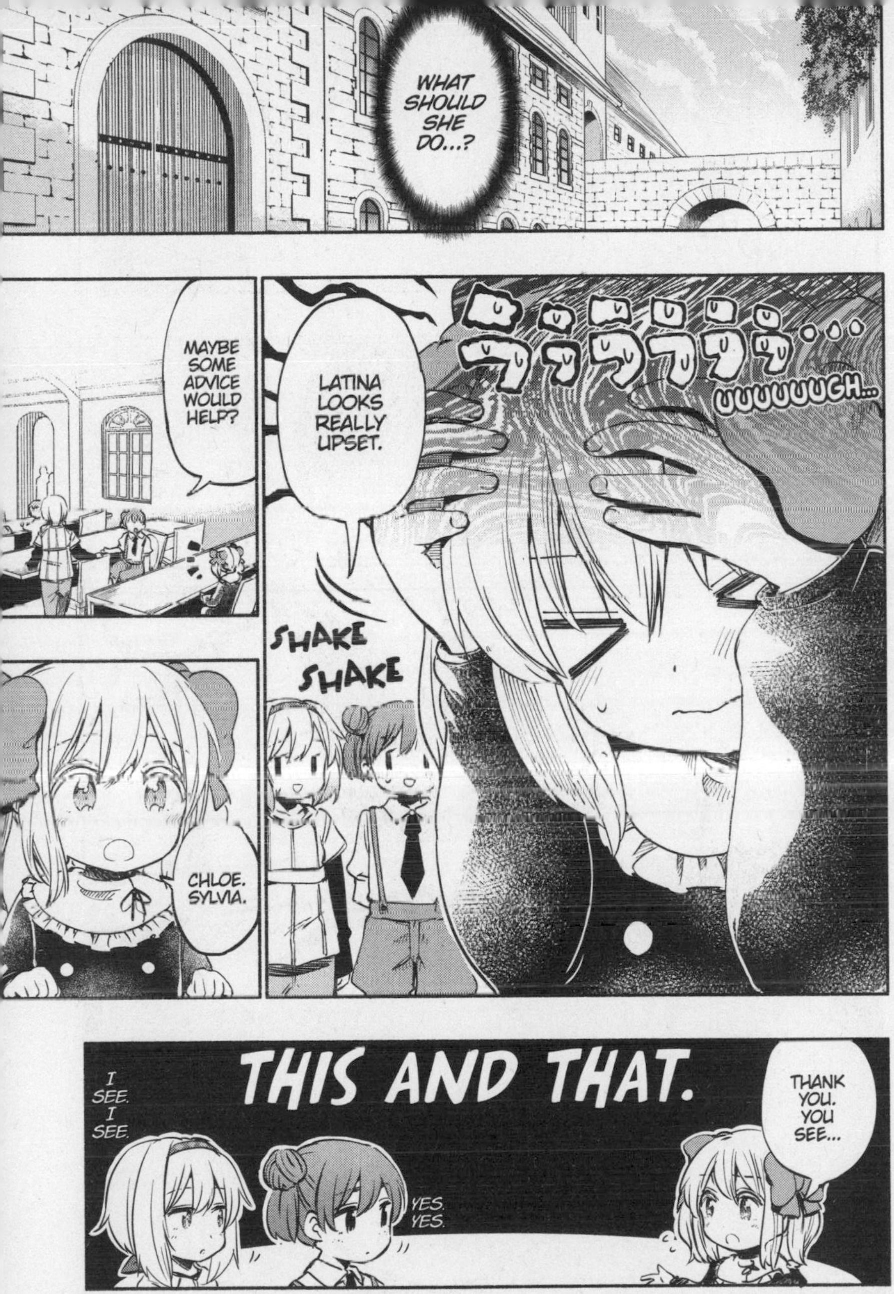
WHAT SHOULD SHE DO...?
UUUUUUGH...
LATINA LOOKS REALLY UPSET.
SHAKE SHAKE
MAYBE SOME ADVICE WOULD HELP?
CHLOE. SYLVIA.
THIS AND THAT.
THANK YOU. YOU SEE...
YES. YES.
I SEE. I SEE.

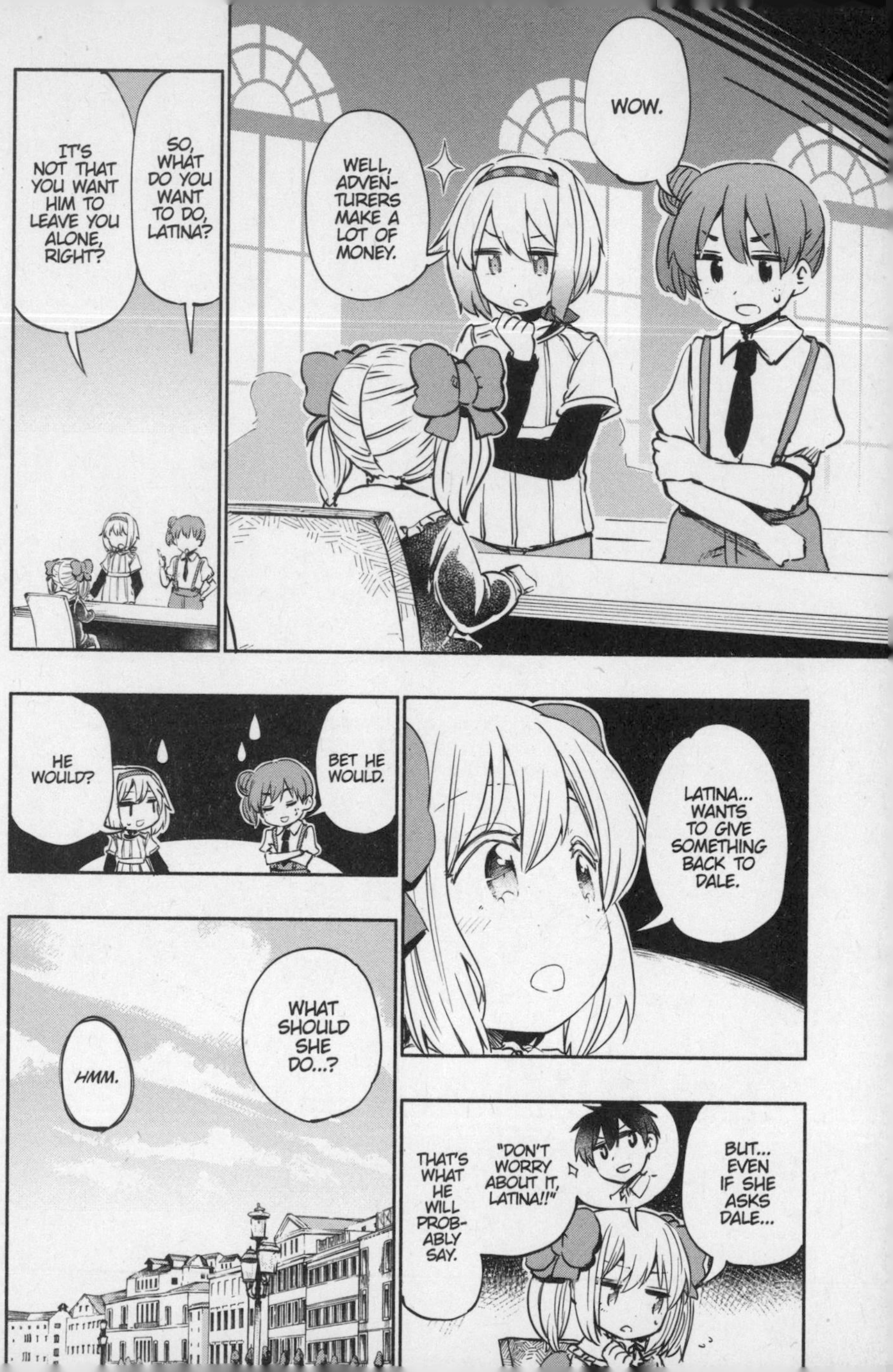
WOW.
WELL, ADVENTURERS MAKE A LOT OF MONEY.
SO, WHAT DO YOU WANT TO DO, LATINA?
IT'S NOT THAT YOU WANT HIM TO LEAVE YOU ALONE, RIGHT?
LATINA... WANTS TO GIVE SOMETHING BACK TO DALE.
BUT... EVEN IF SHE ASKS DALE...
"DON'T WORRY ABOUT IT, LATINA!!"
THAT'S WHAT HE WILL PROBABLY SAY.
BET HE WOULD.
HE WOULD?
WHAT SHOULD SHE DO...?
HMM.

If It's For My Daughter I'd Even Defeat a Demon Lord

If It's For My Daughter, I'd Even Defeat a Demon Lord.

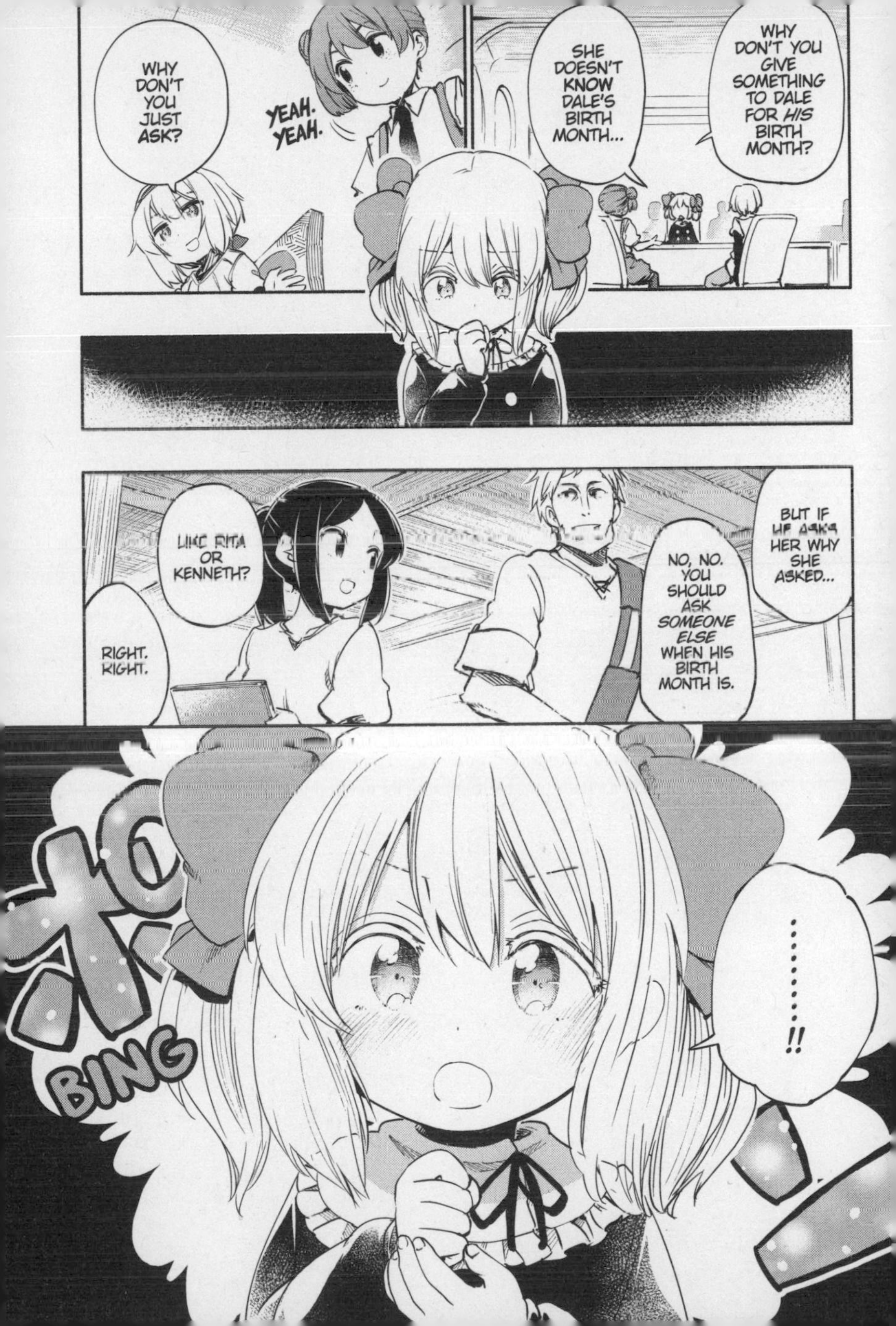
WHY DON'T YOU GIVE SOMETHING TO DALE FOR *HIS* BIRTH MONTH?
SHE DOESN'T KNOW DALE'S BIRTH MONTH...
WHY DON'T YOU JUST ASK?
YEAH. YEAH.
BUT IF HE ASKS HER WHY SHE ASKED...
NO, NO. YOU SHOULD ASK *SOMEONE ELSE* WHEN HIS BIRTH MONTH IS.
LIKE RITA OR KENNETH?
RIGHT. RIGHT.
........!!
BING

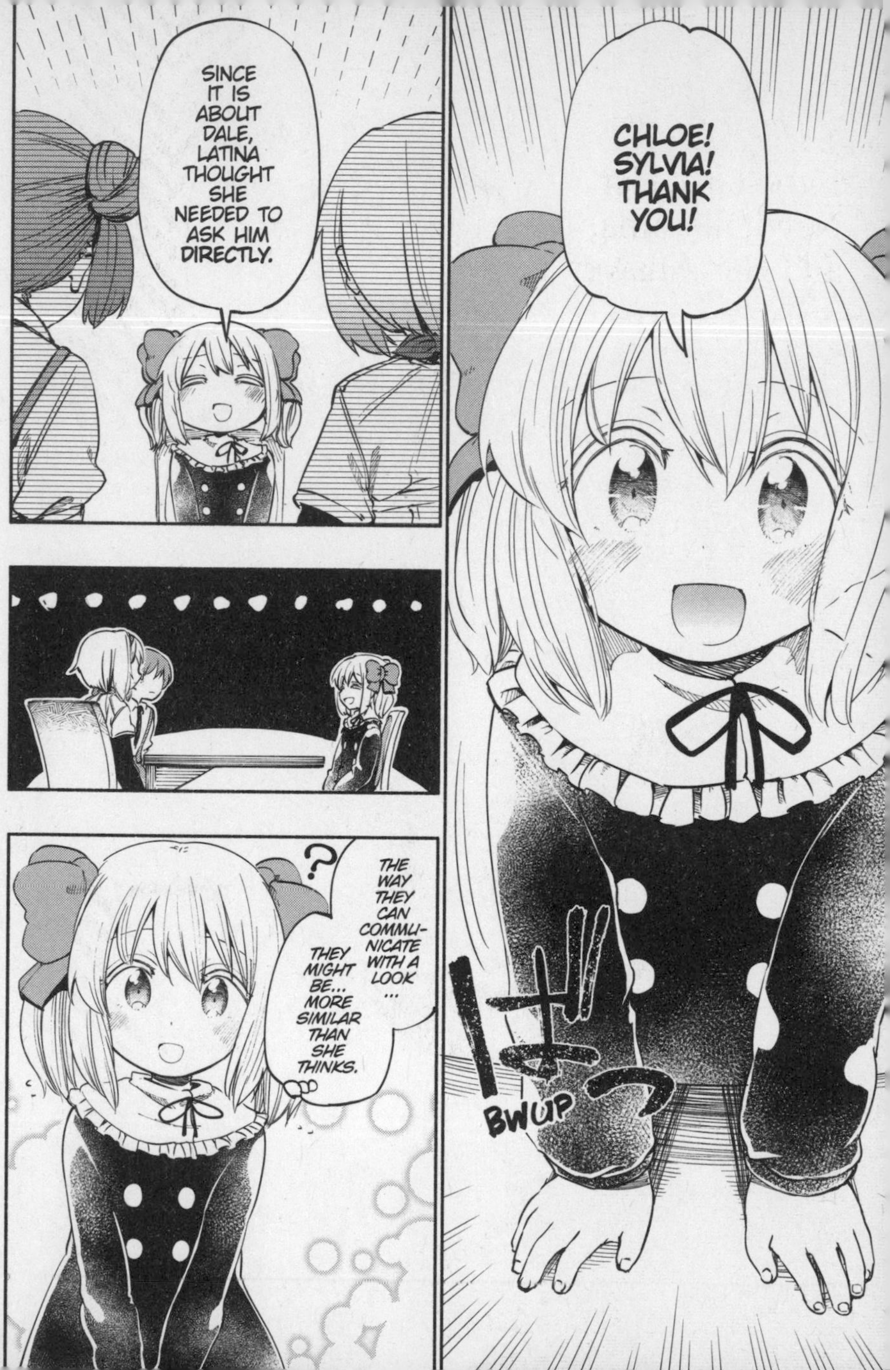
CHLOE! SYLVIA! THANK YOU!
BWUP
SINCE IT IS ABOUT DALE, LATINA THOUGHT SHE NEEDED TO ASK HIM DIRECTLY.
?
THE WAY THEY CAN COMMUNICATE WITH A LOOK ...
THEY MIGHT BE... MORE SIMILAR THAN SHE THINKS.

19. Little Girl, Her New Dilemma, and Her Answer

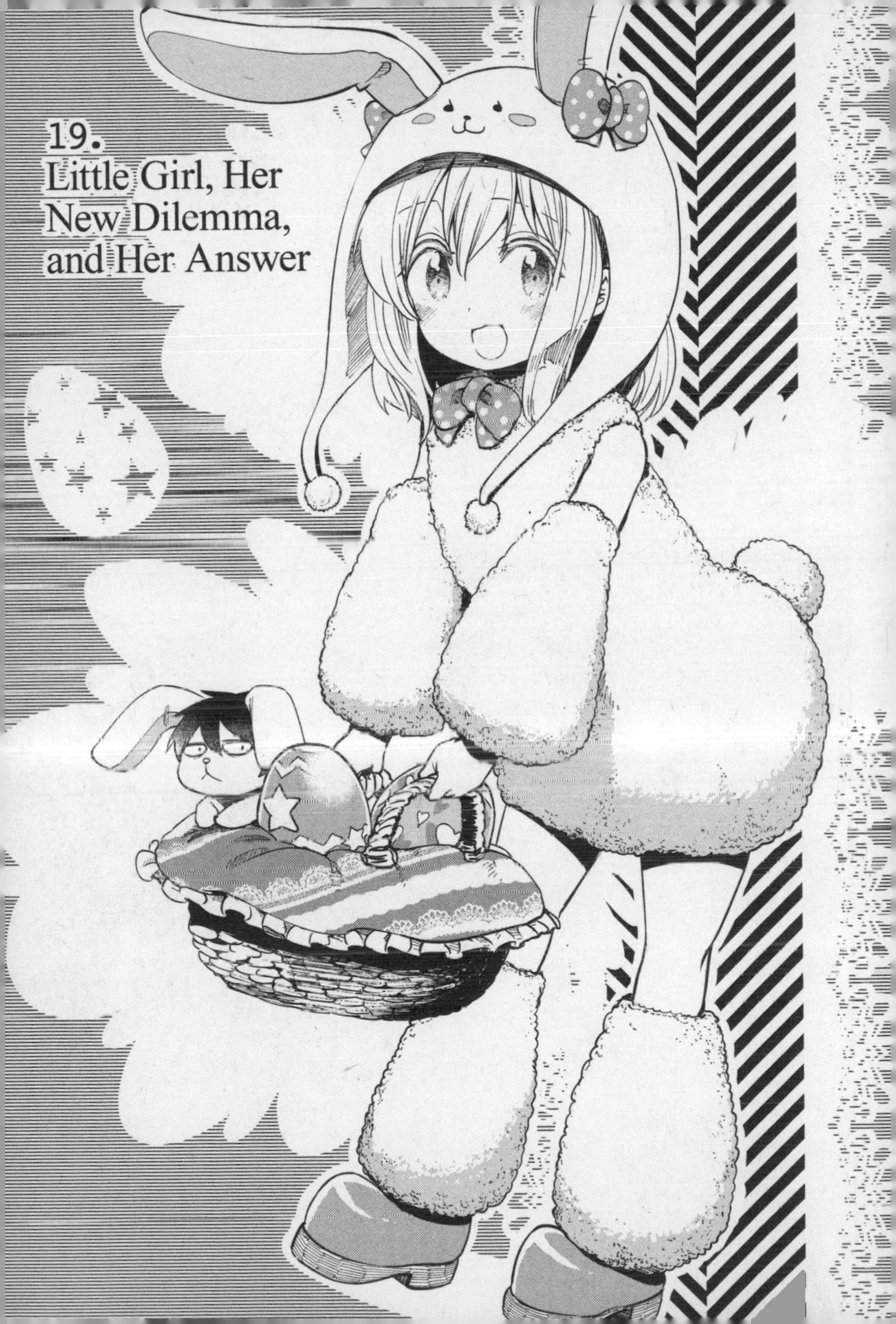

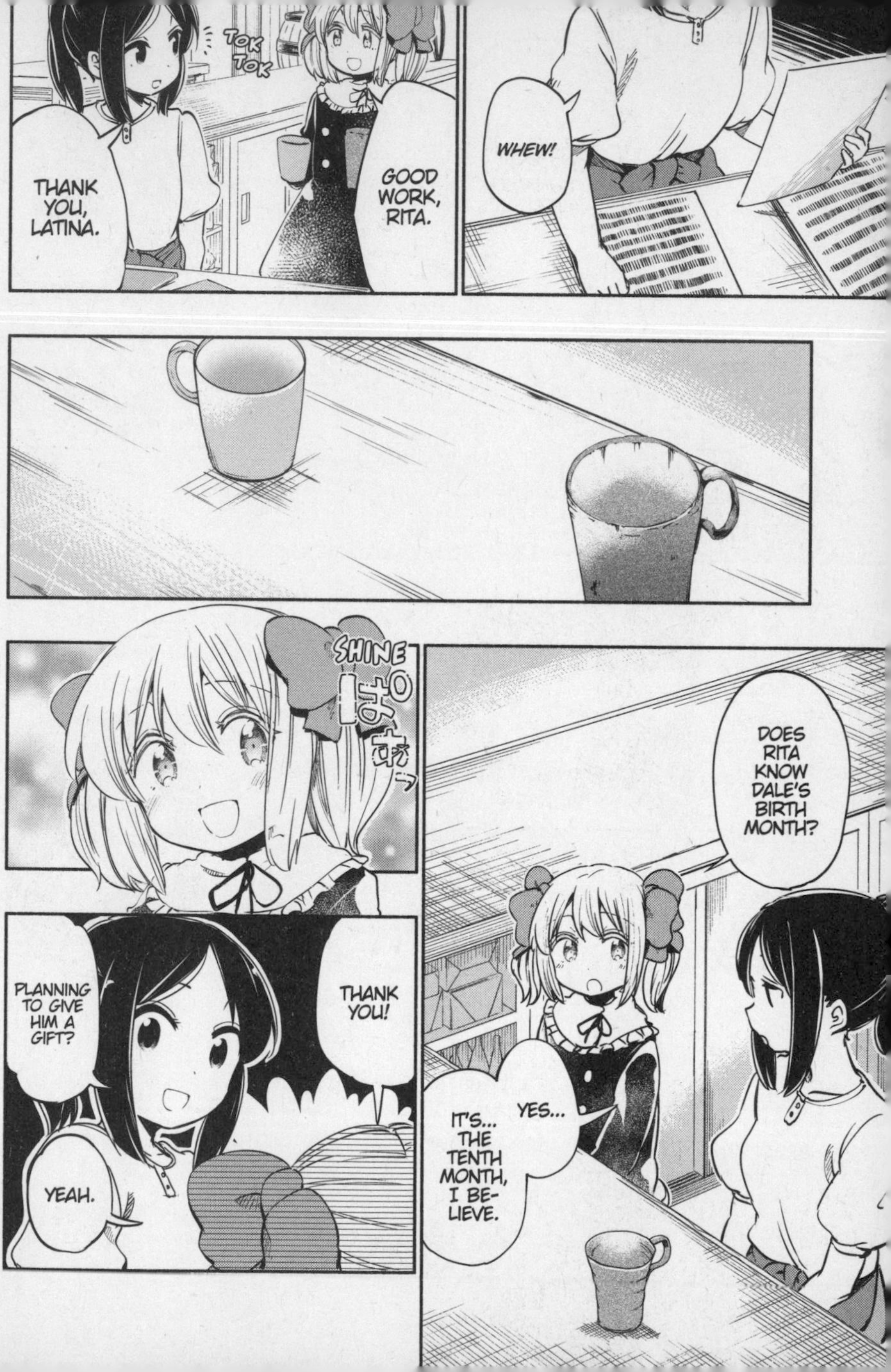
WHEW!
TOK TOK
GOOD WORK, RITA.
THANK YOU, LATINA.
DOES RITA KNOW DALE'S BIRTH MONTH?
YES...
IT'S... THE TENTH MONTH, I BE-LIEVE.
SHINE
THANK YOU!
PLANNING TO GIVE HIM A GIFT?
YEAH.

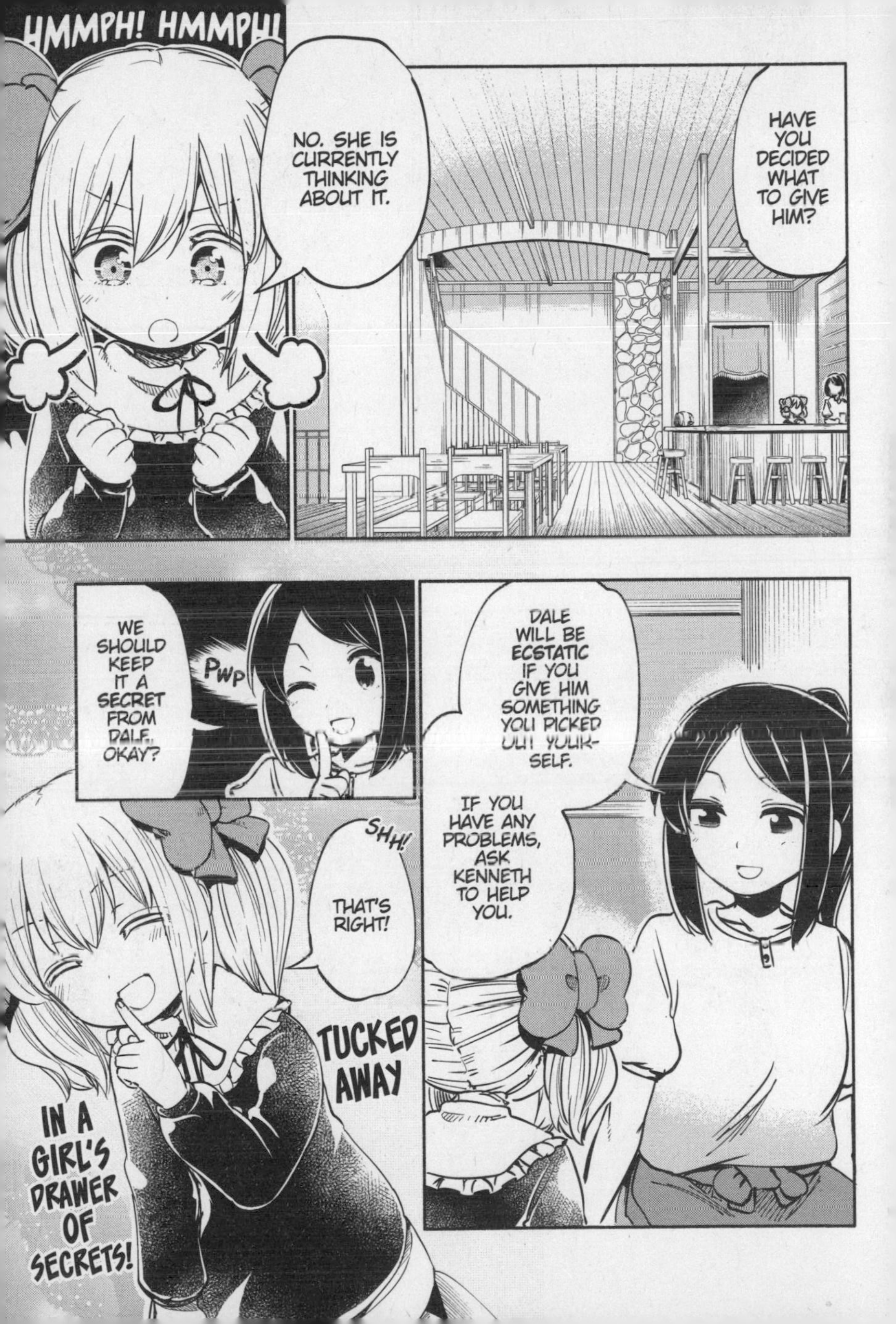
HAVE YOU DECIDED WHAT TO GIVE HIM?
NO. SHE IS CURRENTLY THINKING ABOUT IT.
HMMPH! HMMPH!
DALE WILL BE ECSTATIC IF YOU GIVE HIM SOMETHING YOU PICKED OUT YOUR-SELF.
IF YOU HAVE ANY PROBLEMS, ASK KENNETH TO HELP YOU.
WE SHOULD KEEP IT A SECRET FROM DALE, OKAY?
PWP
SHH!
THAT'S RIGHT!
TUCKED AWAY
IN A GIRL'S DRAWER OF SECRETS!

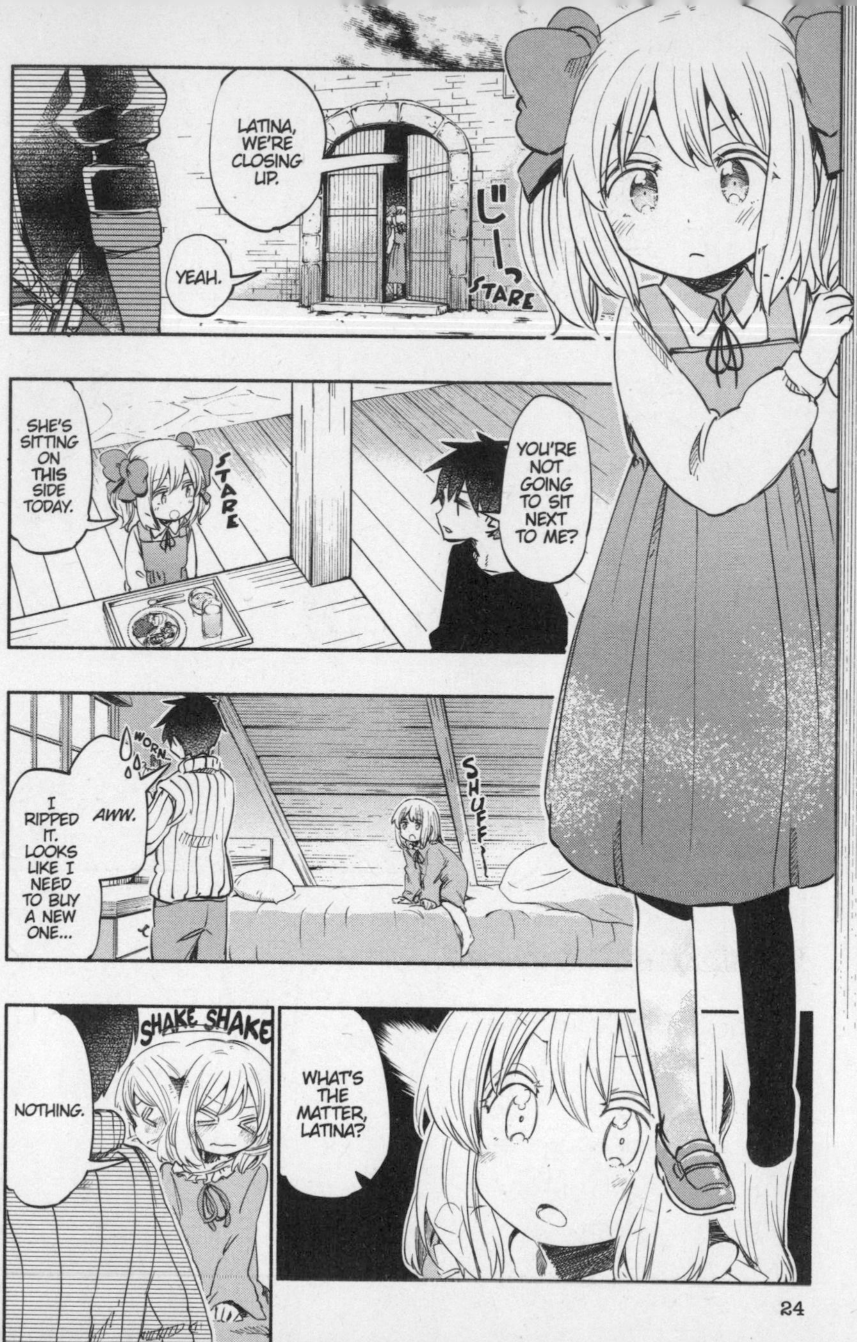
じーっ
STARE
LATINA, WE'RE CLOSING UP.
YEAH.
YOU'RE NOT GOING TO SIT NEXT TO ME?
STARE
SHE'S SITTING ON THIS SIDE TODAY.
SHUFF
WORN...
AWW.
I RIPPED IT. LOOKS LIKE I NEED TO BUY A NEW ONE...
WHAT'S THE MATTER, LATINA?
SHAKE SHAKE
NOTHING.

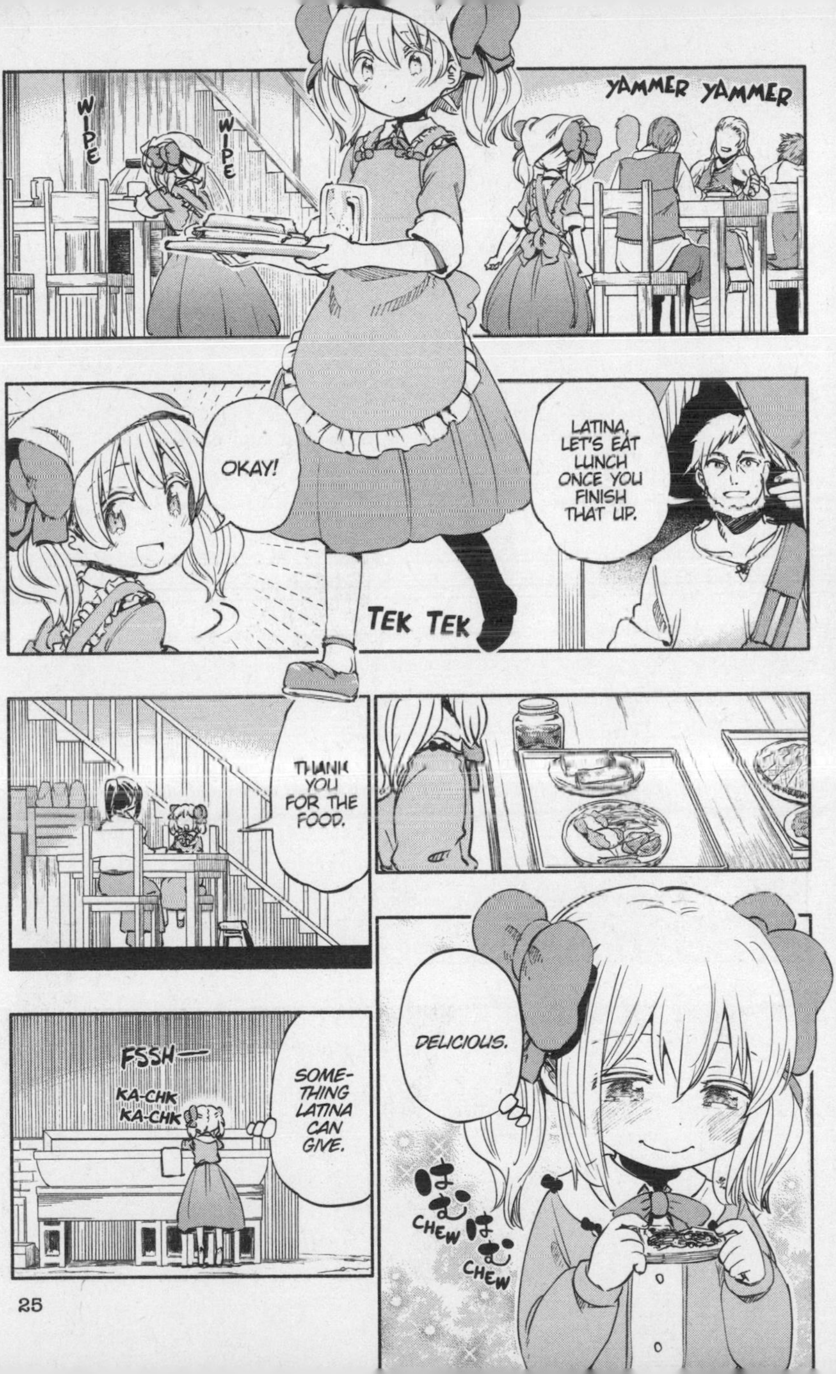
YAMMER YAMMER
WIPE WIPE
LATINA, LET'S EAT LUNCH ONCE YOU FINISH THAT UP.
OKAY!
TEK TEK
THANK YOU FOR THE FOOD.
DELICIOUS.
はむ CHEW はむ CHEW
SOME-THING LATINA CAN GIVE.
FSSH—
KA-CHK KA-CHK

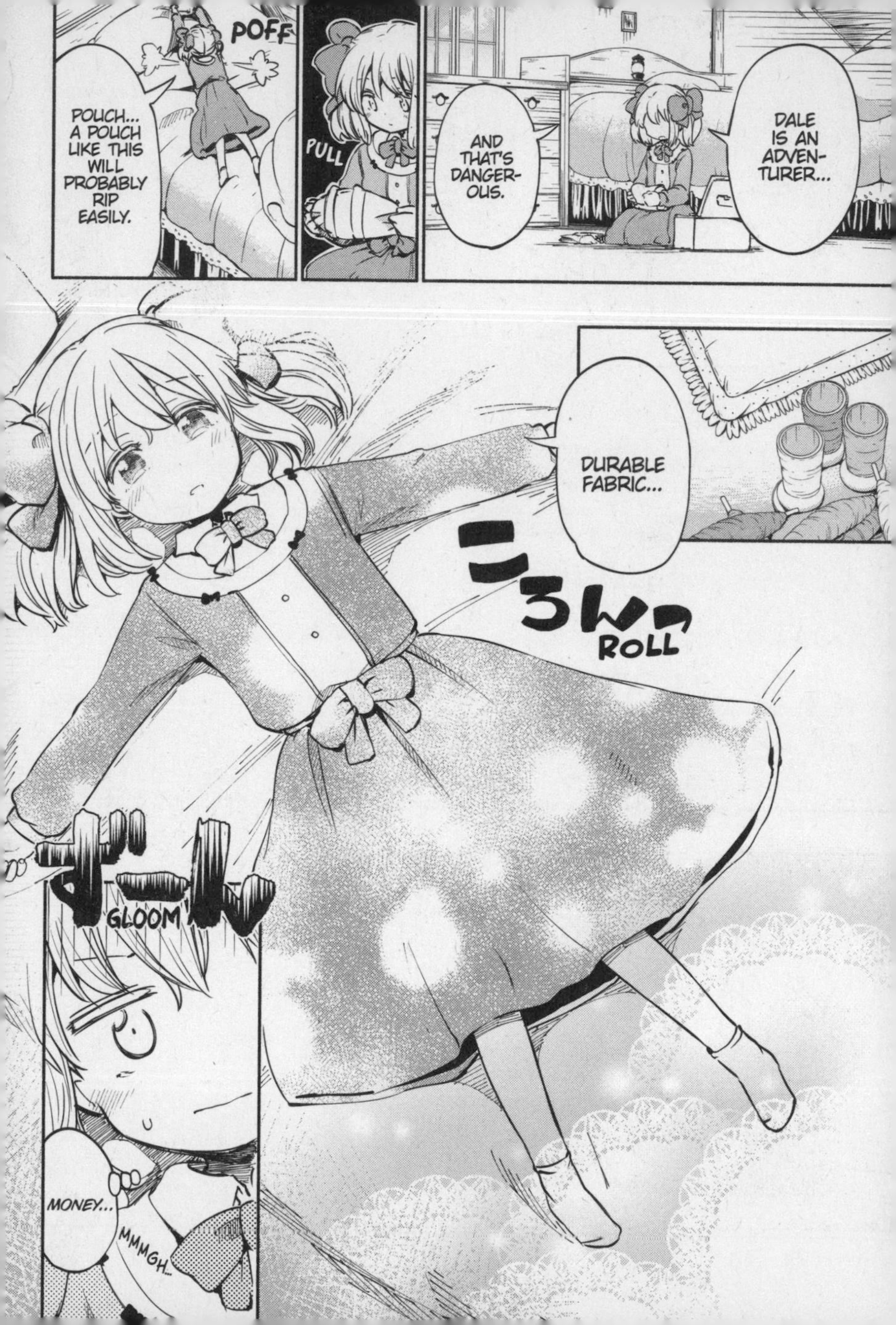
DALE IS AN ADVENTURER...
AND THAT'S DANGEROUS.
PULL
POFF
POUCH... A POUCH LIKE THIS WILL PROBABLY RIP EASILY.
DURABLE FABRIC...
ROLL
GLOOM
MONEY...
MMMGH...

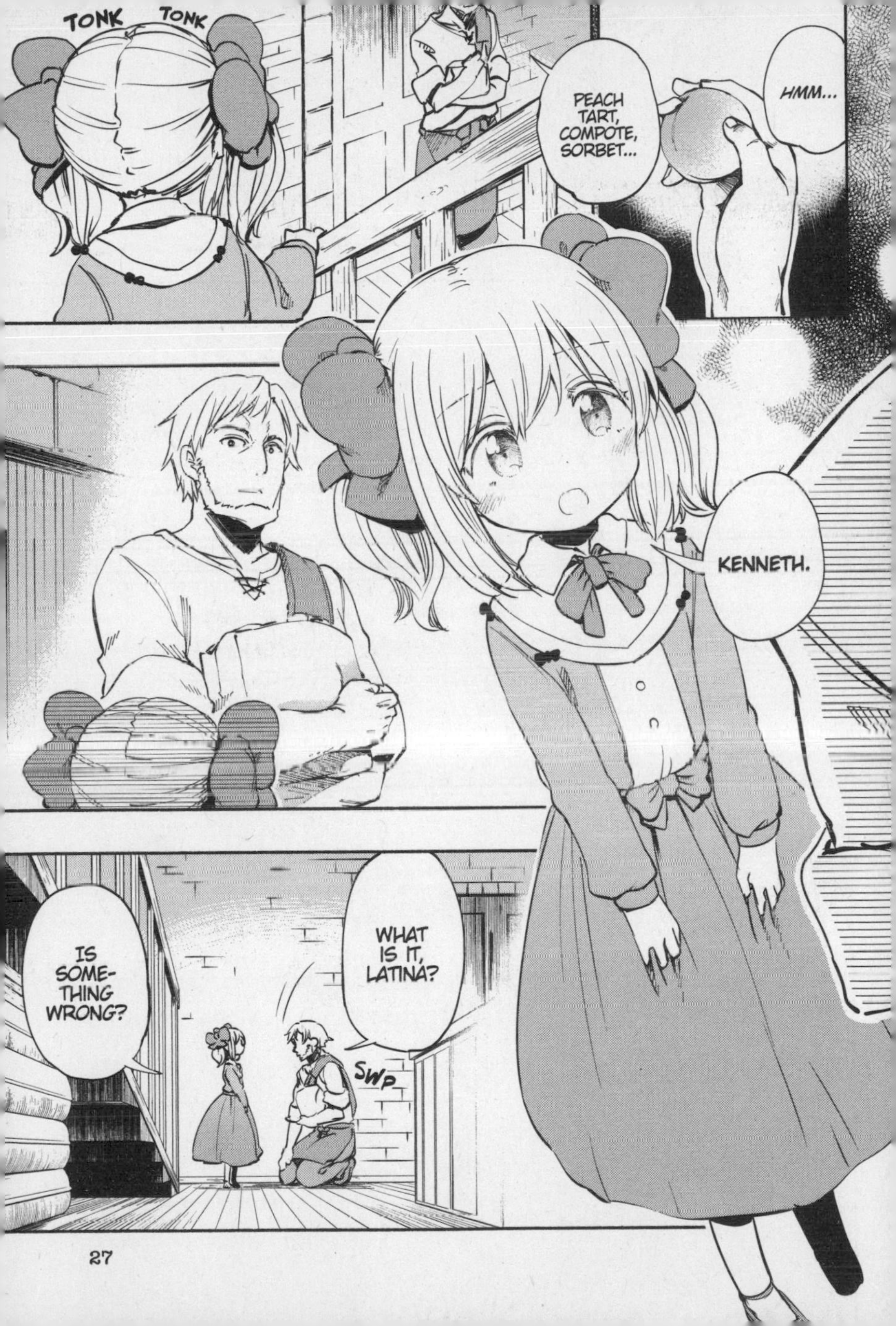
HMM...
PEACH TART, COMPOTE, SORBET...
TONK TONK
KENNETH.
WHAT IS IT, LATINA?
SWP
IS SOMETHING WRONG?

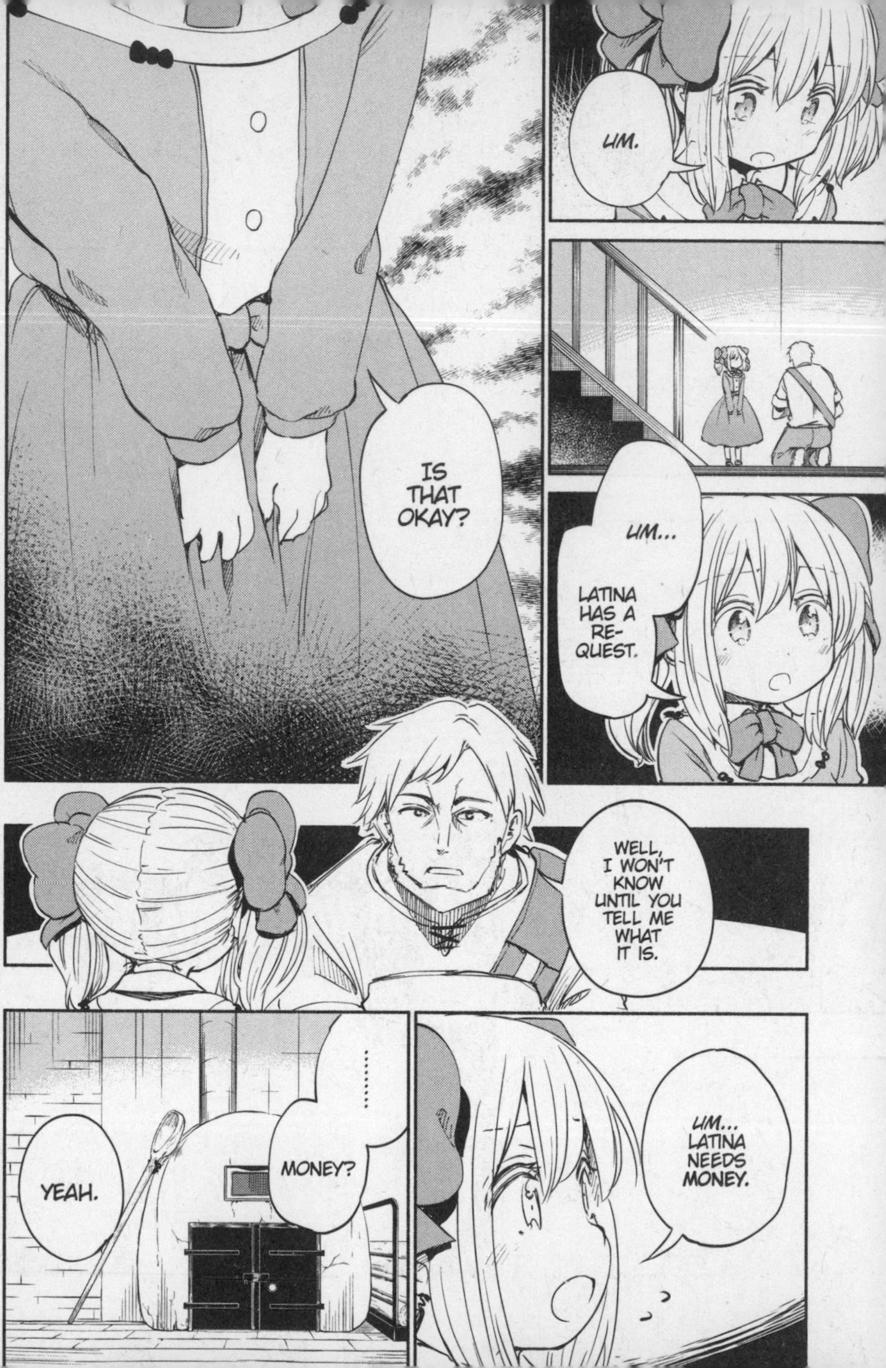
UM.
UM...
LATINA HAS A RE-QUEST.
IS THAT OKAY?
WELL, I WON'T KNOW UNTIL YOU TELL ME WHAT IT IS.
UM... LATINA NEEDS MONEY.
......
MONEY?
YEAH.

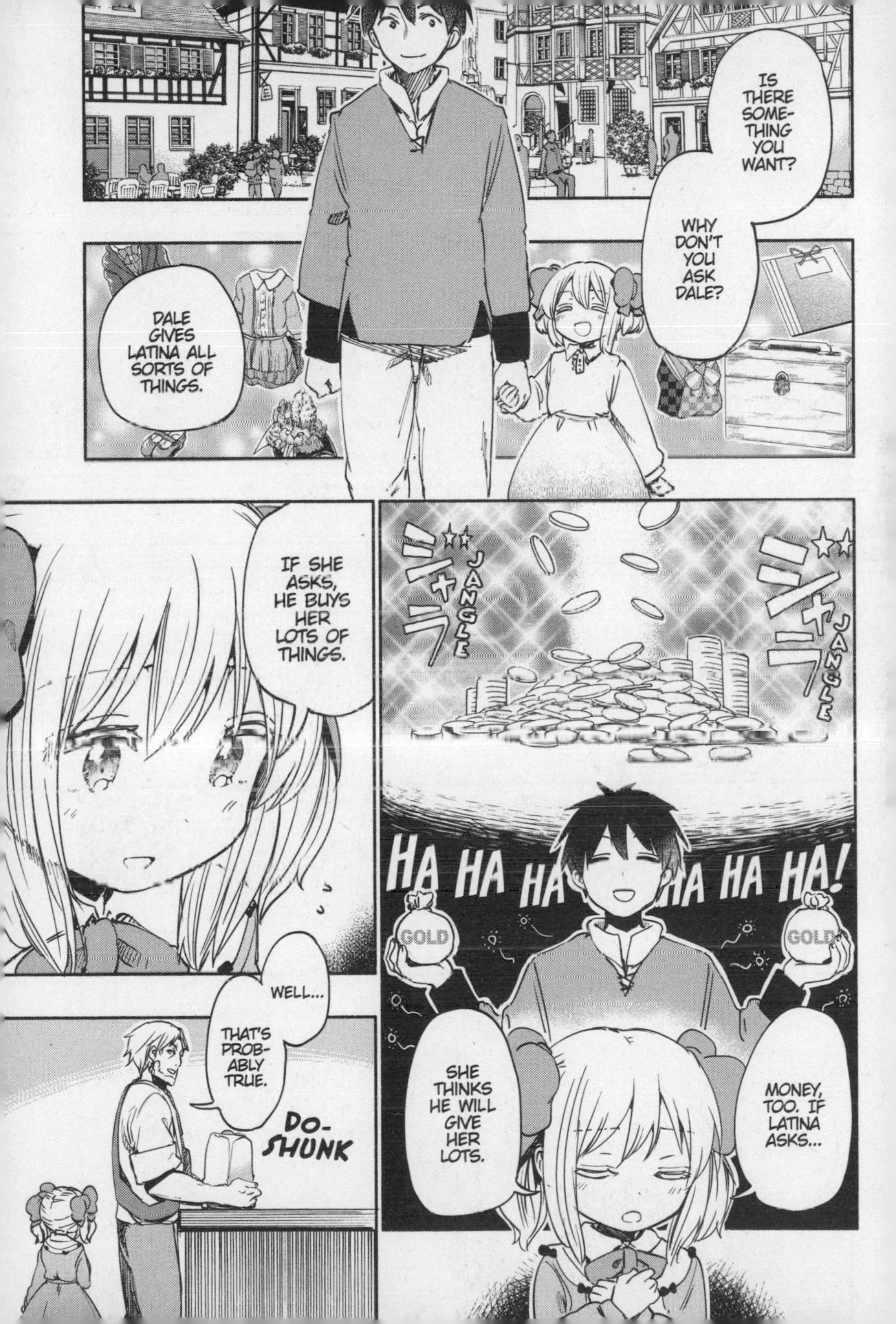
IS THERE SOMETHING YOU WANT?
WHY DON'T YOU ASK DALE?
DALE GIVES LATINA ALL SORTS OF THINGS.
シャラ
JANGLE
シャラ
JANGLE
HA HA HA HA HA HA!
GOLD
GOLD
MONEY, TOO. IF LATINA ASKS...
SHE THINKS HE WILL GIVE HER LOTS.
IF SHE ASKS, HE BUYS HER LOTS OF THINGS.
WELL...
THAT'S PROBABLY TRUE.
DO-SHUNK

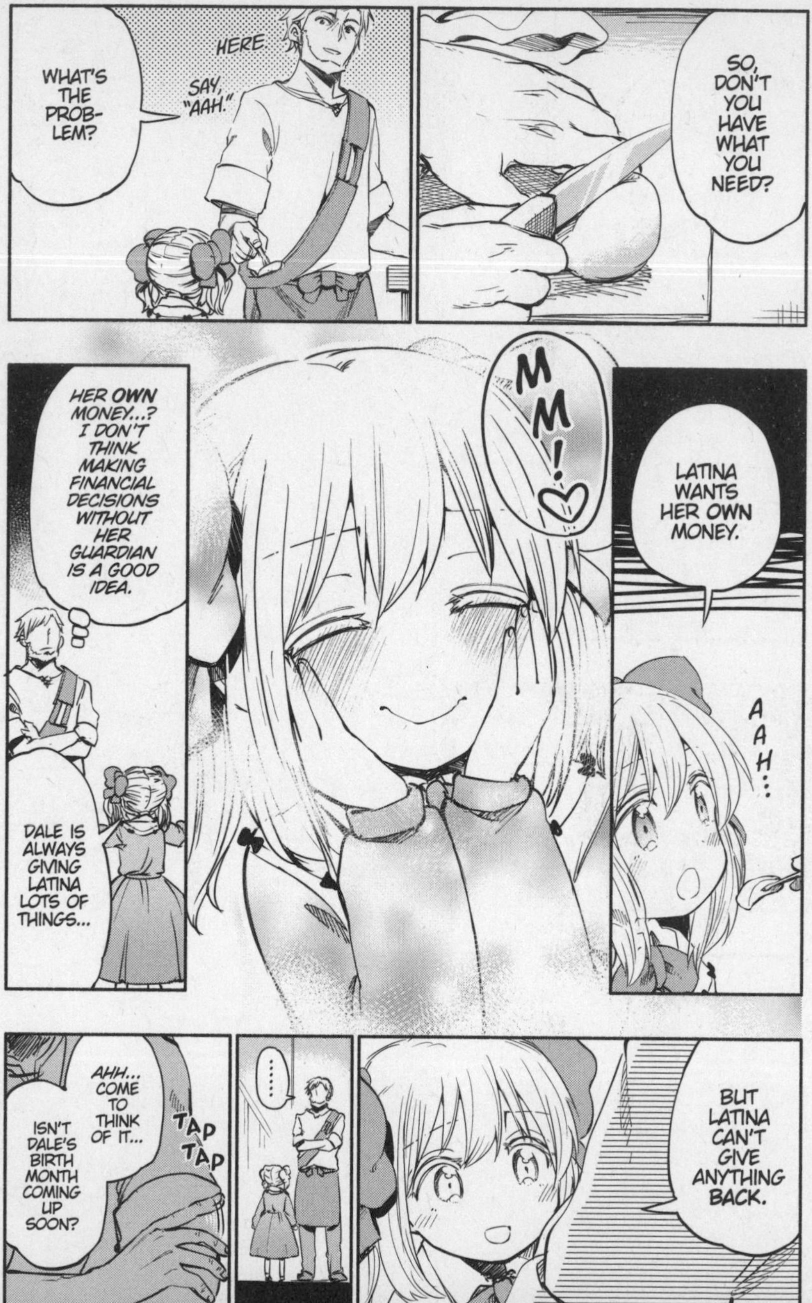
SO, DON'T YOU HAVE WHAT YOU NEED?
HERE.
SAY, "AAH."
WHAT'S THE PROB-LEM?
LATINA WANTS HER OWN MONEY.
AAH...
MM!♥
HER OWN MONEY...? I DON'T THINK MAKING FINANCIAL DECISIONS WITHOUT HER GUARDIAN IS A GOOD IDEA.
DALE IS ALWAYS GIVING LATINA LOTS OF THINGS...
BUT LATINA CAN'T GIVE ANYTHING BACK.
......
AHH... COME TO THINK OF IT...
TAP TAP
ISN'T DALE'S BIRTH MONTH COMING UP SOON?

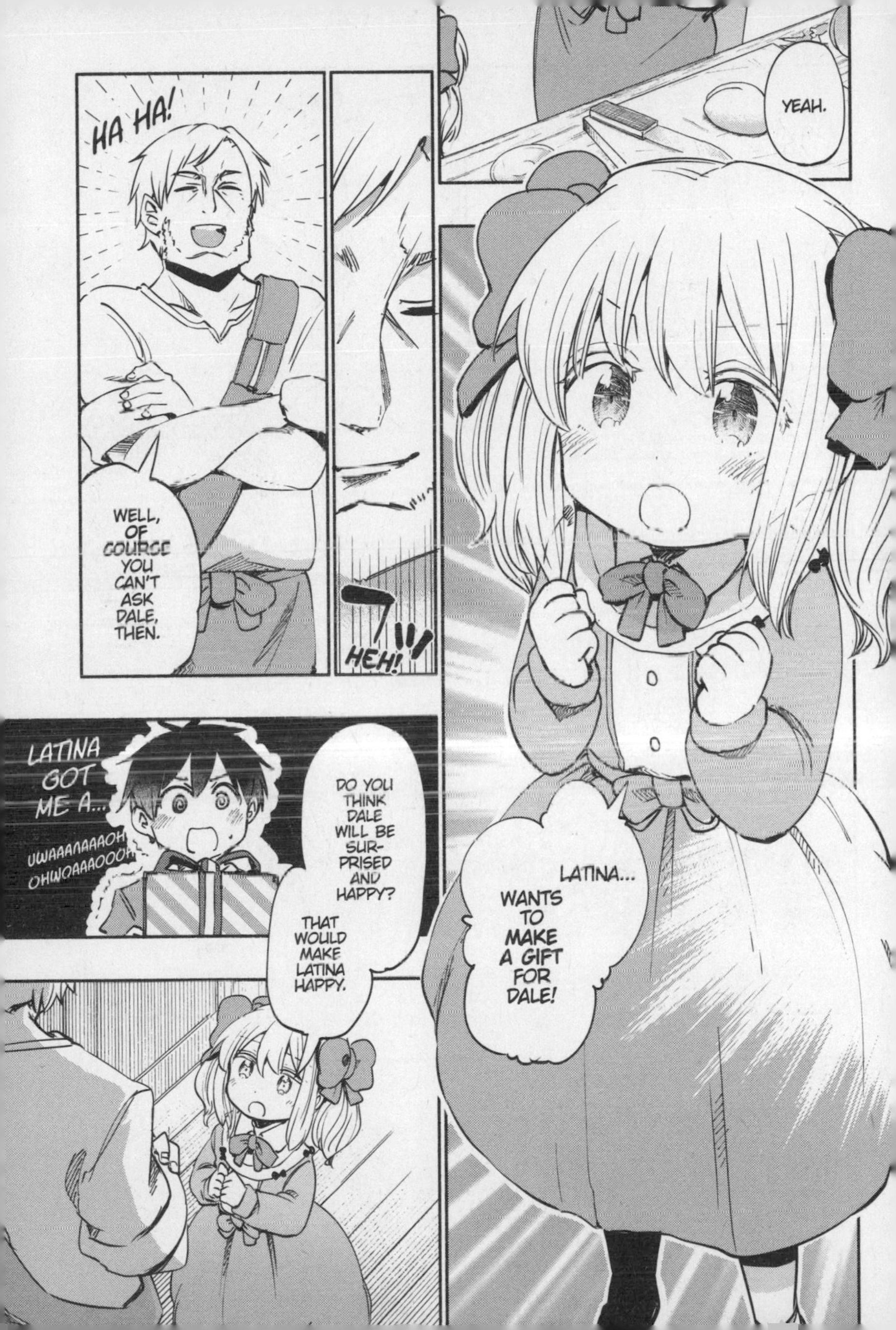
YEAH.
LATINA... WANTS TO MAKE A GIFT FOR DALE!
HEH!
HA HA!
WELL, OF COURSE YOU CAN'T ASK DALE, THEN.
LATINA GOT ME A...
UWAAANAAAOH OHWOAAAOOOH
DO YOU THINK DALE WILL BE SUR-PRISED AND HAPPY?
THAT WOULD MAKE LATINA HAPPY.

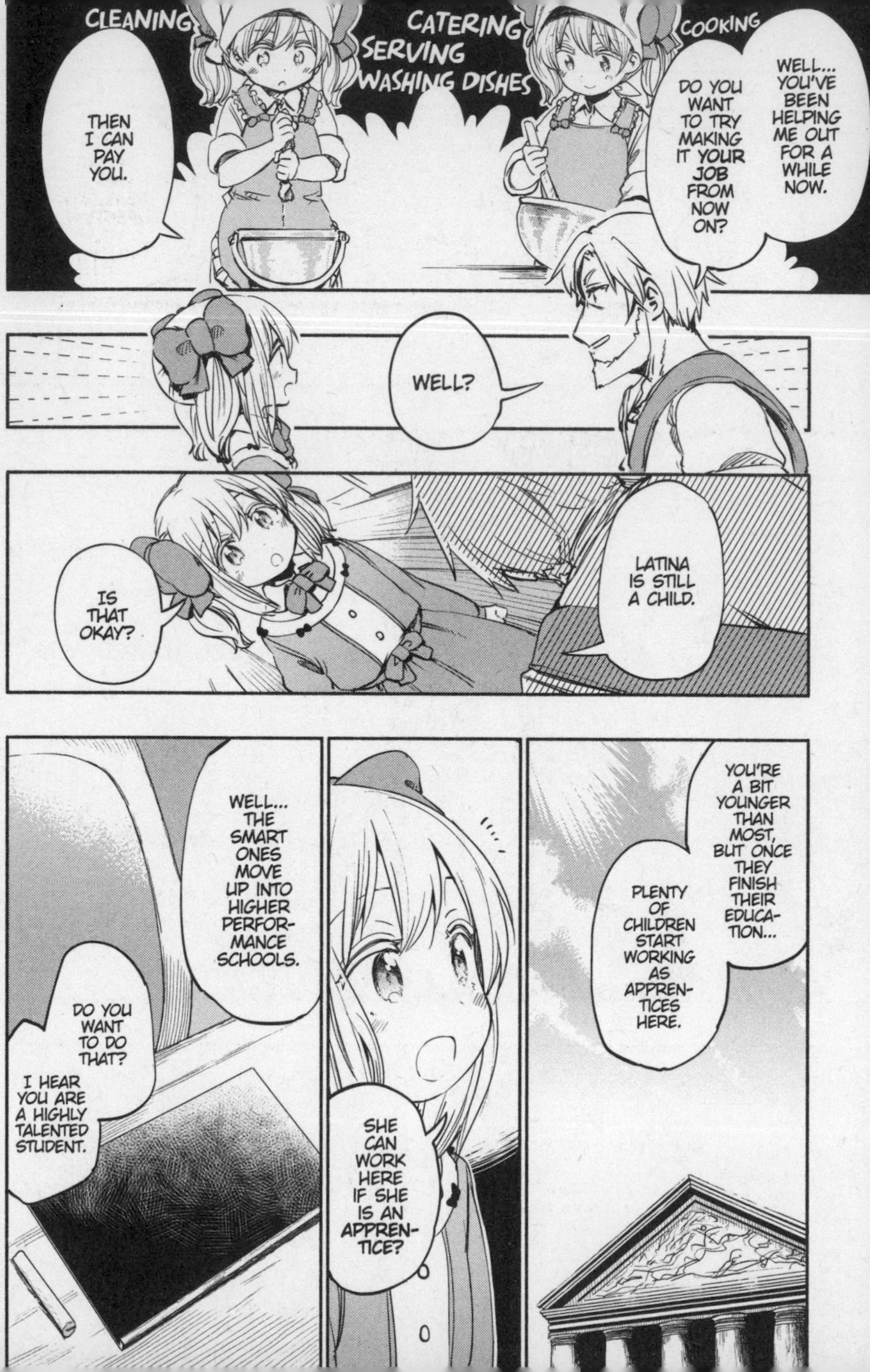
WELL... YOU'VE BEEN HELPING ME OUT FOR A WHILE NOW.
DO YOU WANT TO TRY MAKING IT YOUR JOB FROM NOW ON?
COOKING
CATERING
SERVING
WASHING DISHES
CLEANING
THEN I CAN PAY YOU.
WELL?
LATINA IS STILL A CHILD.
IS THAT OKAY?
YOU'RE A BIT YOUNGER THAN MOST, BUT ONCE THEY FINISH THEIR EDUCA-TION...
PLENTY OF CHILDREN START WORKING AS APPREN-TICES HERE.
SHE CAN WORK HERE IF SHE IS AN APPREN-TICE?
WELL... THE SMART ONES MOVE UP INTO HIGHER PERFOR-MANCE SCHOOLS.
DO YOU WANT TO DO THAT?
I HEAR YOU ARE A HIGHLY TALENTED STUDENT.

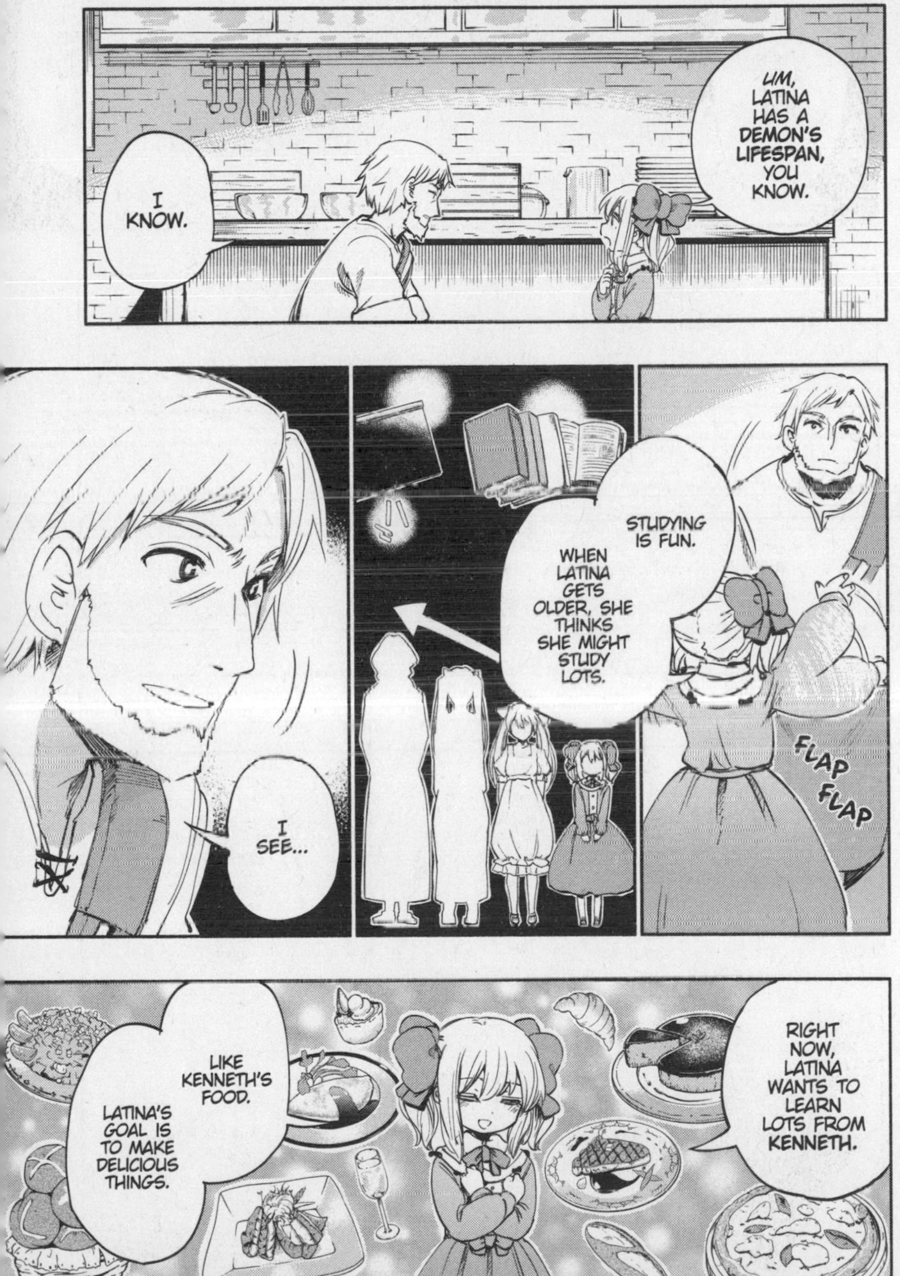
UM, LATINA HAS A DEMON'S LIFESPAN, YOU KNOW.
I KNOW.
STUDYING IS FUN.
WHEN LATINA GETS OLDER, SHE THINKS SHE MIGHT STUDY LOTS.
FLAP FLAP
I SEE...
RIGHT NOW, LATINA WANTS TO LEARN LOTS FROM KENNETH.
LATINA'S GOAL IS TO MAKE DELICIOUS THINGS.
LIKE KENNETH'S FOOD.

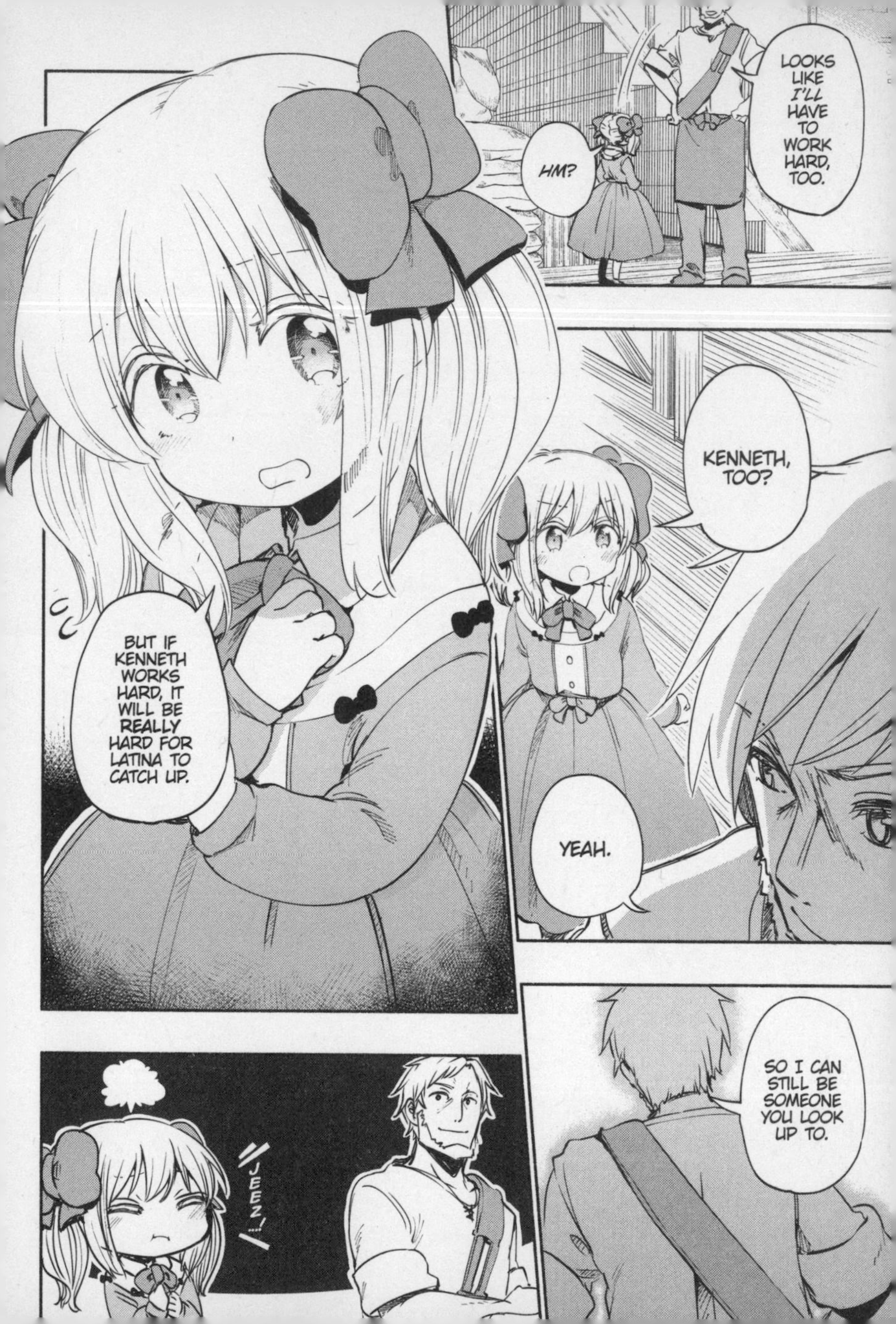
LOOKS LIKE I'LL HAVE TO WORK HARD, TOO.
HM?
KENNETH, TOO?
YEAH.
BUT IF KENNETH WORKS HARD, IT WILL BE REALLY HARD FOR LATINA TO CATCH UP.
SO I CAN STILL BE SOMEONE YOU LOOK UP TO.
JEEZ...!

If It's For My Daughter, I'd Even Defeat a Demon Lord

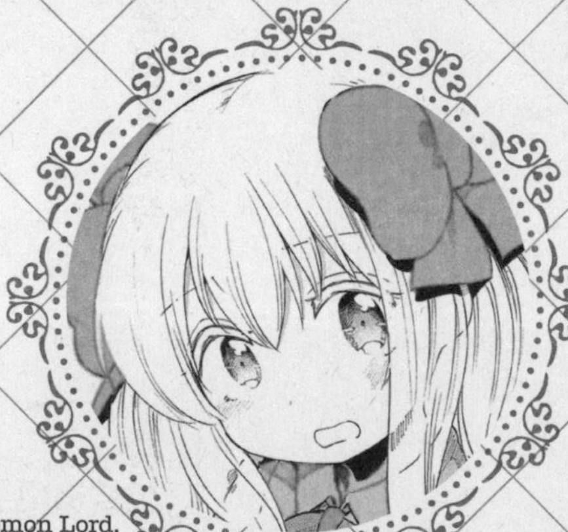

If It's For My Daughter, I'd Even Defeat a Demon Lord.

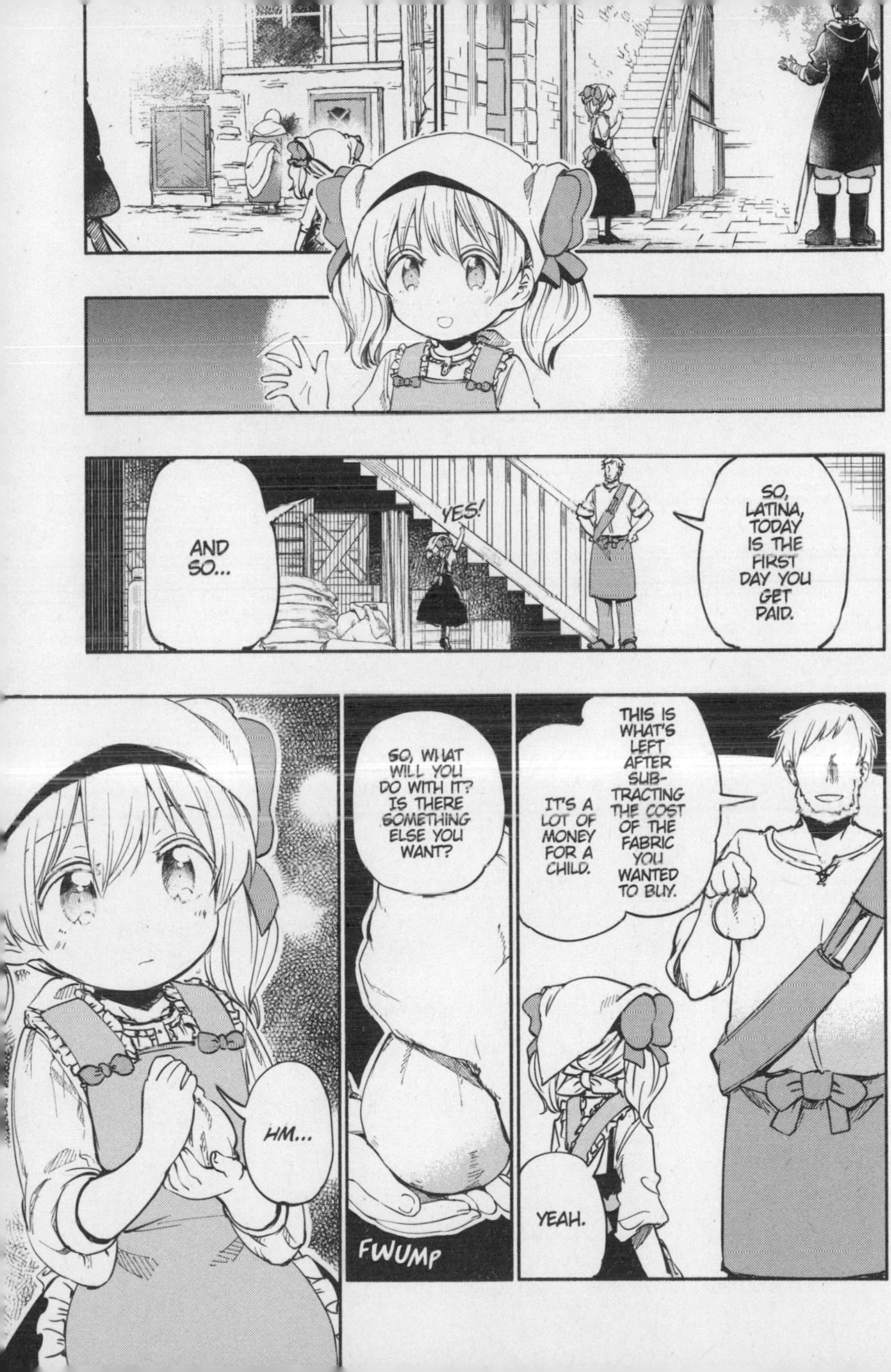
SO, LATINA, TODAY IS THE FIRST DAY YOU GET PAID.
YES!
AND SO...
THIS IS WHAT'S LEFT AFTER SUB-TRACTING THE COST OF THE FABRIC YOU WANTED TO BUY.
IT'S A LOT OF MONEY FOR A CHILD.
YEAH.
SO, WHAT WILL YOU DO WITH IT? IS THERE SOMETHING ELSE YOU WANT?
FWUMP
HM...

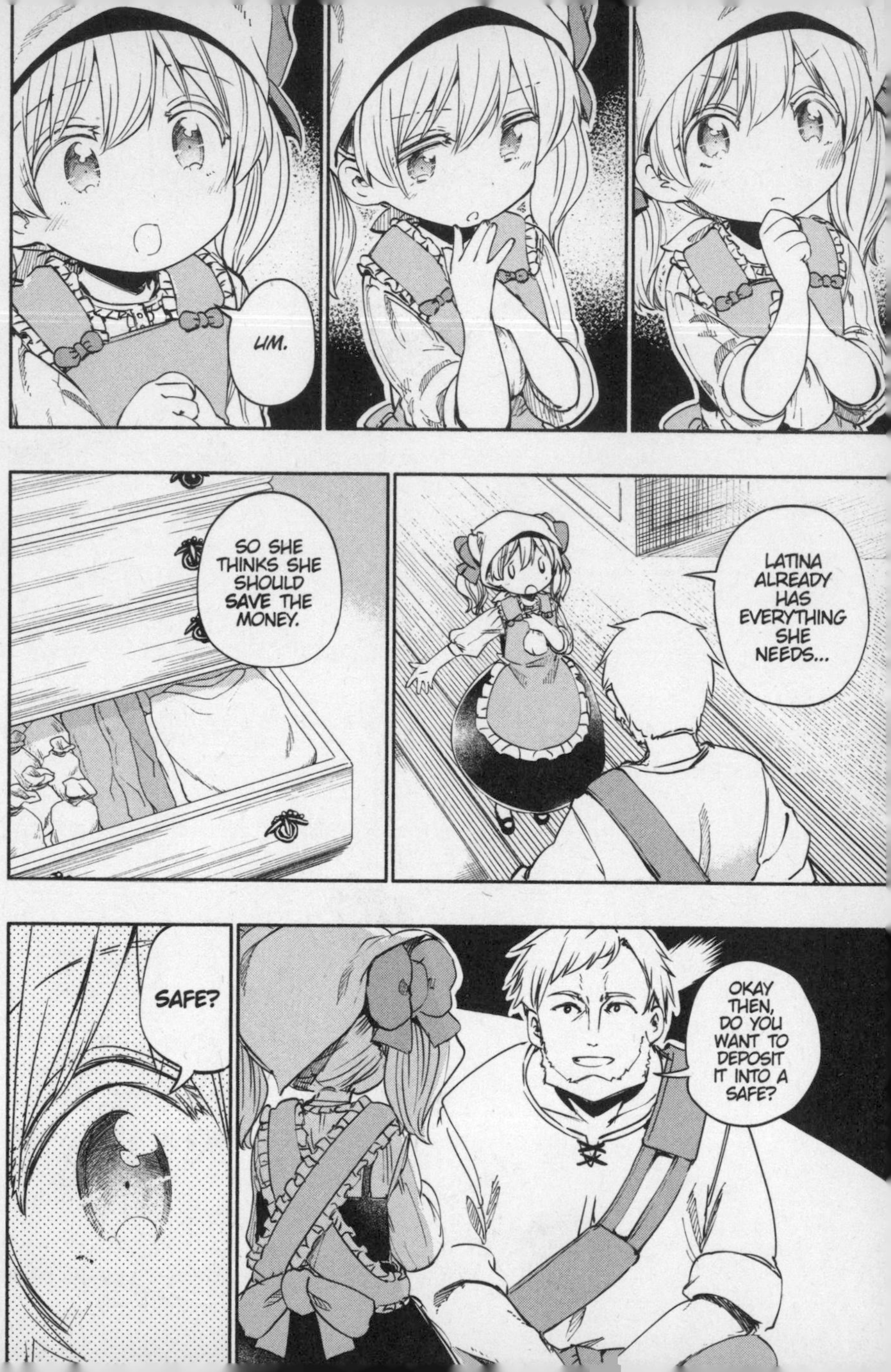
UM.
LATINA ALREADY HAS EVERYTHING SHE NEEDS...
SO SHE THINKS SHE SHOULD SAVE THE MONEY.
OKAY THEN, DO YOU WANT TO DEPOSIT IT INTO A SAFE?
SAFE?

20. Little Girl's First Deposit

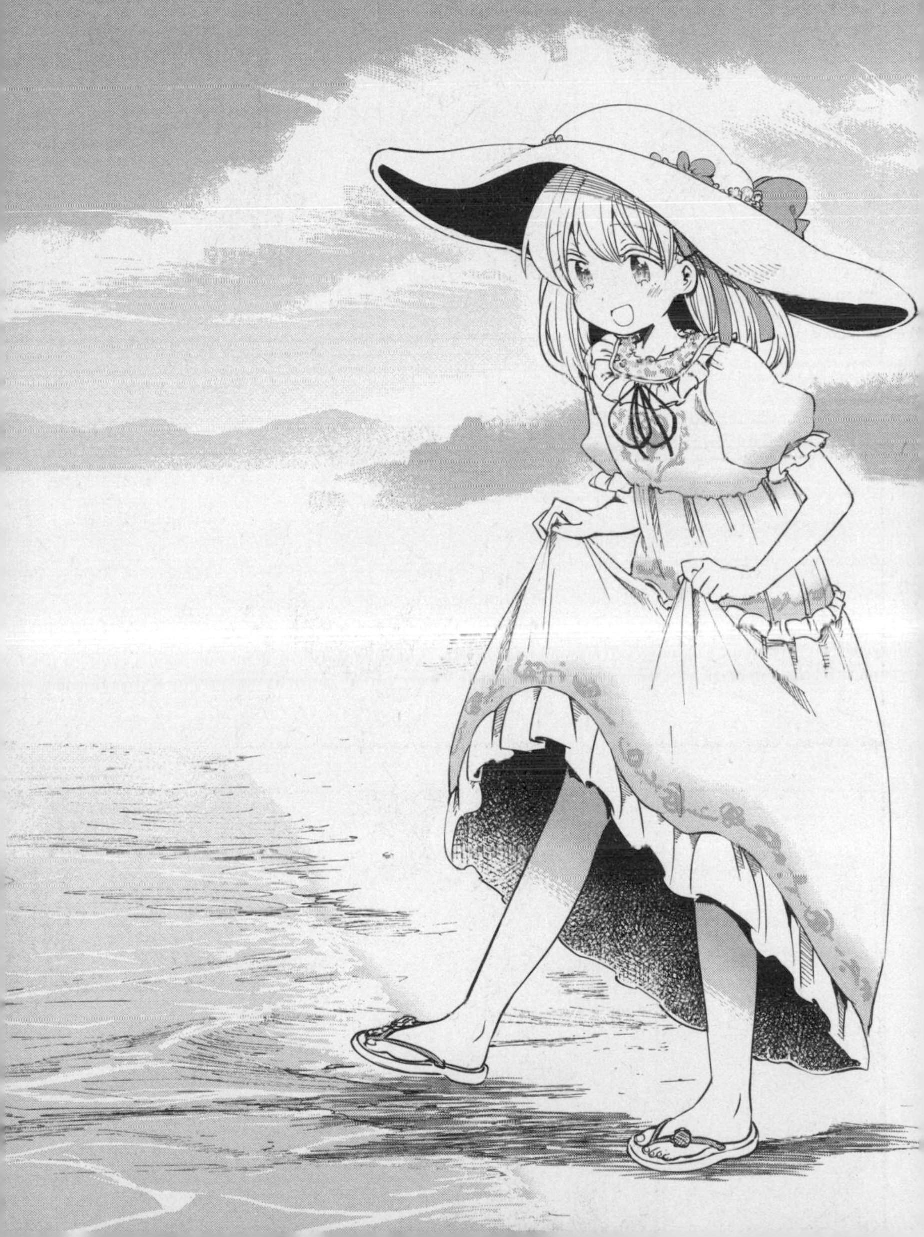

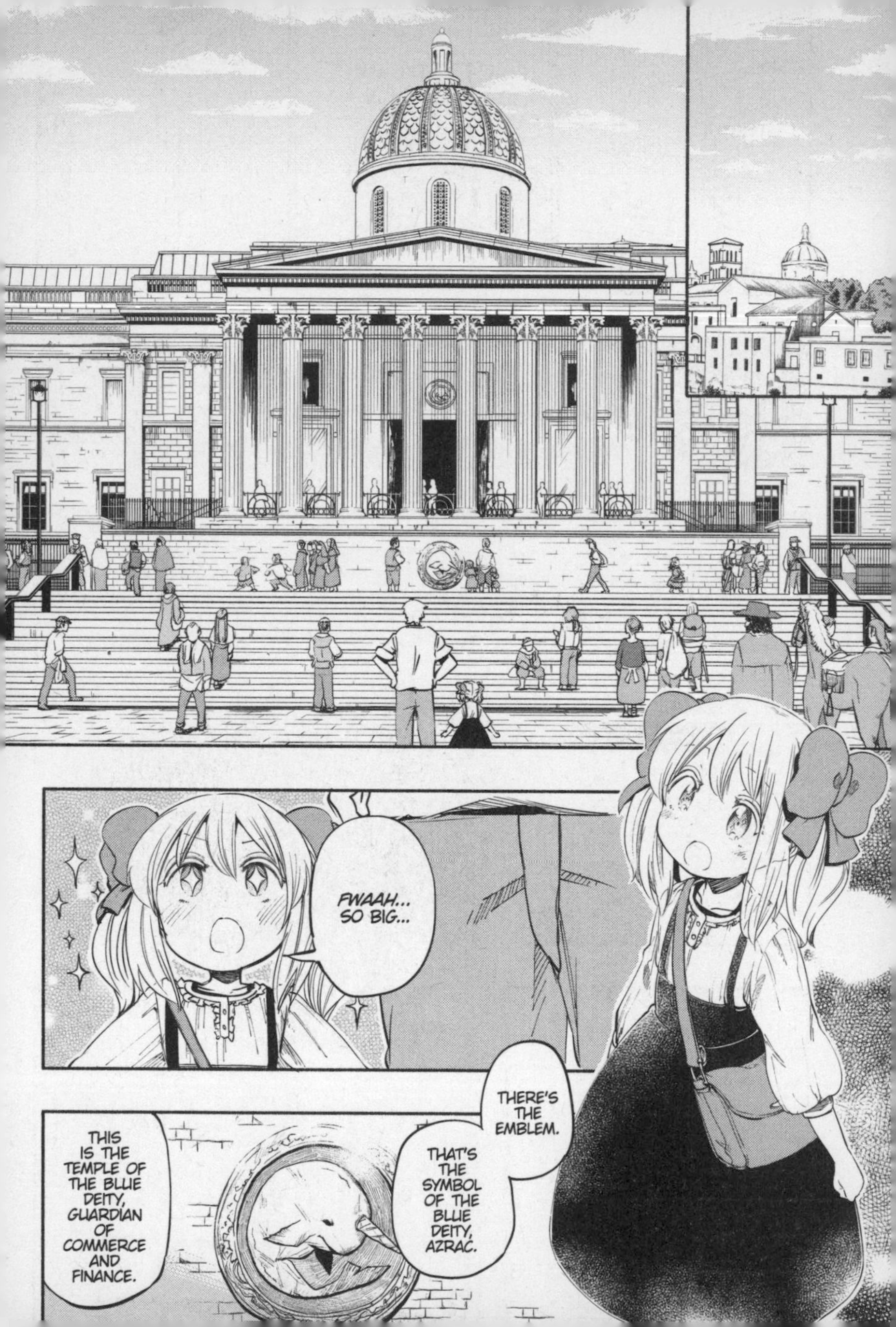
FWAAH... SO BIG...
THERE'S THE EMBLEM.
THAT'S THE SYMBOL OF THE BLUE DEITY, AZRAC.
THIS IS THE TEMPLE OF THE BLUE DEITY, GUARDIAN OF COMMERCE AND FINANCE.

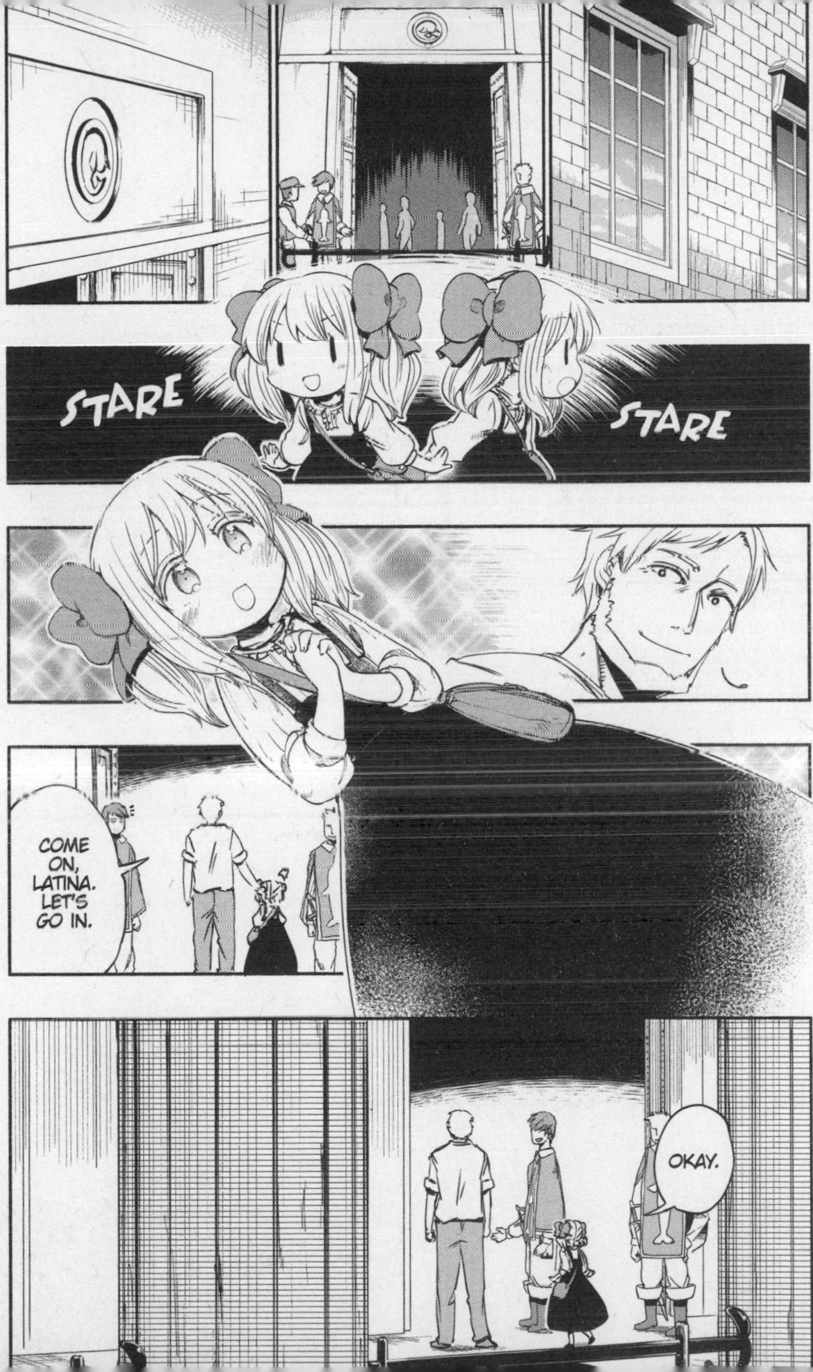
STARE
STARE
COME ON, LATINA. LET'S GO IN.
OKAY.

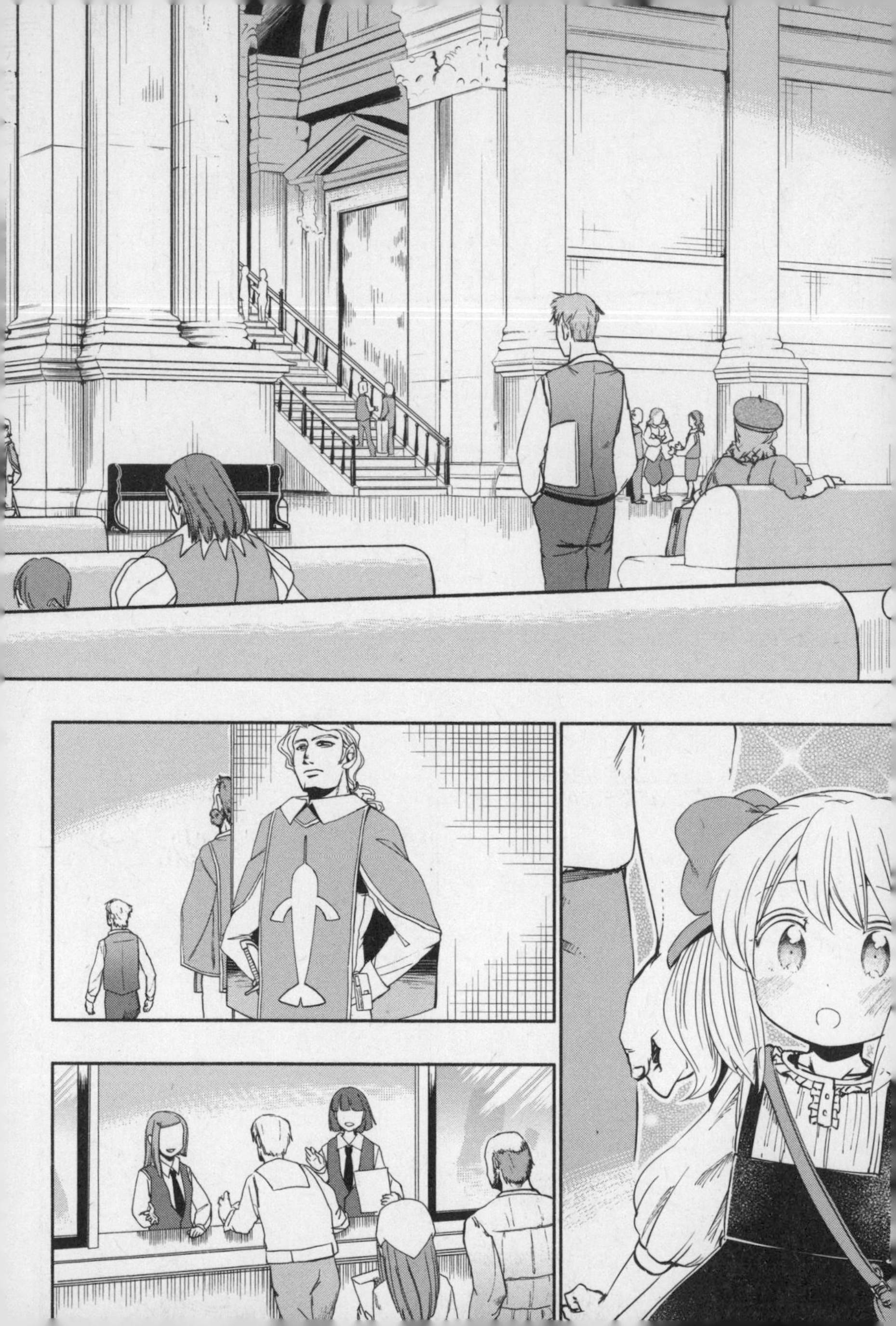

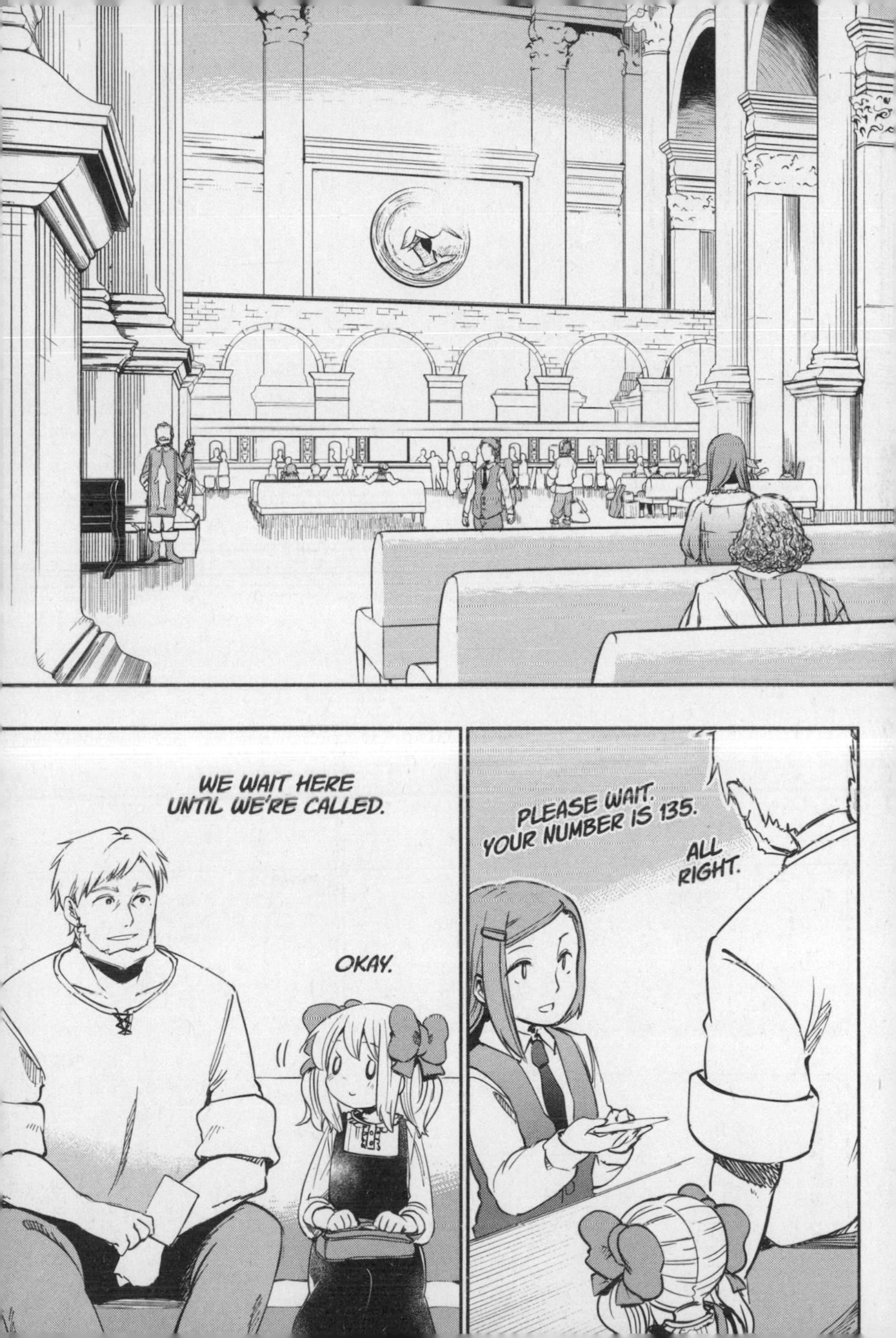
PLEASE WAIT. YOUR NUMBER IS 135.
ALL RIGHT.
WE WAIT HERE UNTIL WE'RE CALLED.
OKAY.

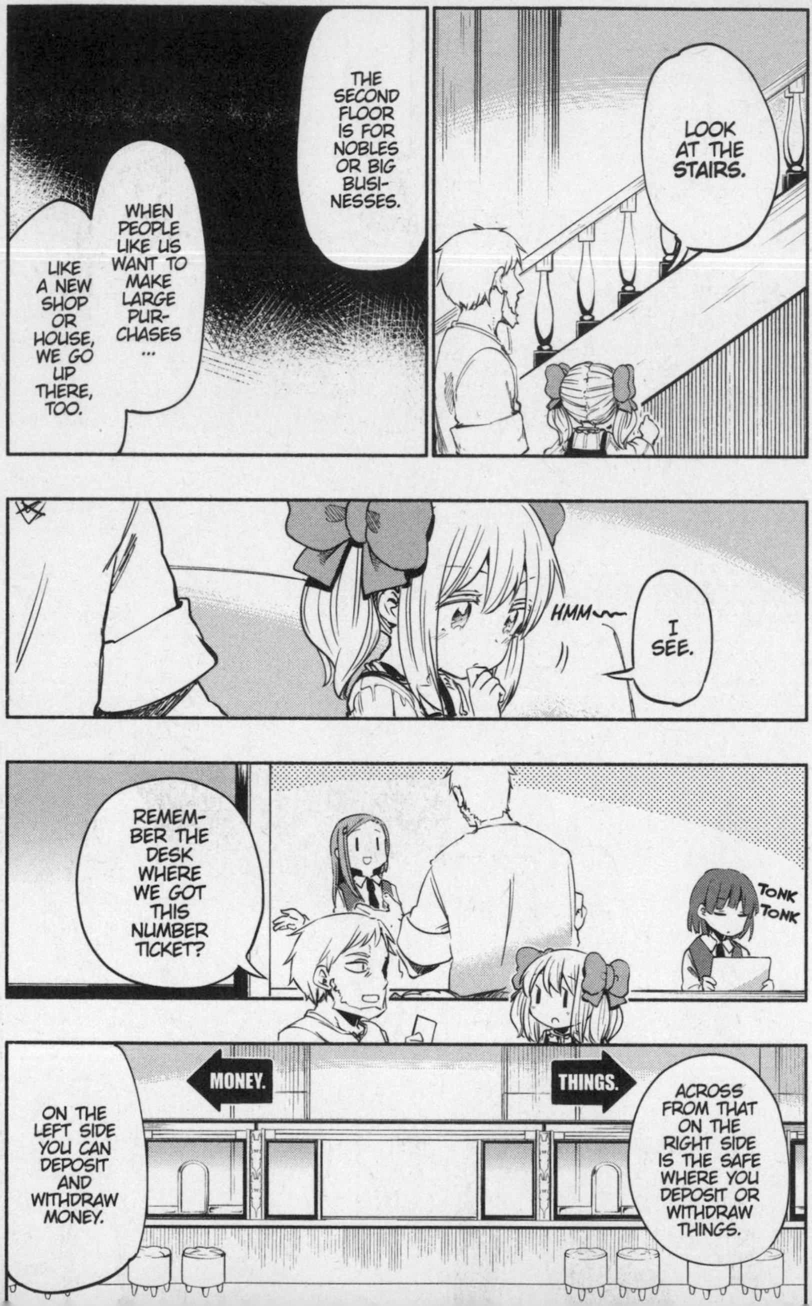
LOOK AT THE STAIRS.
THE SECOND FLOOR IS FOR NOBLES OR BIG BUSI-NESSES.
WHEN PEOPLE LIKE US WANT TO MAKE LARGE PUR-CHASES ...
LIKE A NEW SHOP OR HOUSE, WE GO UP THERE, TOO.
I SEE.
HMM~~
TONK TONK
REMEM-BER THE DESK WHERE WE GOT THIS NUMBER TICKET?
THINGS.
MONEY.
ON THE LEFT SIDE YOU CAN DEPOSIT AND WITHDRAW MONEY.
ACROSS FROM THAT ON THE RIGHT SIDE IS THE SAFE WHERE YOU DEPOSIT OR WITHDRAW THINGS.

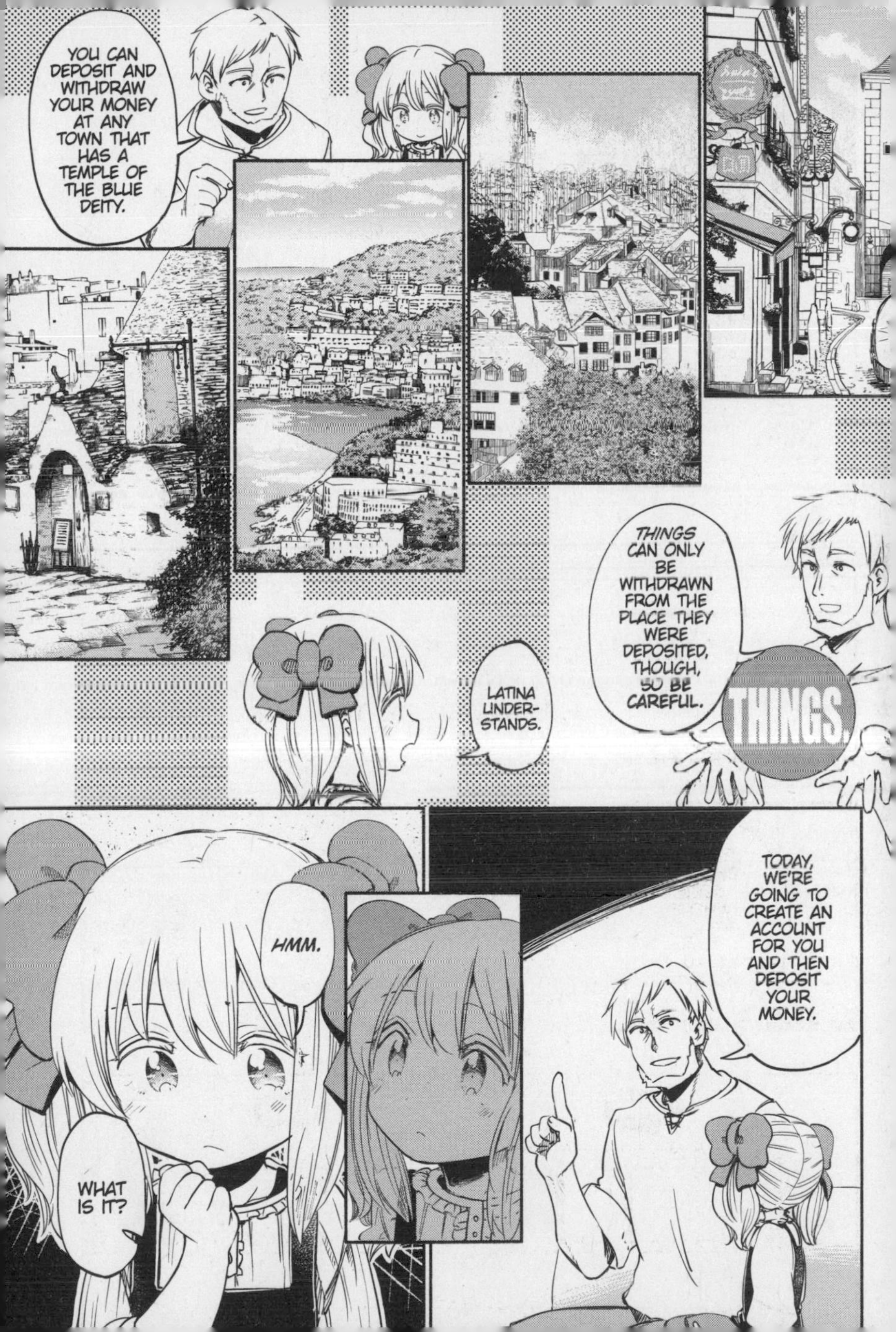
YOU CAN DEPOSIT AND WITHDRAW YOUR MONEY AT ANY TOWN THAT HAS A TEMPLE OF THE BLUE DEITY.
THINGS CAN ONLY BE WITHDRAWN FROM THE PLACE THEY WERE DEPOSITED, THOUGH, SO BE CAREFUL.
THINGS.
LATINA UNDER-STANDS.
TODAY, WE'RE GOING TO CREATE AN ACCOUNT FOR YOU AND THEN DEPOSIT YOUR MONEY.
HMM.
WHAT IS IT?

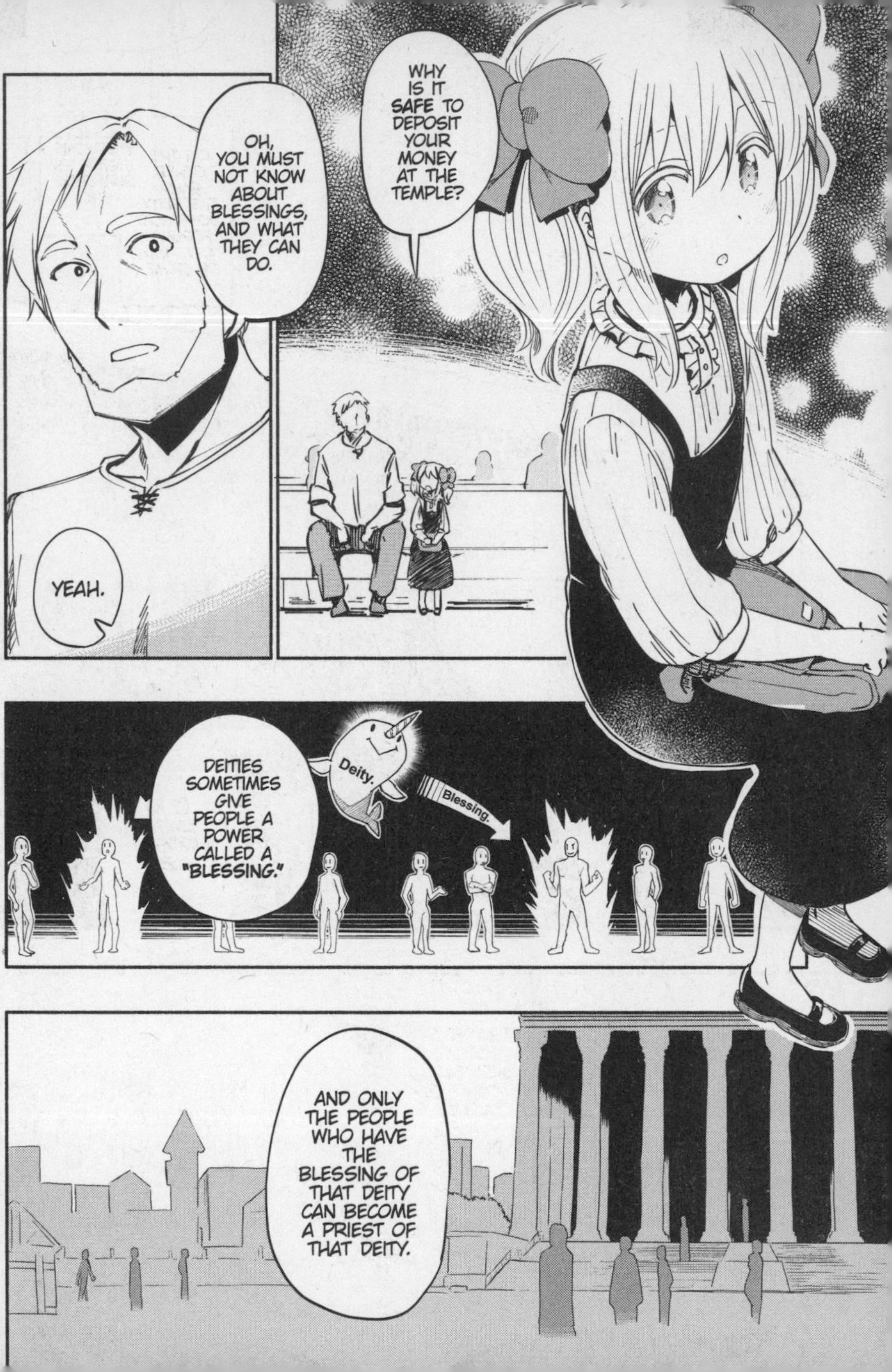

WHY IS IT SAFE TO DEPOSIT YOUR MONEY AT THE TEMPLE?
OH, YOU MUST NOT KNOW ABOUT BLESSINGS, AND WHAT THEY CAN DO.
YEAH.
Deity.
Blessing.
DEITIES SOMETIMES GIVE PEOPLE A POWER CALLED A "BLESSING."
AND ONLY THE PEOPLE WHO HAVE THE BLESSING OF THAT DEITY CAN BECOME A PRIEST OF THAT DEITY.

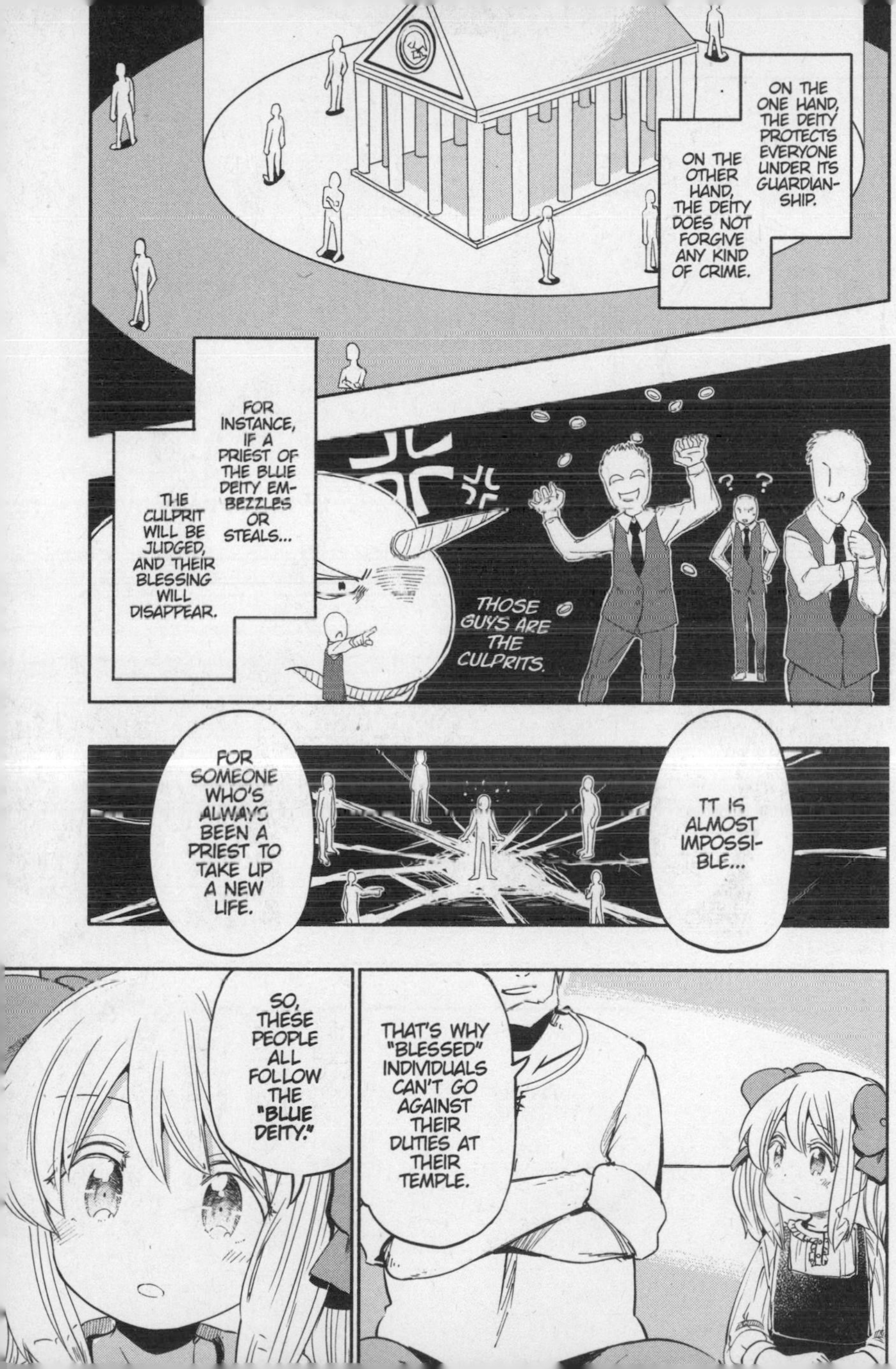
ON THE ONE HAND, THE DEITY PROTECTS EVERYONE UNDER ITS GUARDIANSHIP.
ON THE OTHER HAND, THE DEITY DOES NOT FORGIVE ANY KIND OF CRIME.
FOR INSTANCE, IF A PRIEST OF THE BLUE DEITY EMBEZZLES OR STEALS...
THE CULPRIT WILL BE JUDGED, AND THEIR BLESSING WILL DISAPPEAR.
THOSE GUYS ARE THE CULPRITS.
IT IS ALMOST IMPOSSIBLE...
FOR SOMEONE WHO'S ALWAYS BEEN A PRIEST TO TAKE UP A NEW LIFE.
THAT'S WHY "BLESSED" INDIVIDUALS CAN'T GO AGAINST THEIR DUTIES AT THEIR TEMPLE.
SO, THESE PEOPLE ALL FOLLOW THE "BLUE DEITY."

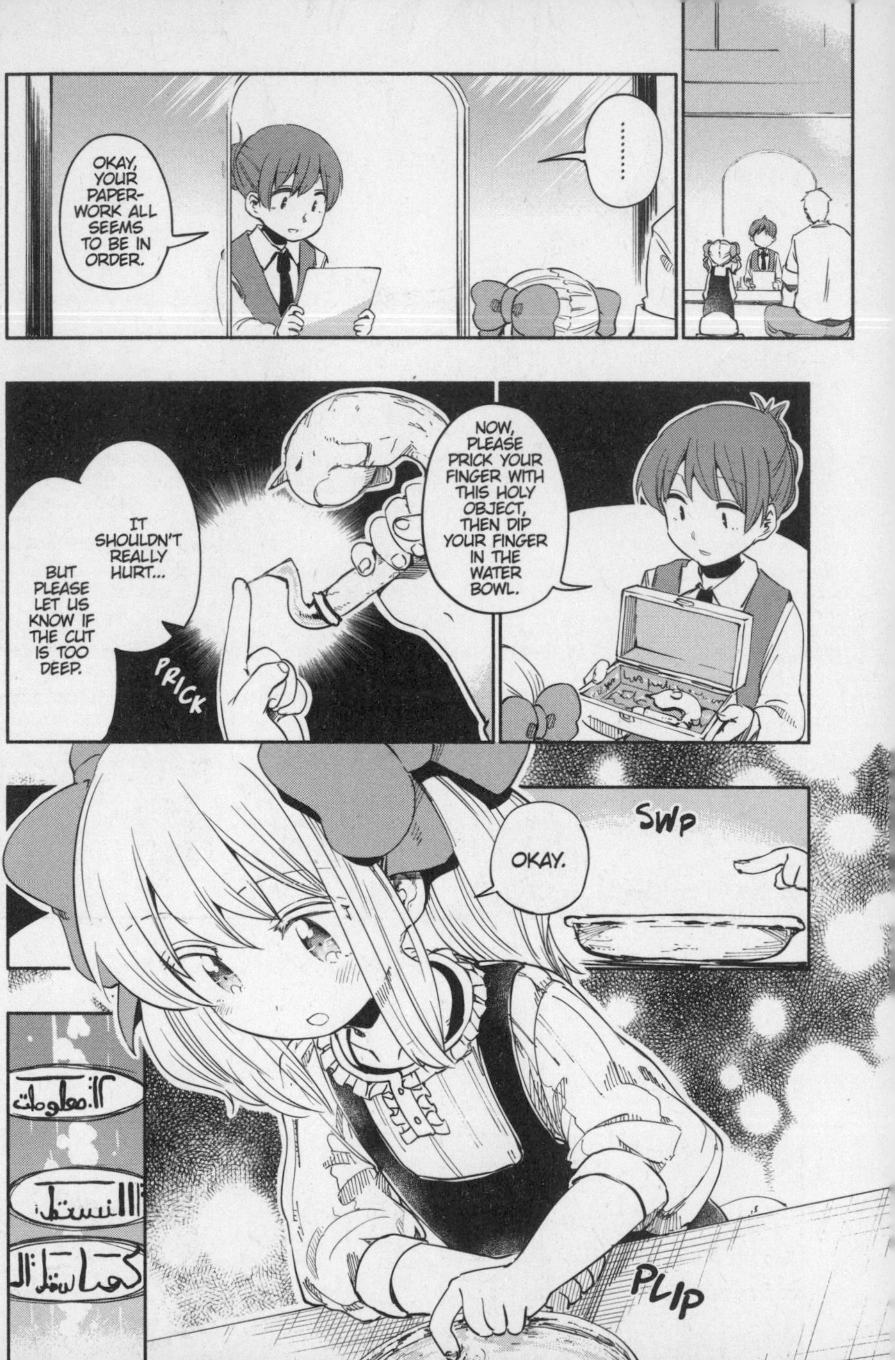
......
OKAY, YOUR PAPER-WORK ALL SEEMS TO BE IN ORDER.
NOW, PLEASE PRICK YOUR FINGER WITH THIS HOLY OBJECT, THEN DIP YOUR FINGER IN THE WATER BOWL.
IT SHOULDN'T REALLY HURT...
BUT PLEASE LET US KNOW IF THE CUT IS TOO DEEP.
PRICK
SWP
OKAY.
PLIP

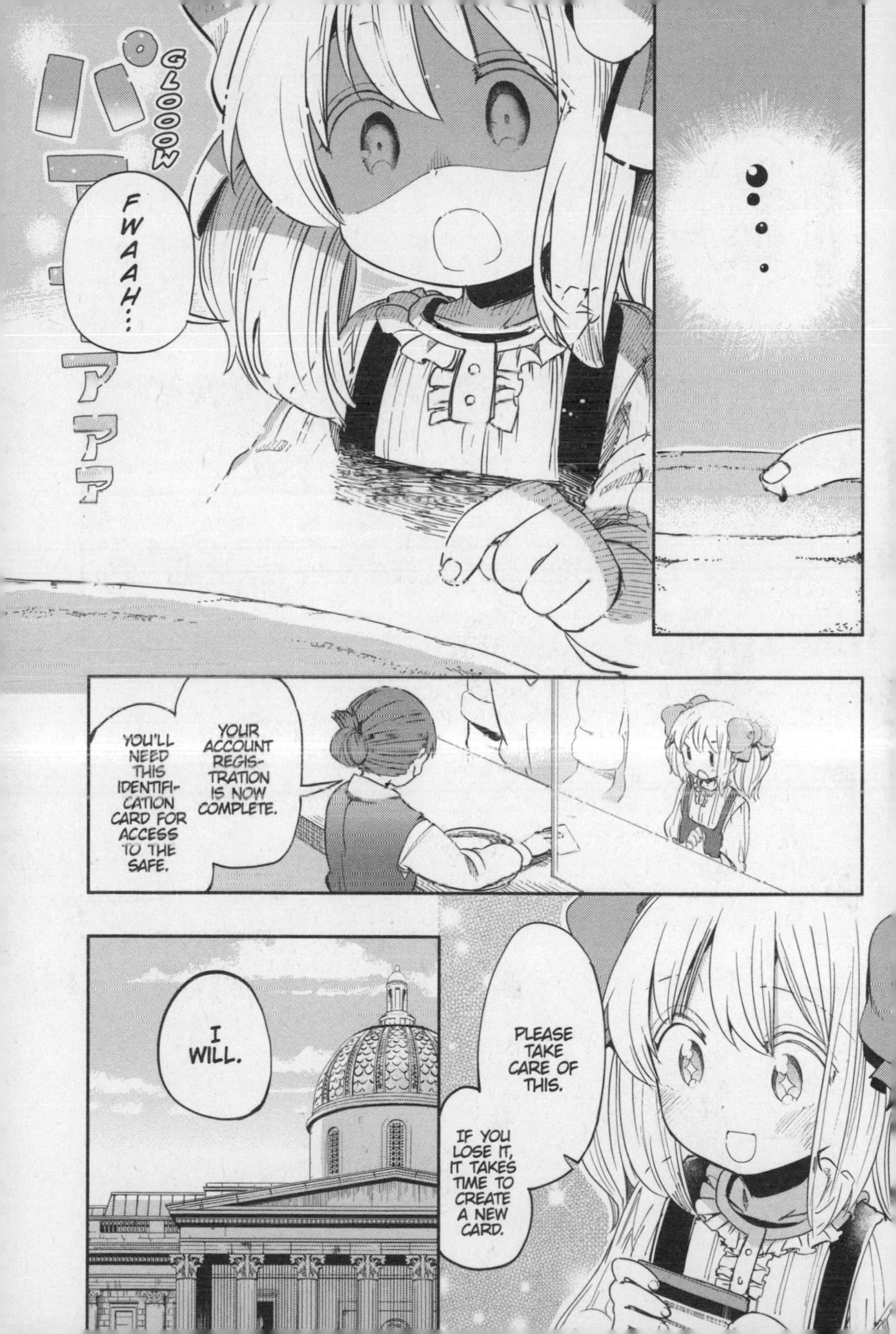
GLOOOW
FWAAH...
YOUR ACCOUNT REGIS- TRATION IS NOW COMPLETE.
YOU'LL NEED THIS IDENTIFI- CATION CARD FOR ACCESS TO THE SAFE.
PLEASE TAKE CARE OF THIS.
IF YOU LOSE IT, IT TAKES TIME TO CREATE A NEW CARD.
I WILL.

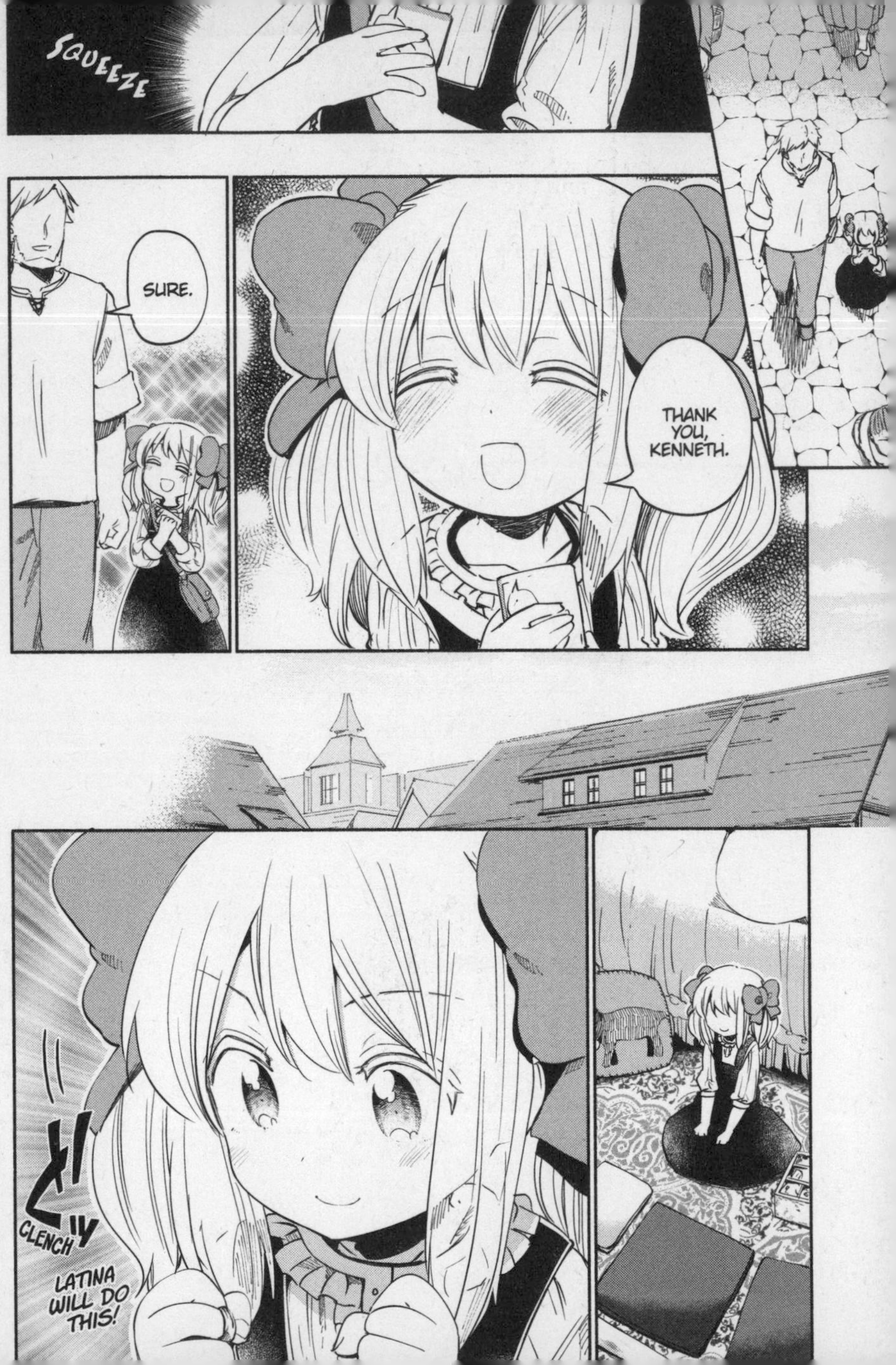
SQUEEZE
THANK YOU, KENNETH.
SURE.
CLENCH
LATINA WILL DO THIS!

If It's For My Daughter I'd Even Defeat a Demon Lord

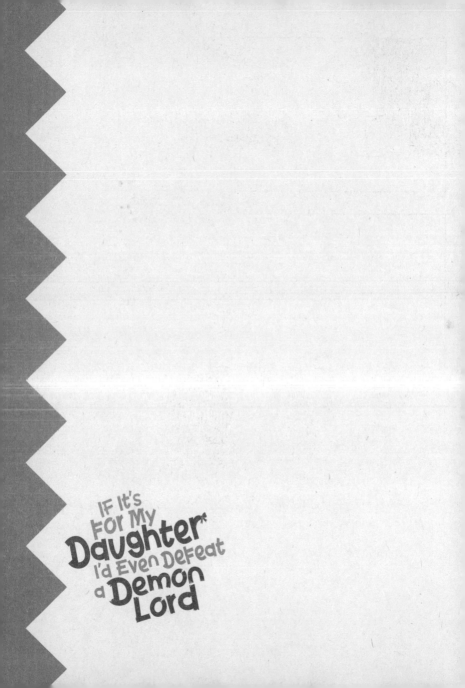

If It's For My Daughter, I'd Even Defeat a Demon Lord.

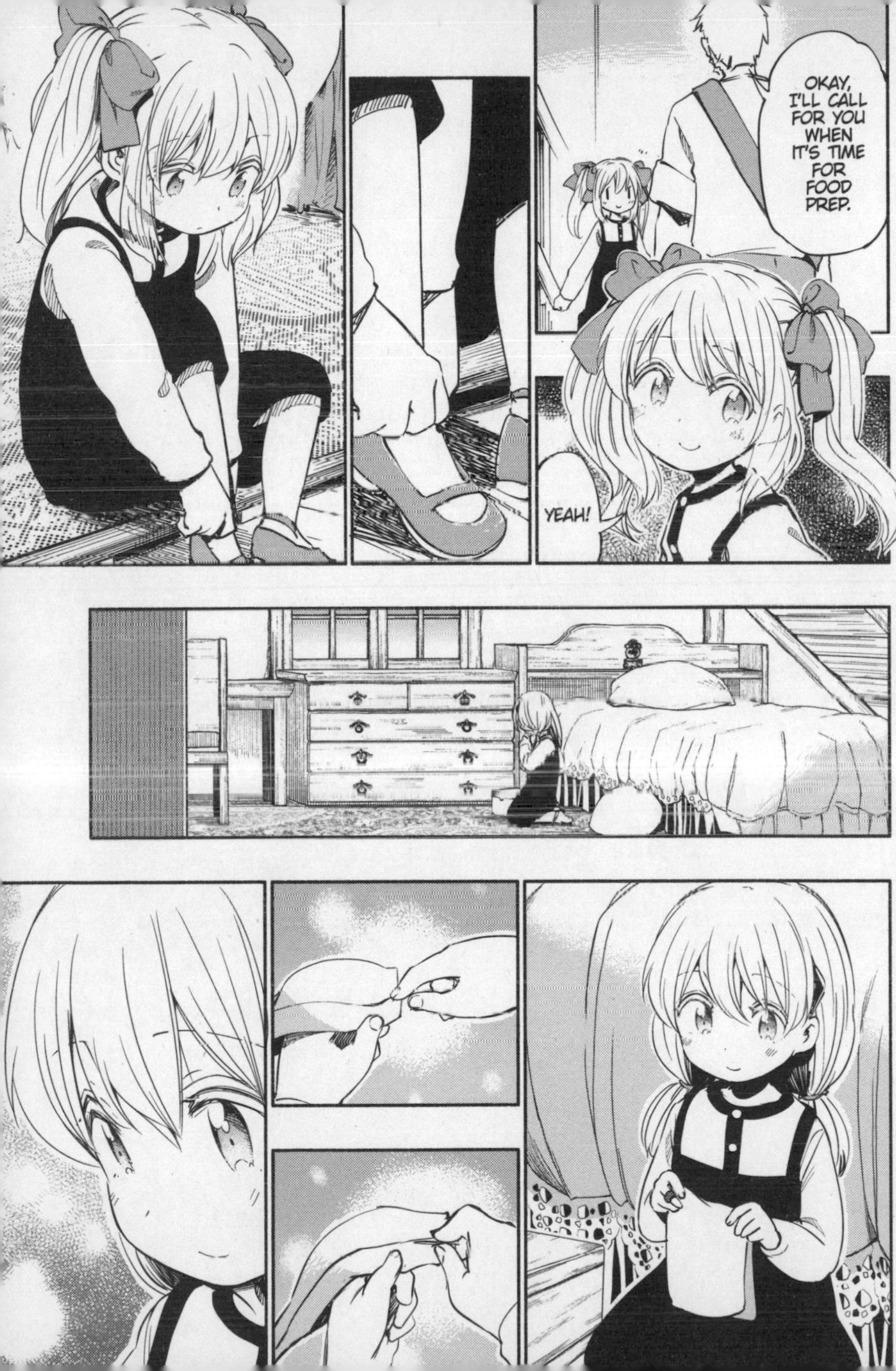
OKAY, I'LL CALL FOR YOU WHEN IT'S TIME FOR FOOD PREP.
YEAH!

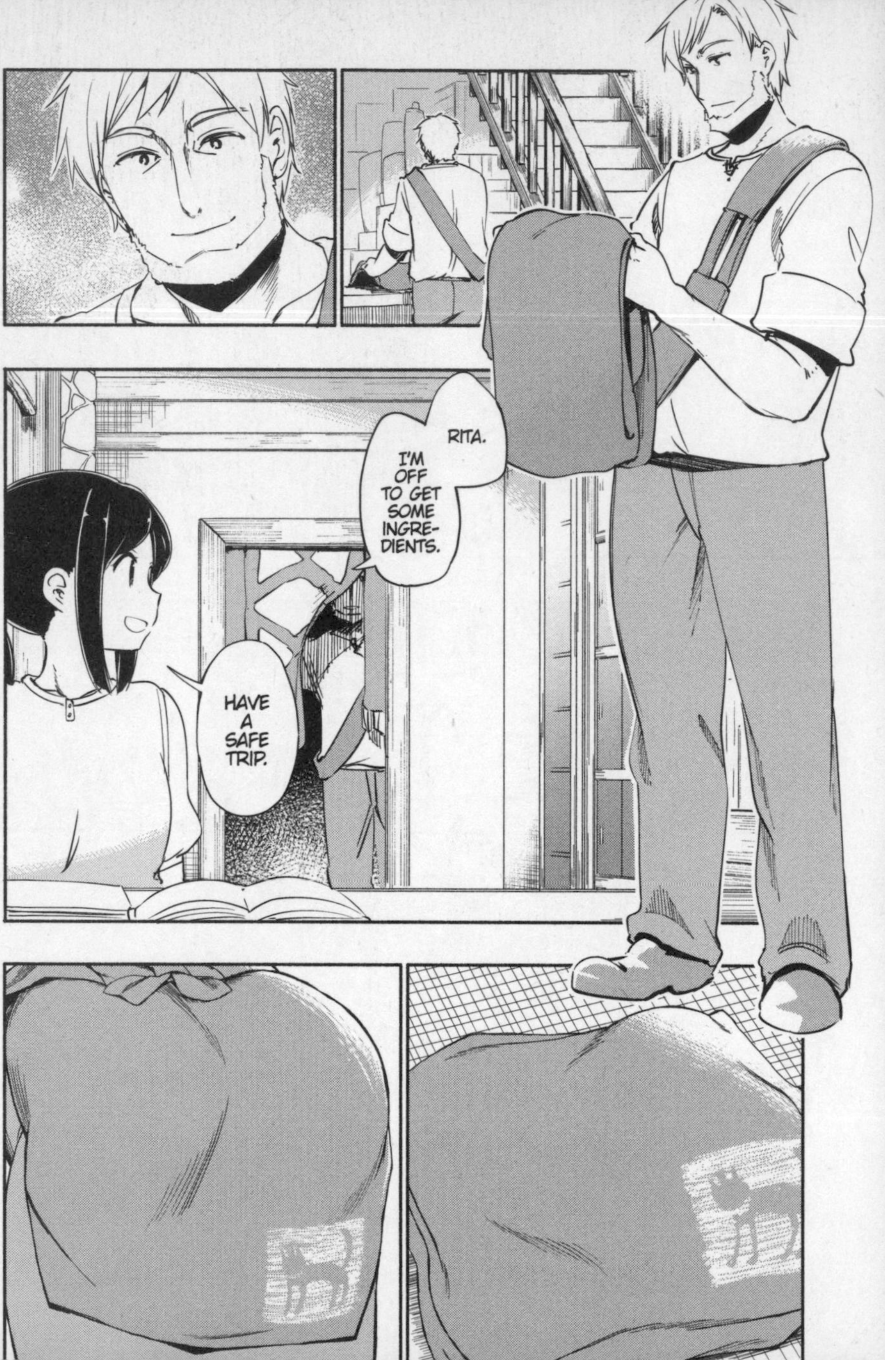
RITA.
I'M OFF TO GET SOME INGRE-DIENTS.
HAVE A SAFE TRIP.

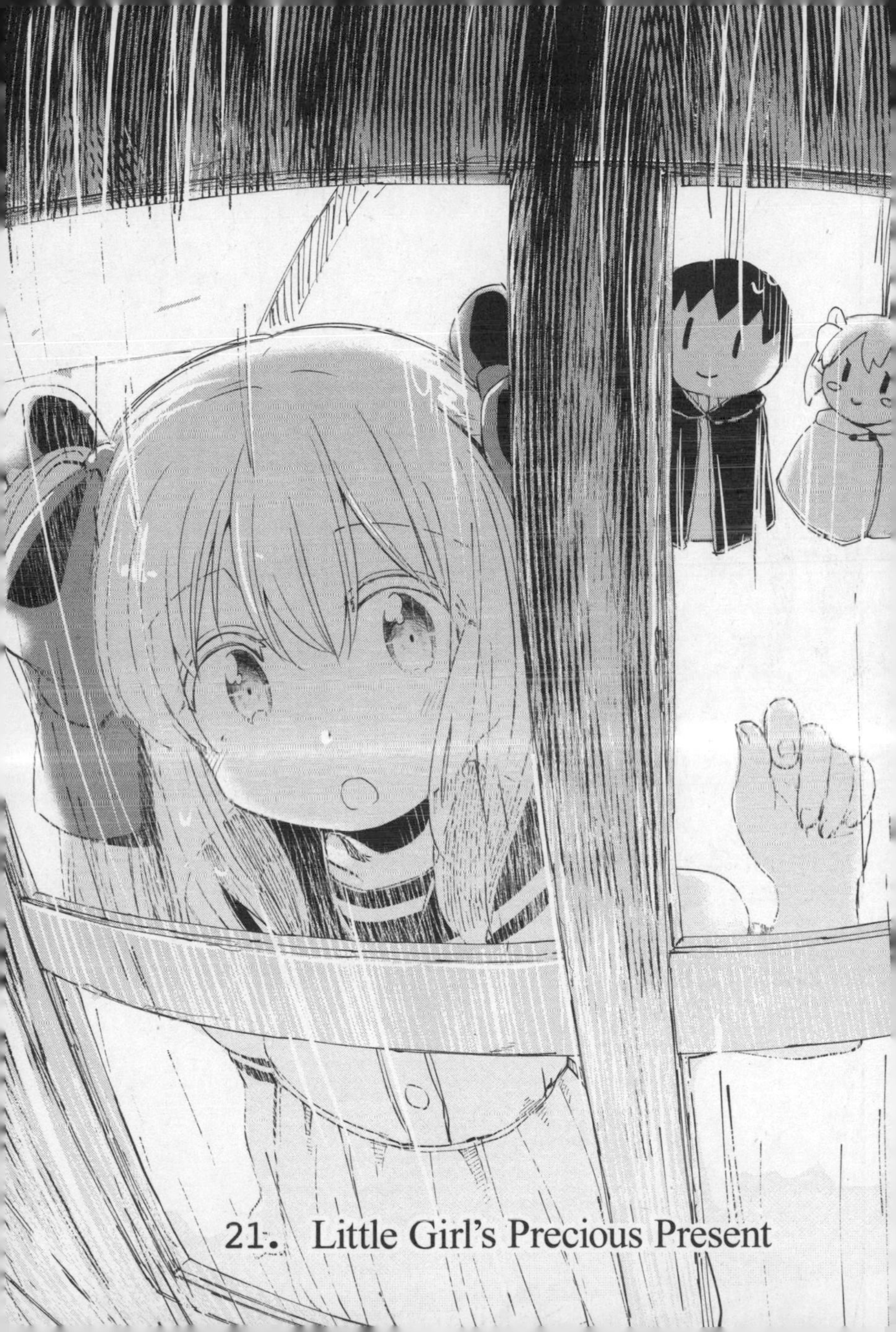

21. Little Girl's Precious Present

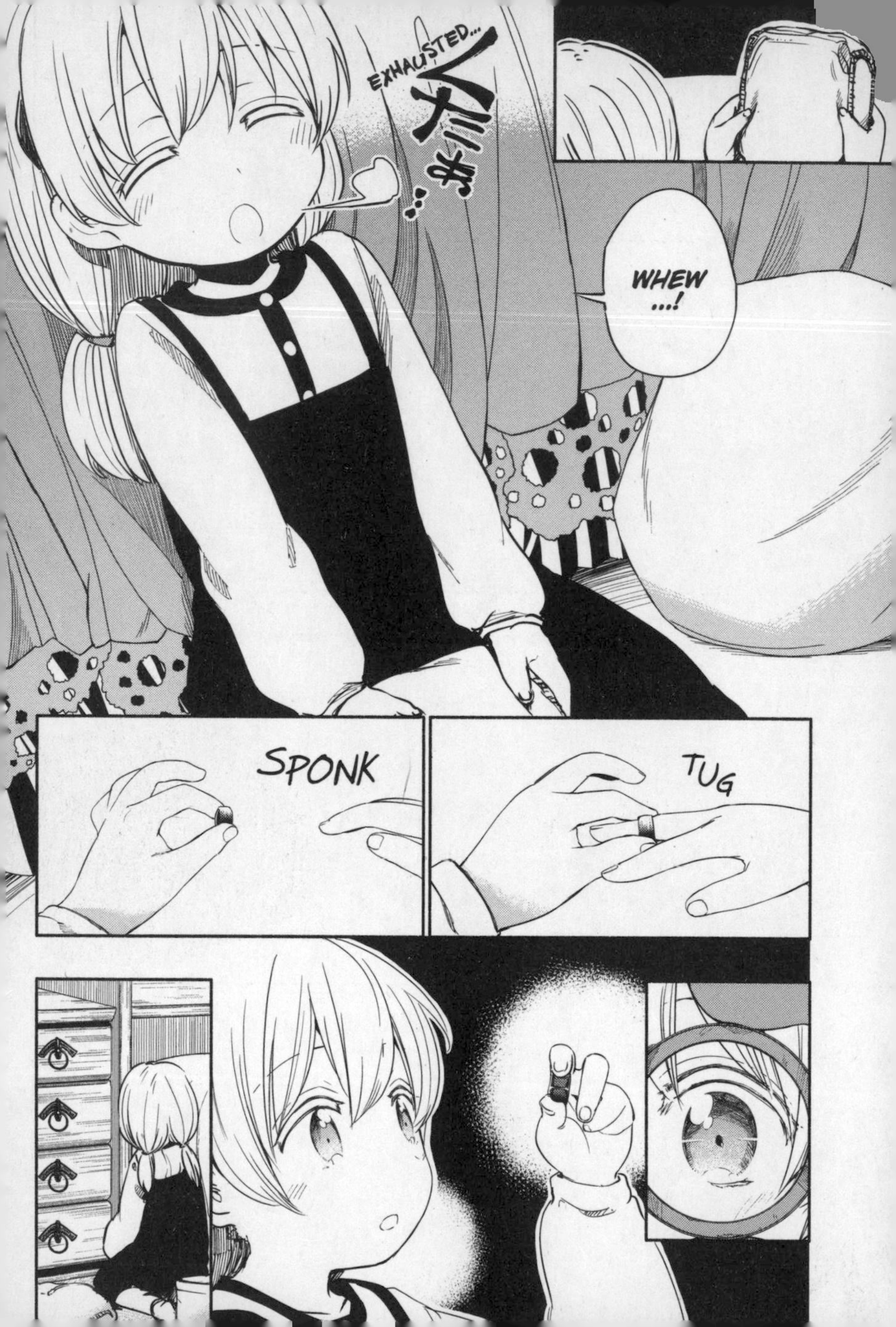
EXHAUSTED...
WHEW ...!
TUG
SPONK

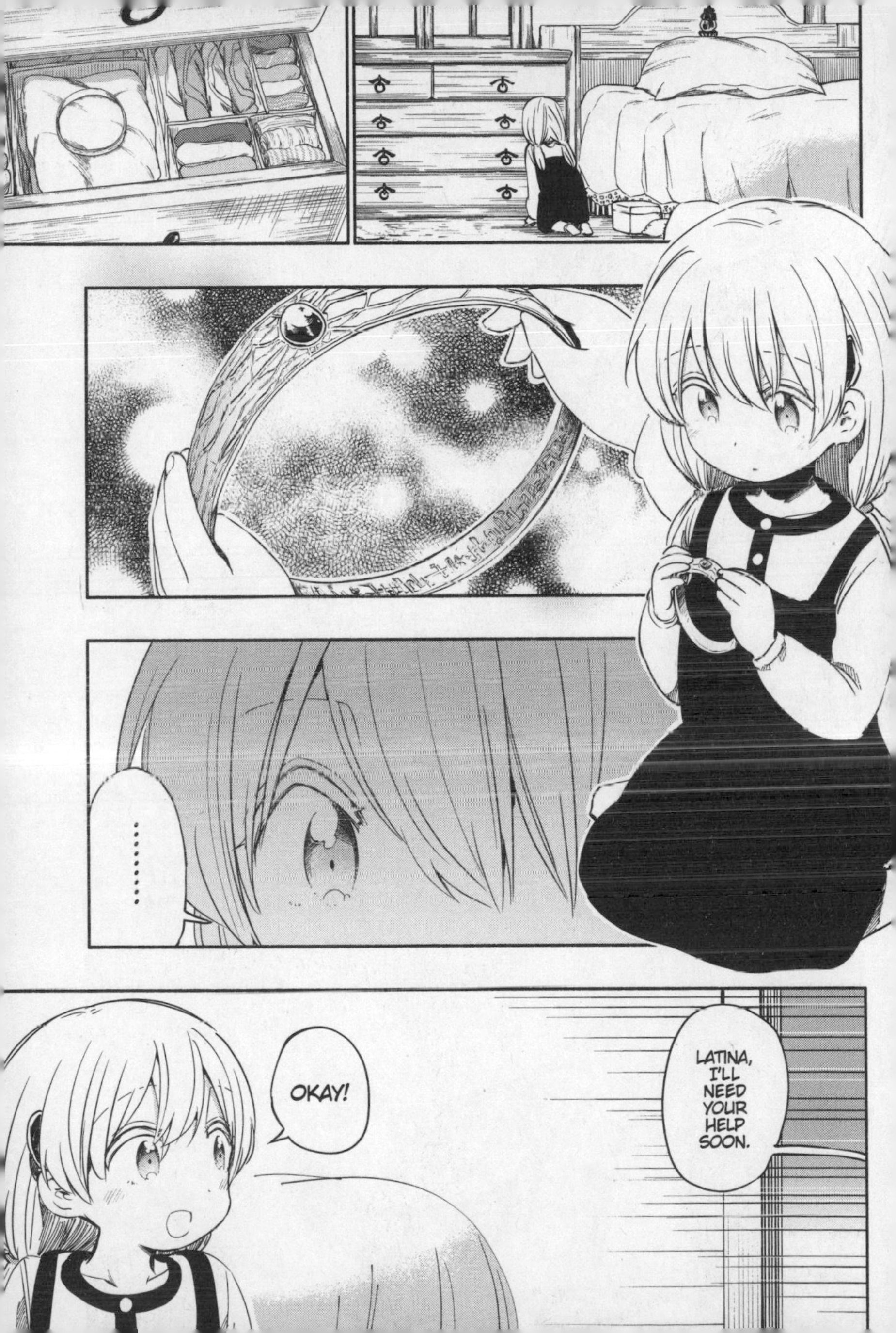
......
LATINA, I'LL NEED YOUR HELP SOON.
OKAY!

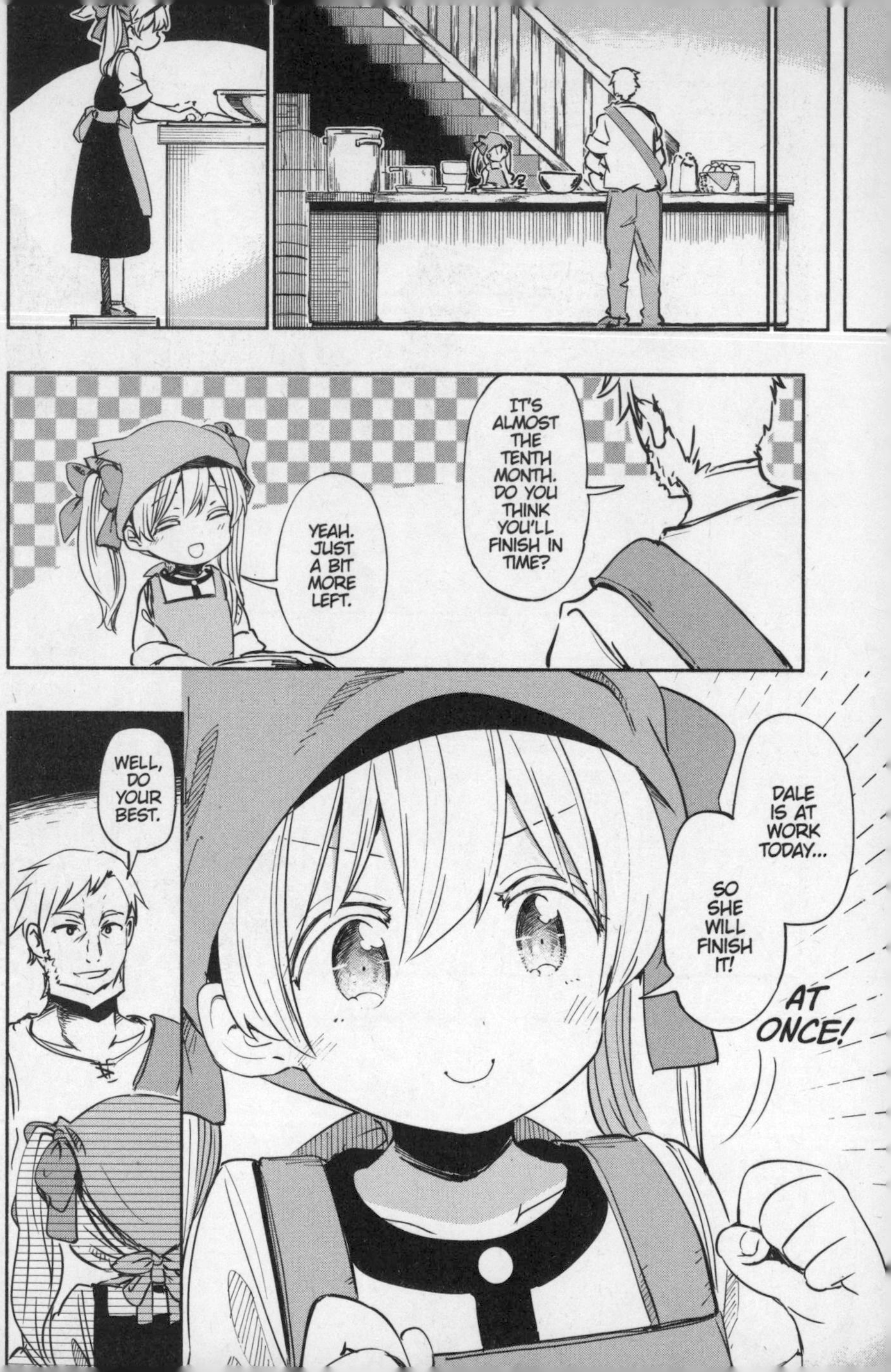
IT'S ALMOST THE TENTH MONTH. DO YOU THINK YOU'LL FINISH IN TIME?
YEAH. JUST A BIT MORE LEFT.
DALE IS AT WORK TODAY...
SO SHE WILL FINISH IT!
AT ONCE!
WELL, DO YOUR BEST.

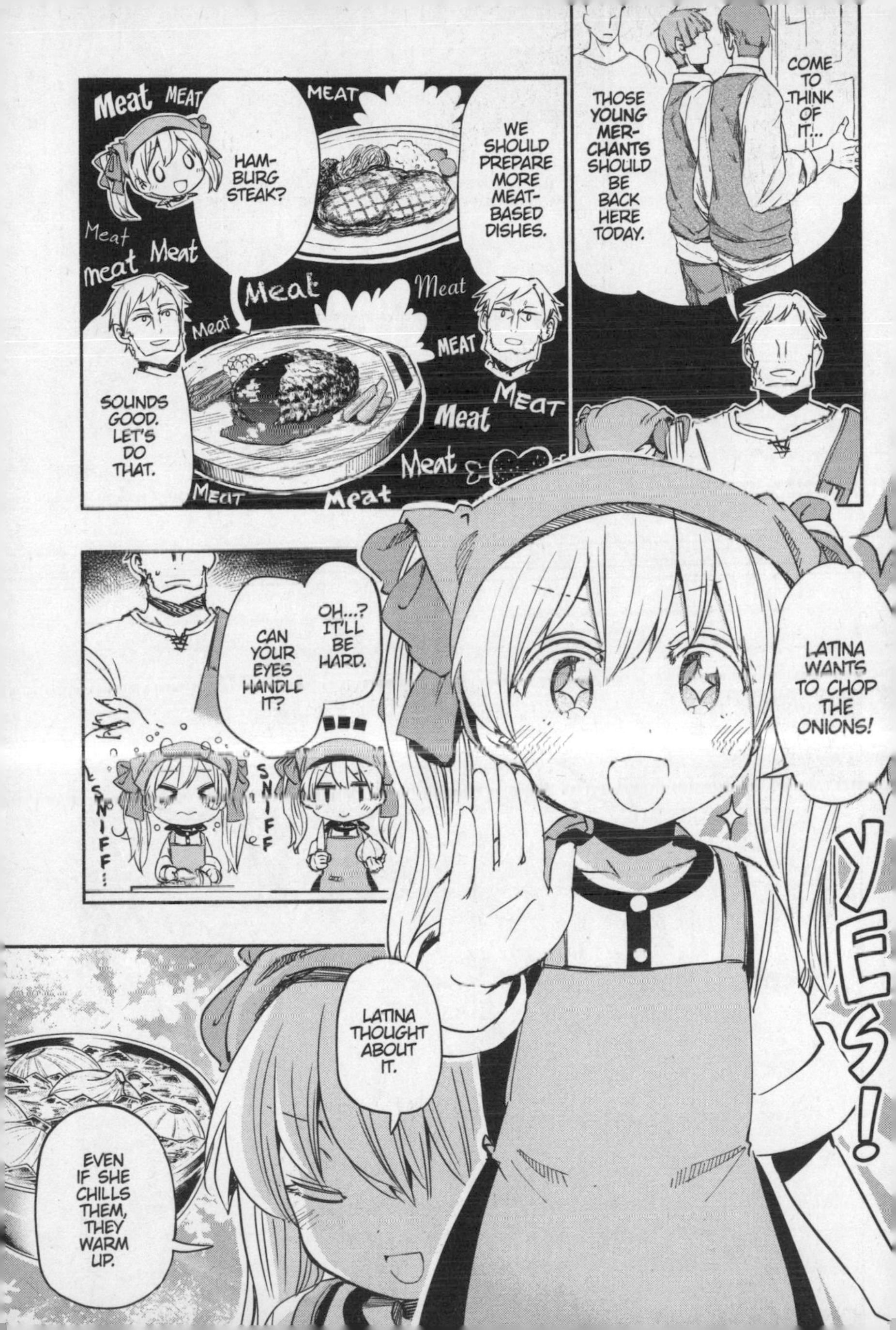
COME TO THINK OF IT...
THOSE YOUNG MER-CHANTS SHOULD BE BACK HERE TODAY.
WE SHOULD PREPARE MORE MEAT-BASED DISHES.
HAM-BURG STEAK?
SOUNDS GOOD. LET'S DO THAT.
Meat MEAT MEAT Meat meat Meat Meat Meat Meat MEAT MEAT Meat Meat MEAT Meat
LATINA WANTS TO CHOP THE ONIONS!
YES!
OH...? IT'LL BE HARD.
CAN YOUR EYES HANDLE IT?
SNIFF
SNIFF...
LATINA THOUGHT ABOUT IT.
EVEN IF SHE CHILLS THEM, THEY WARM UP.

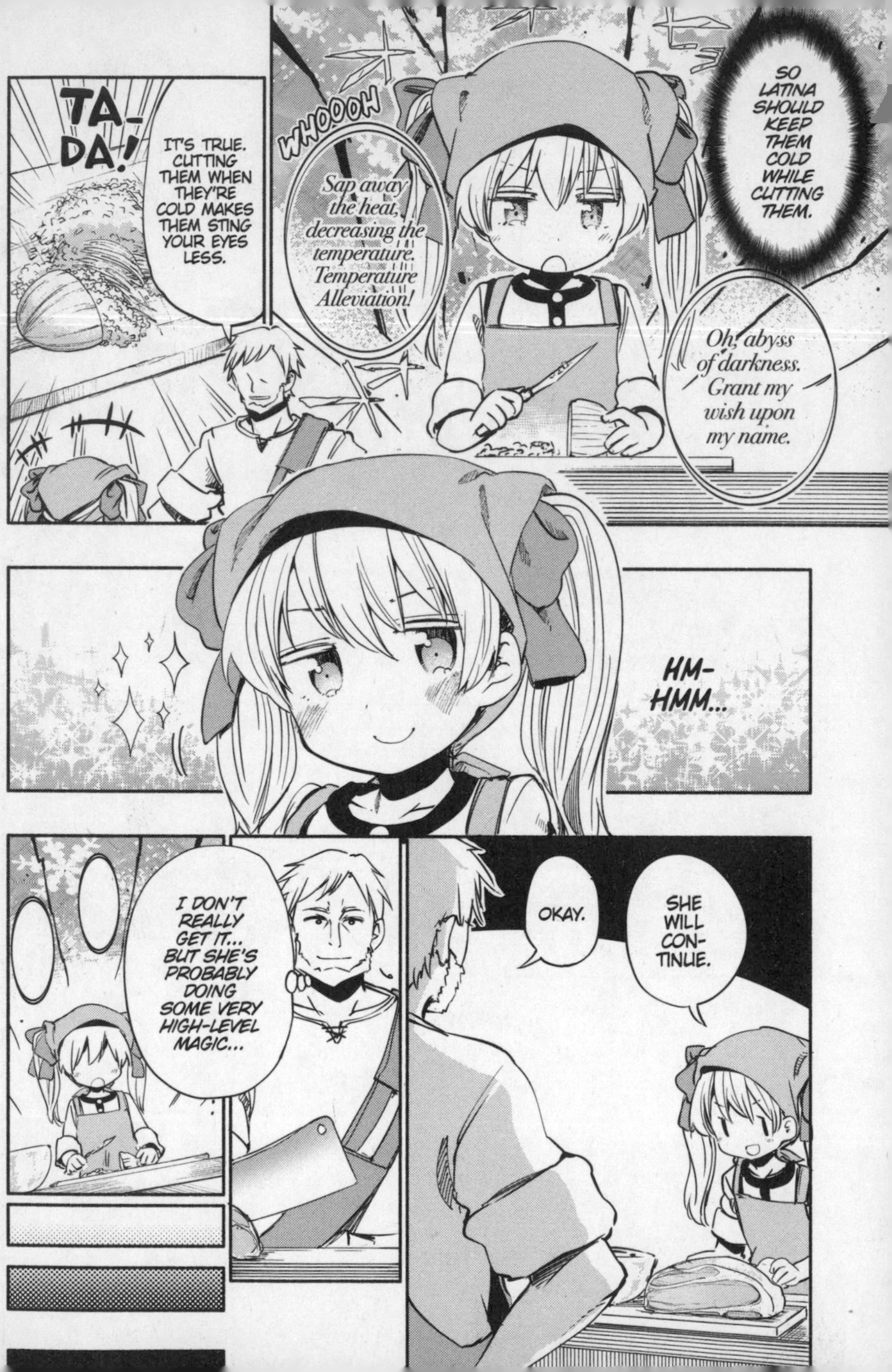
SO LATINA SHOULD KEEP THEM COLD WHILE CUTTING THEM.
Oh, abyss of darkness. Grant my wish upon my name.
WHOOOH
Sap away the heat, decreasing the temperature. Temperature Alleviation!
TA-DA!
IT'S TRUE. CUTTING THEM WHEN THEY'RE COLD MAKES THEM STING YOUR EYES LESS.
HM-HMM...
SHE WILL CON-TINUE.
OKAY.
I DON'T REALLY GET IT... BUT SHE'S PROBABLY DOING SOME VERY HIGH-LEVEL MAGIC...

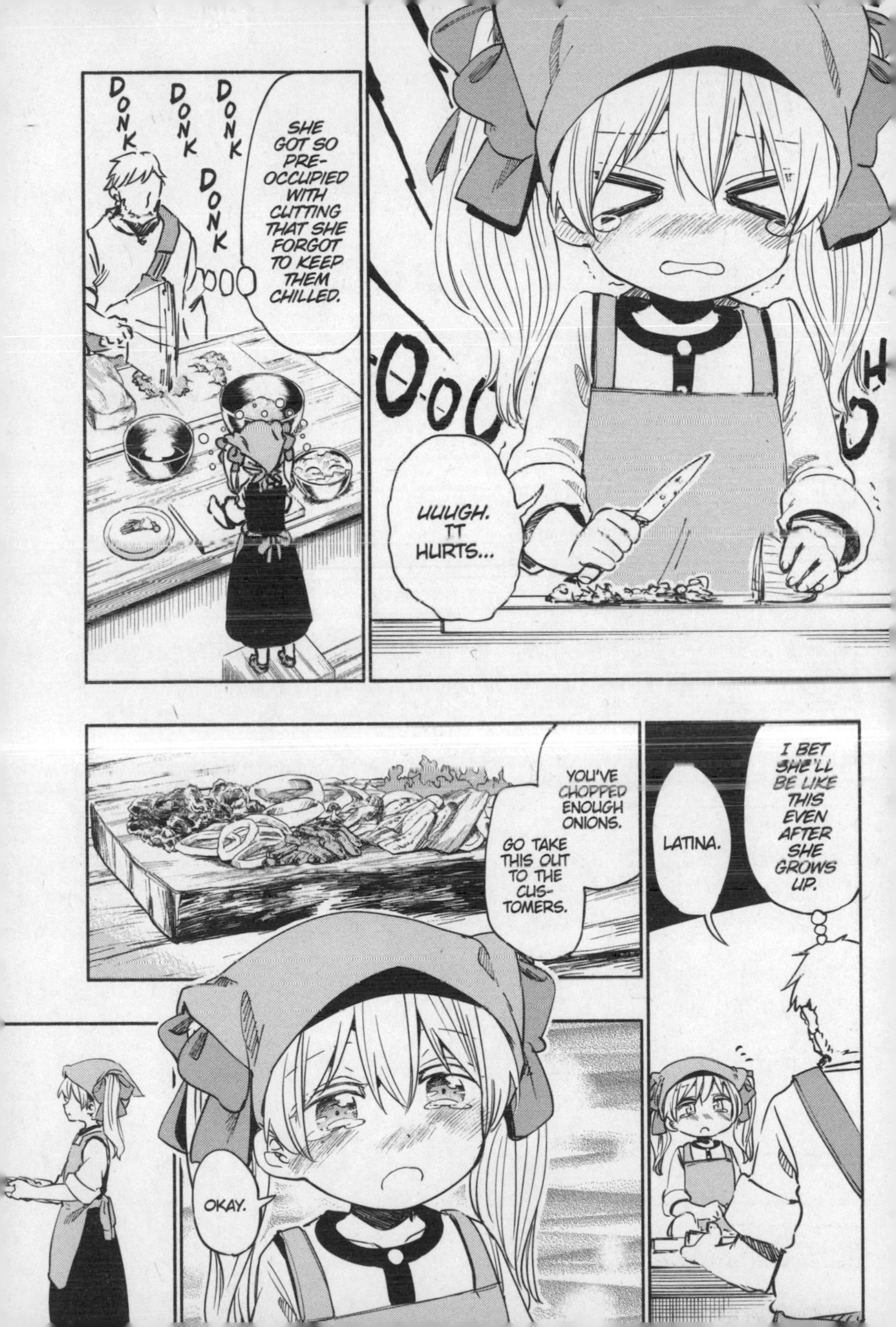
UUUGH. IT HURTS...
SHE GOT SO PRE-OCCUPIED WITH CUTTING THAT SHE FORGOT TO KEEP THEM CHILLED.
DONK DONK DONK DONK
I BET SHE'LL BE LIKE THIS EVEN AFTER SHE GROWS UP.
LATINA.
YOU'VE CHOPPED ENOUGH ONIONS.
GO TAKE THIS OUT TO THE CUSTOMERS.
OKAY.

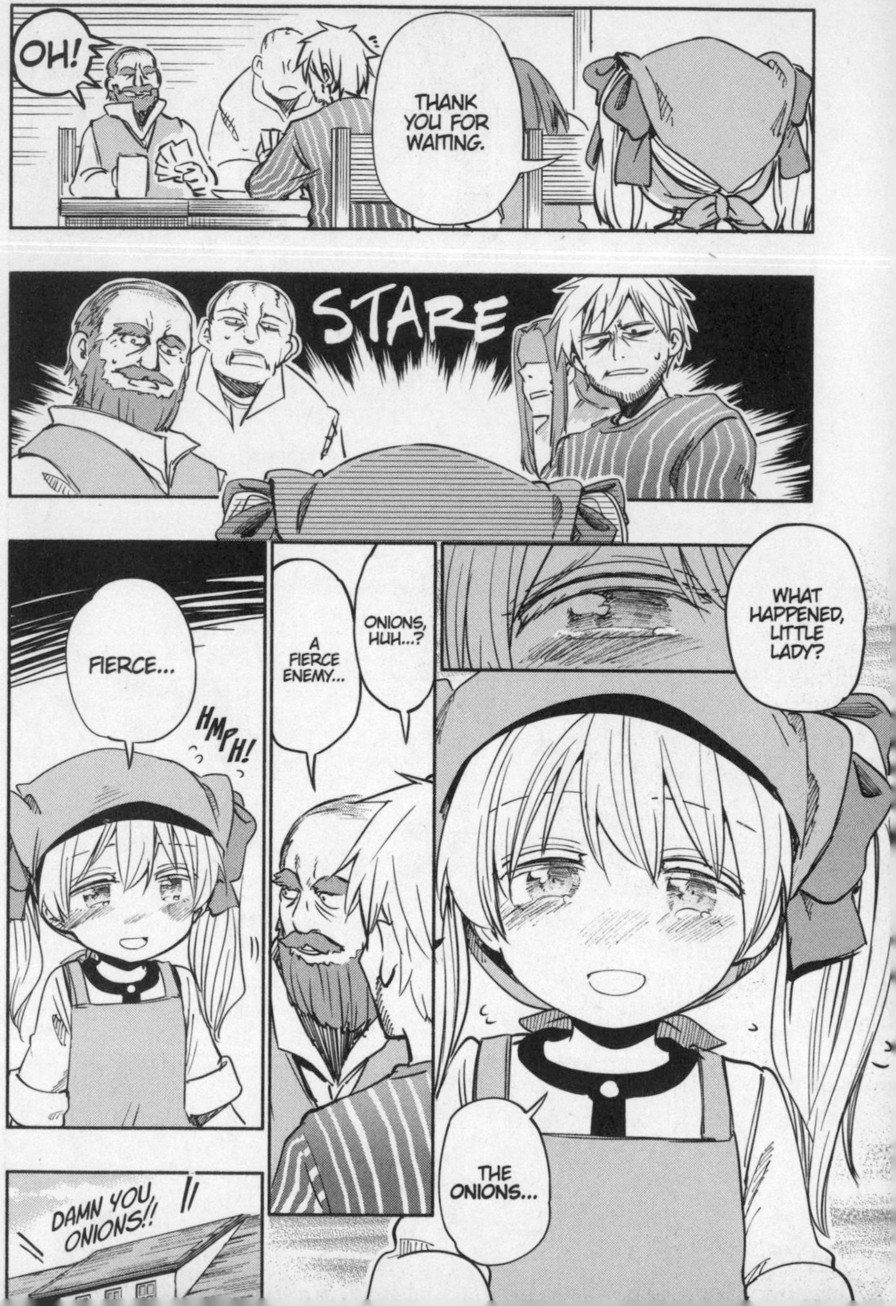
THANK YOU FOR WAITING.
OH!
STARE
WHAT HAPPENED, LITTLE LADY?
THE ONIONS...
ONIONS, HUH...?
A FIERCE ENEMY...
FIERCE...
HMPH!
DAMN YOU, ONIONS!!

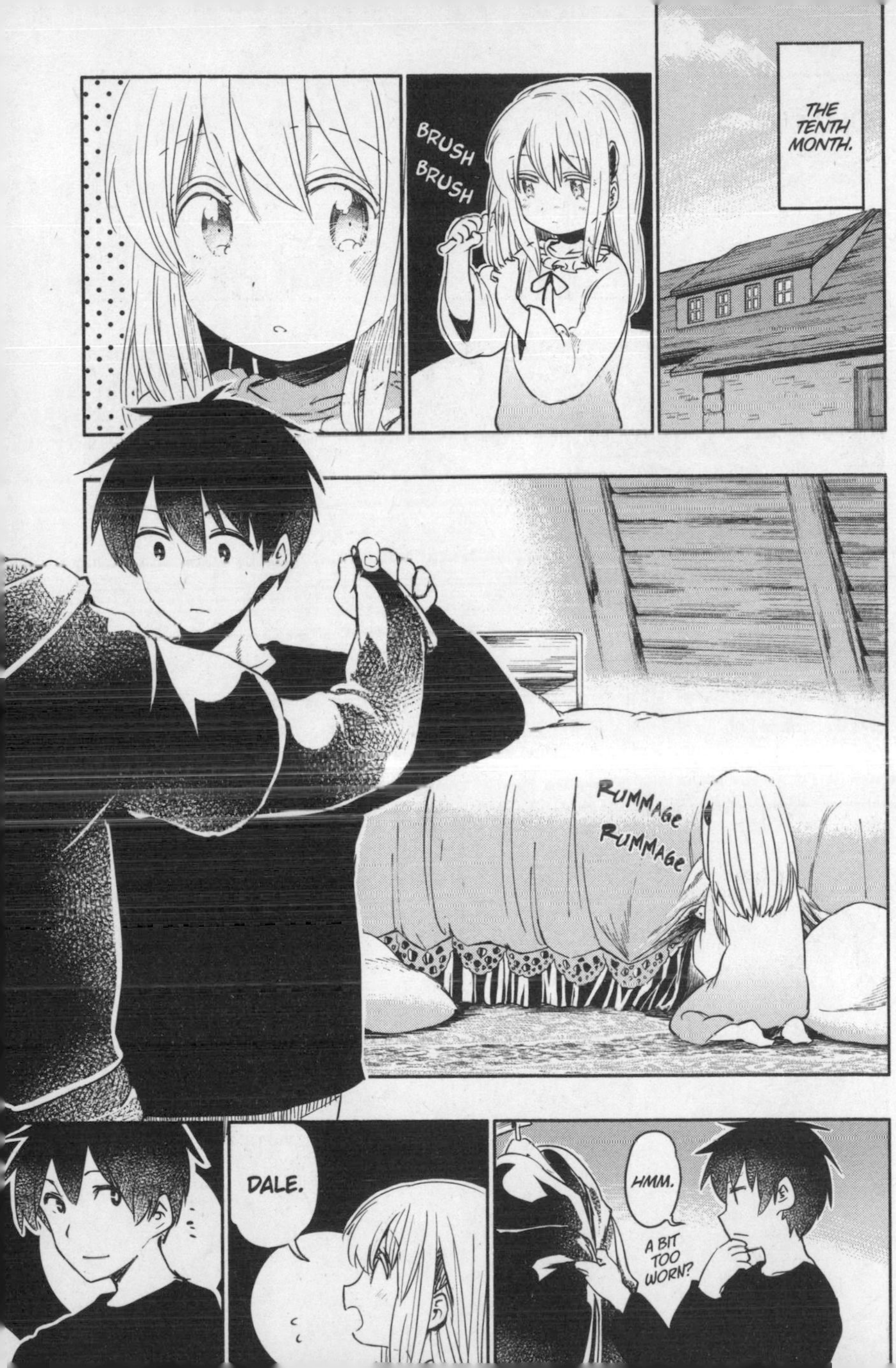
THE TENTH MONTH.
BRUSH BRUSH
RUMMAGE RUMMAGE
HMM.
A BIT TOO WORN?
DALE.

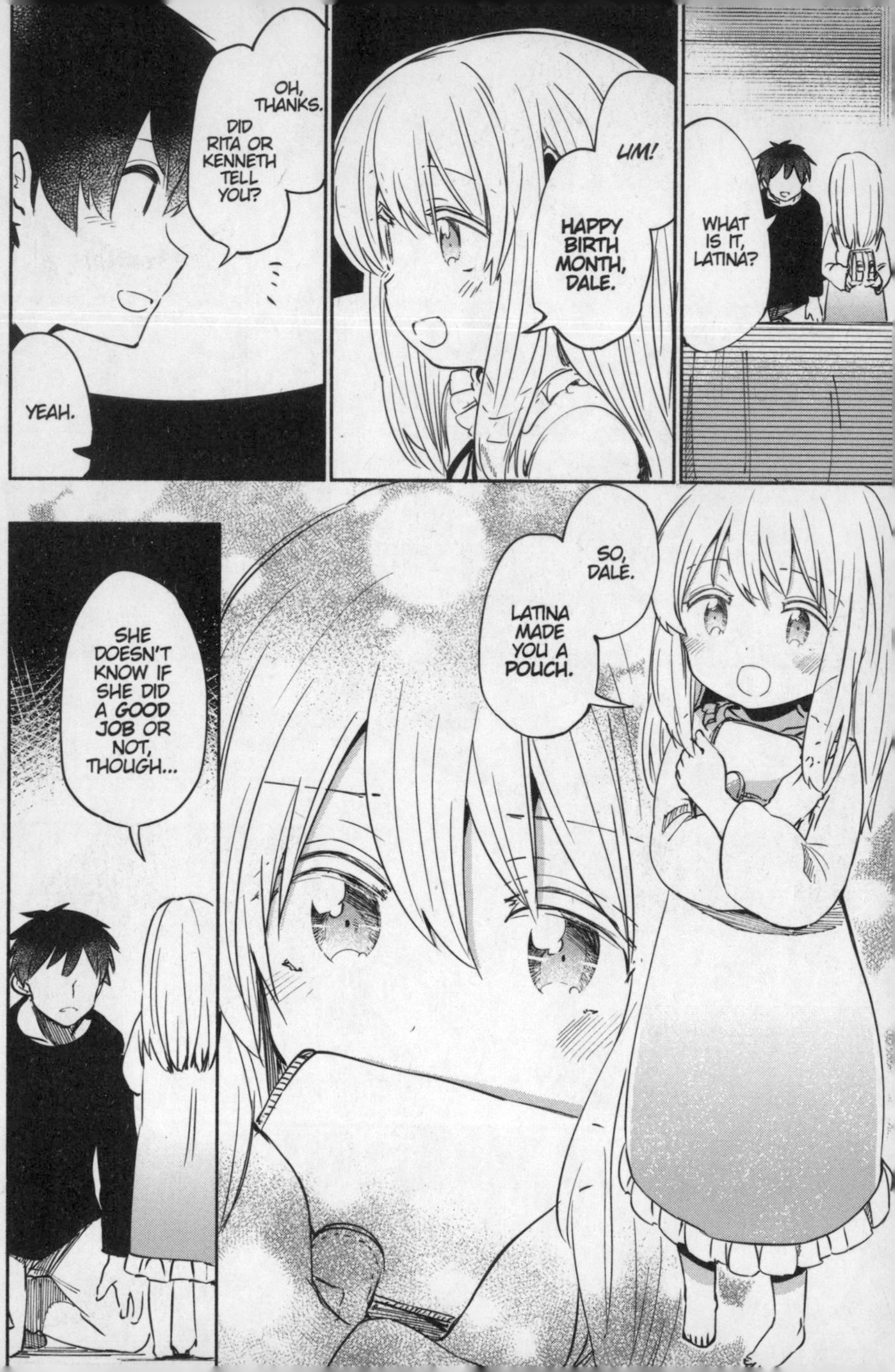
WHAT IS IT, LATINA?
UM!
HAPPY BIRTH MONTH, DALE.
OH, THANKS.
DID RITA OR KENNETH TELL YOU?
YEAH.
SO, DALE.
LATINA MADE YOU A POUCH.
SHE DOESN'T KNOW IF SHE DID A GOOD JOB OR NOT, THOUGH...

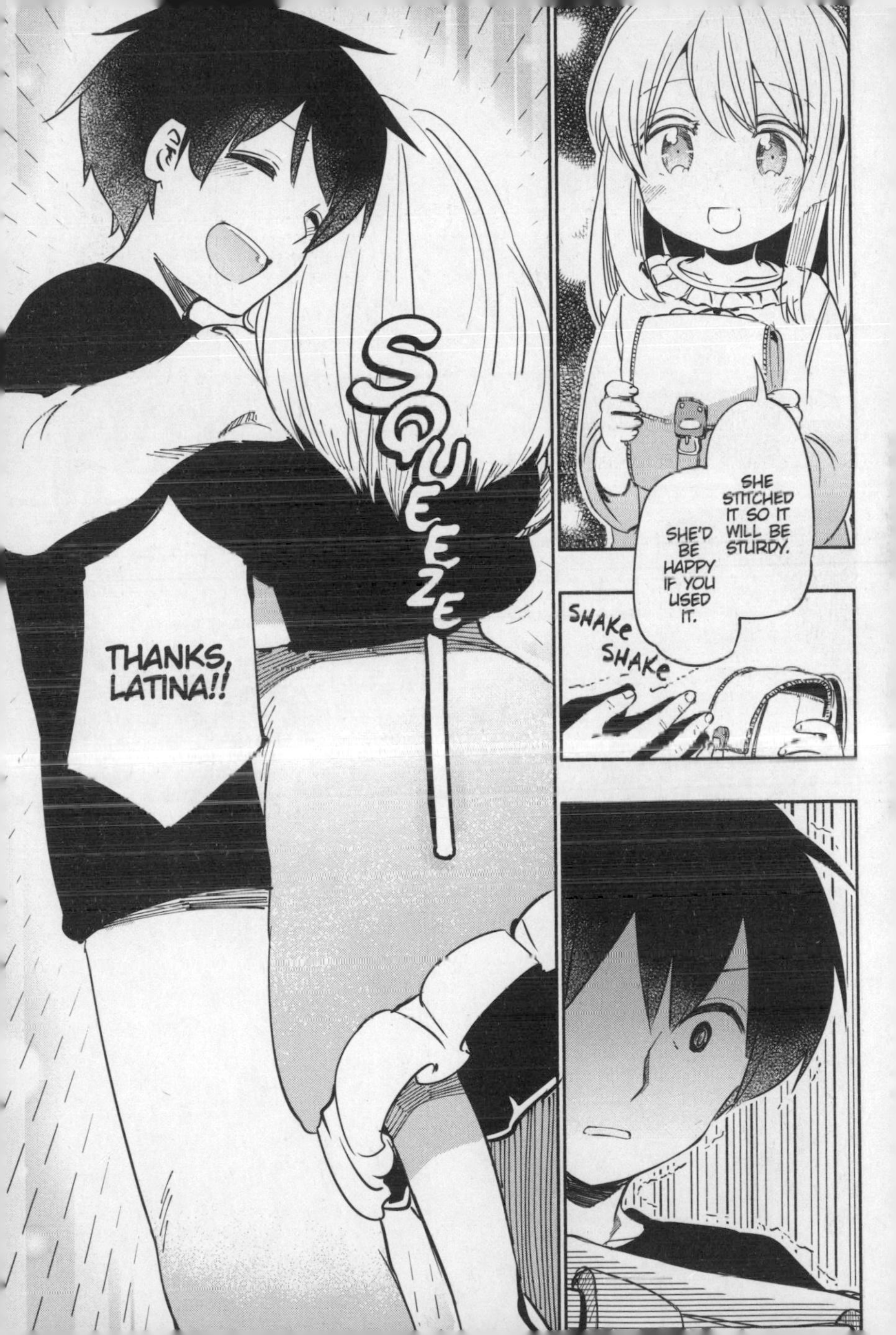
SHE STITCHED IT SO IT WILL BE STURDY.
SHE'D BE HAPPY IF YOU USED IT.
SHAKE SHAKE
SQUEEZE
THANKS, LATINA!!

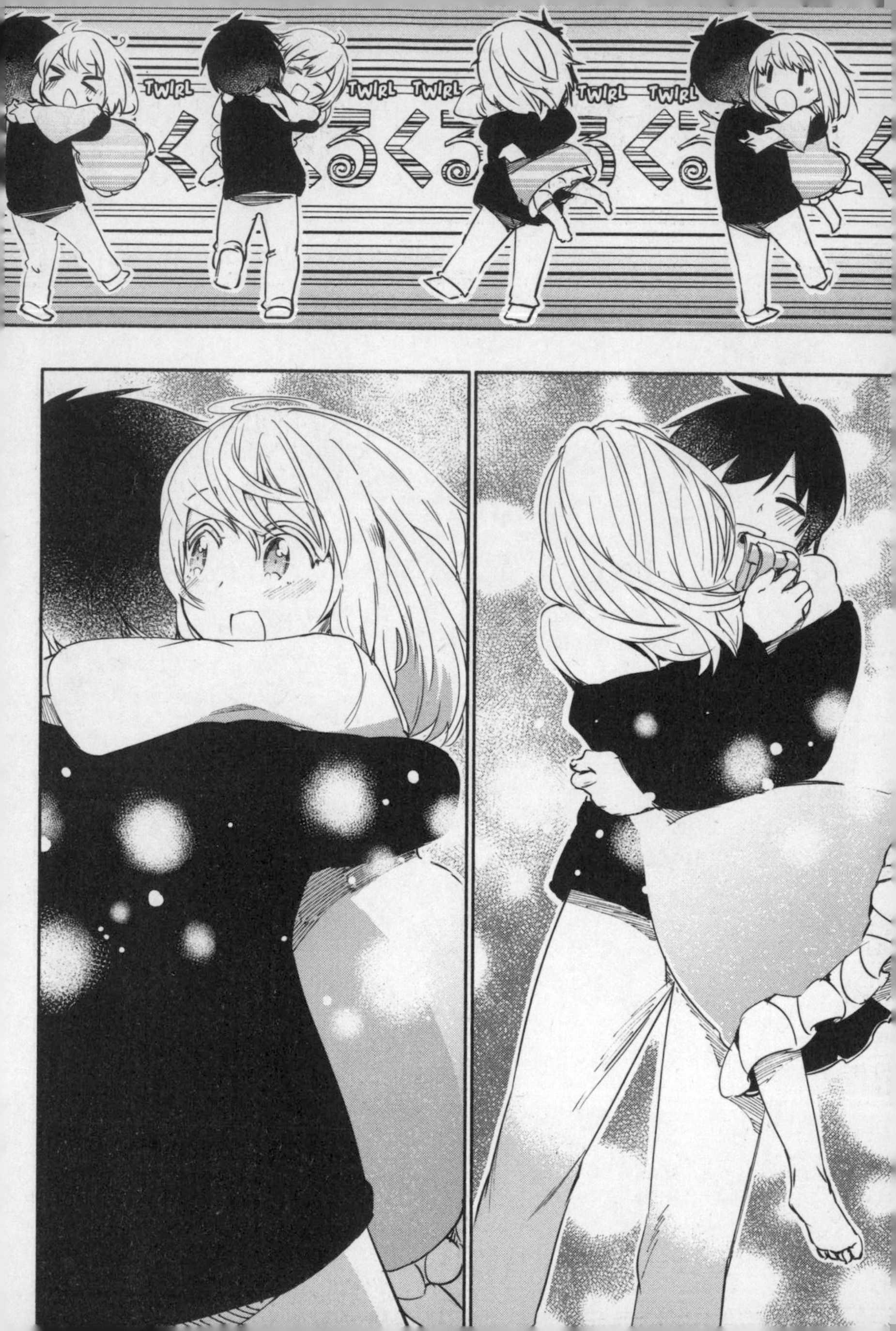
TWIRL
TWIRL
TWIRL
TWIRL
TWIRL

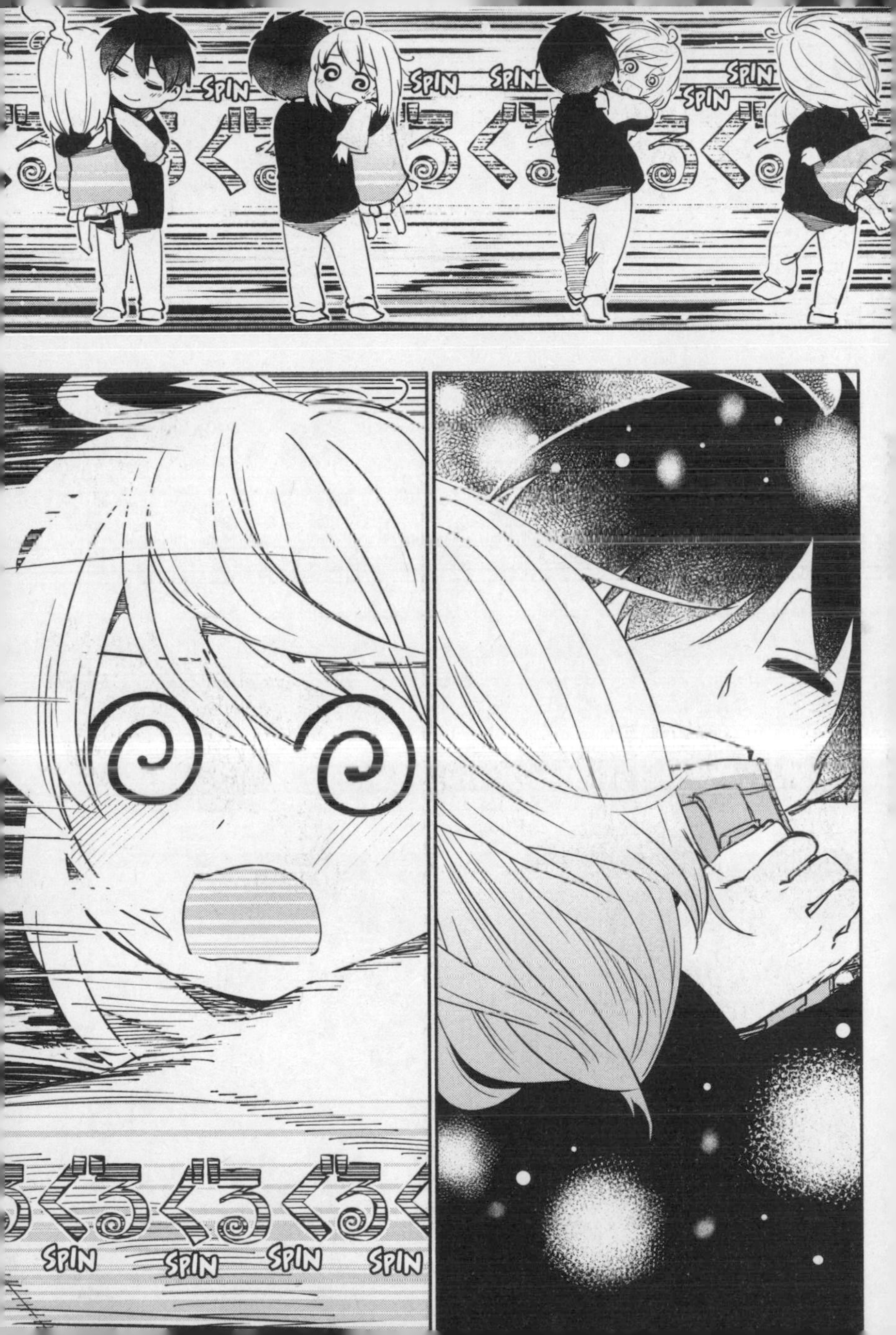
ぐるぐるぐる
SPIN
SPIN
SPIN
SPIN
SPIN
ぐるぐるぐる
SPIN
SPIN
SPIN
SPIN

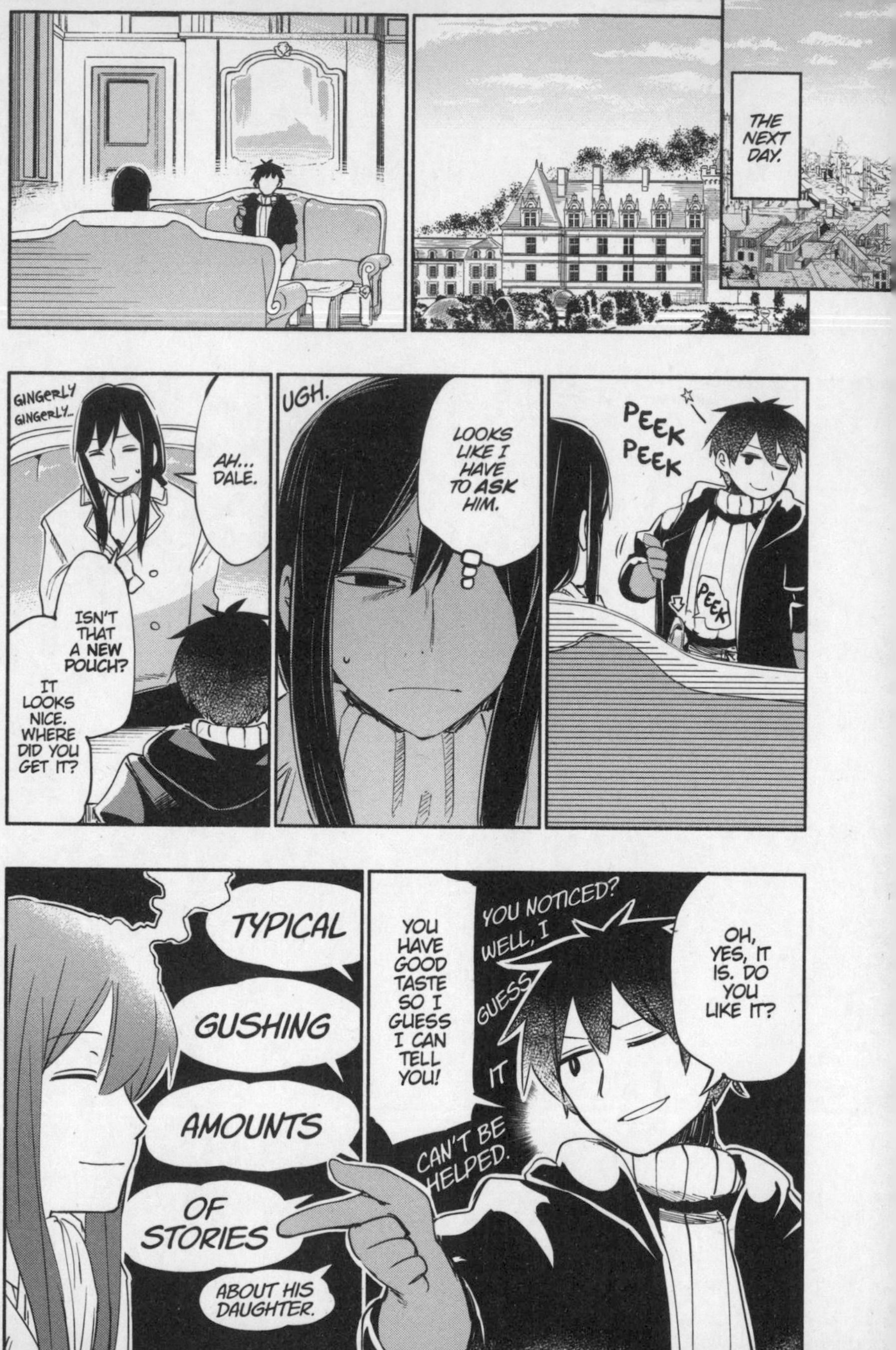
THE NEXT DAY.
PEEK PEEK
PEEK
UGH.
LOOKS LIKE I HAVE TO ASK HIM.
GINGERLY GINGERLY...
AH... DALE.
ISN'T THAT A NEW POUCH?
IT LOOKS NICE. WHERE DID YOU GET IT?
OH, YES, IT IS. DO YOU LIKE IT?
YOU NOTICED? WELL, I GUESS IT CAN'T BE HELPED.
YOU HAVE GOOD TASTE SO I GUESS I CAN TELL YOU!
TYPICAL
GUSHING
AMOUNTS
OF STORIES
ABOUT HIS DAUGHTER.

If It's For My Daughter I'd Even Defeat a Demon Lord

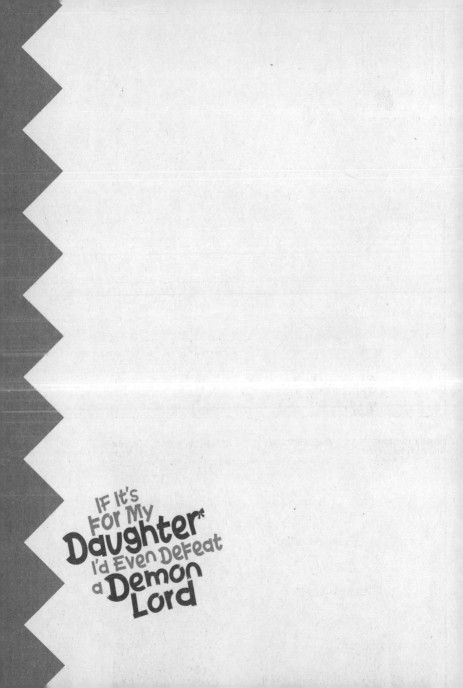

If It's For My Daughter, I'd Even Defeat a Demon Lord.

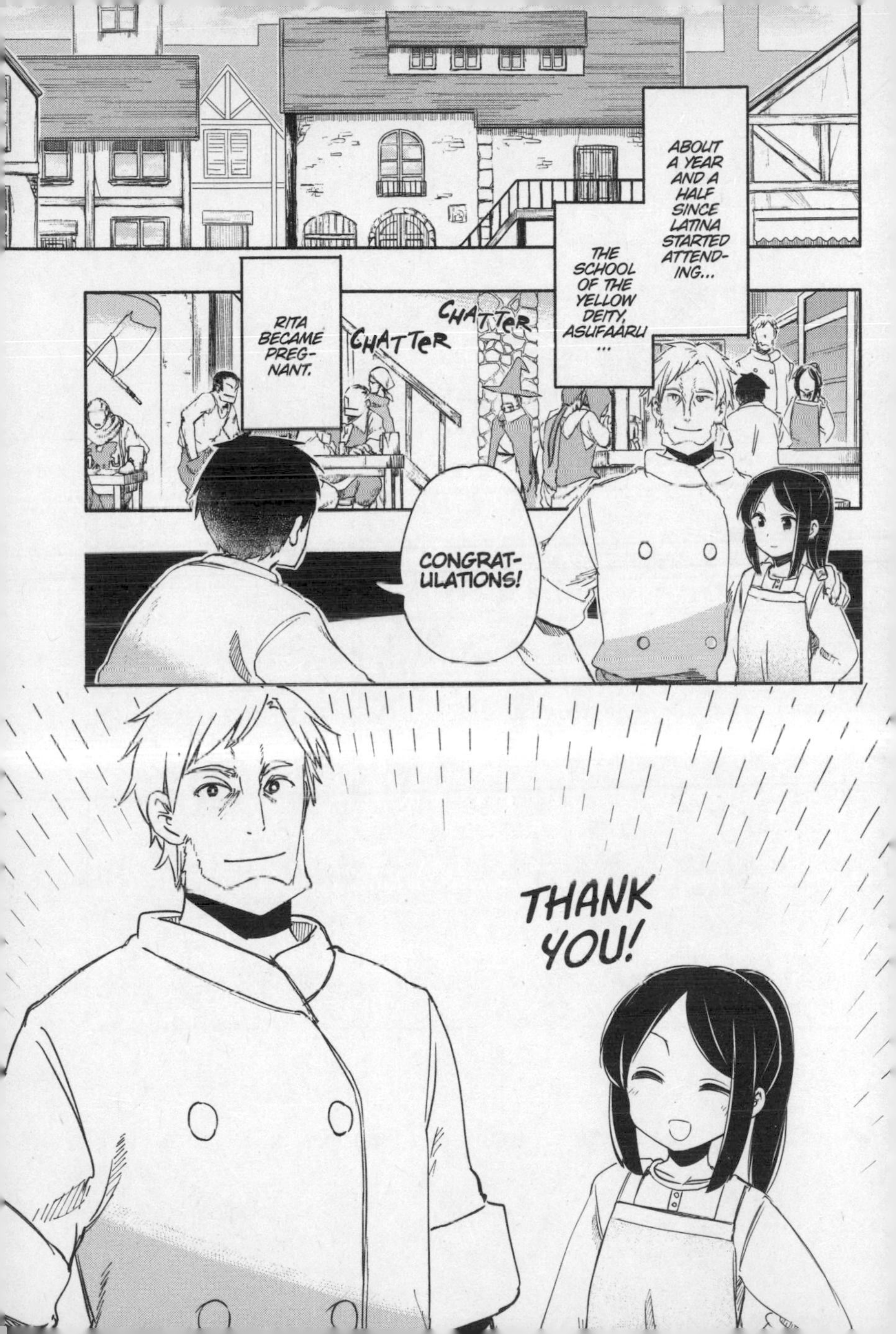
ABOUT A YEAR AND A HALF SINCE LATINA STARTED ATTENDING...
THE SCHOOL OF THE YELLOW DEITY, ASUFAÁRU...
RITA BECAME PREGNANT.
CHATTER
CHATTER
CONGRATULATIONS!
THANK YOU!

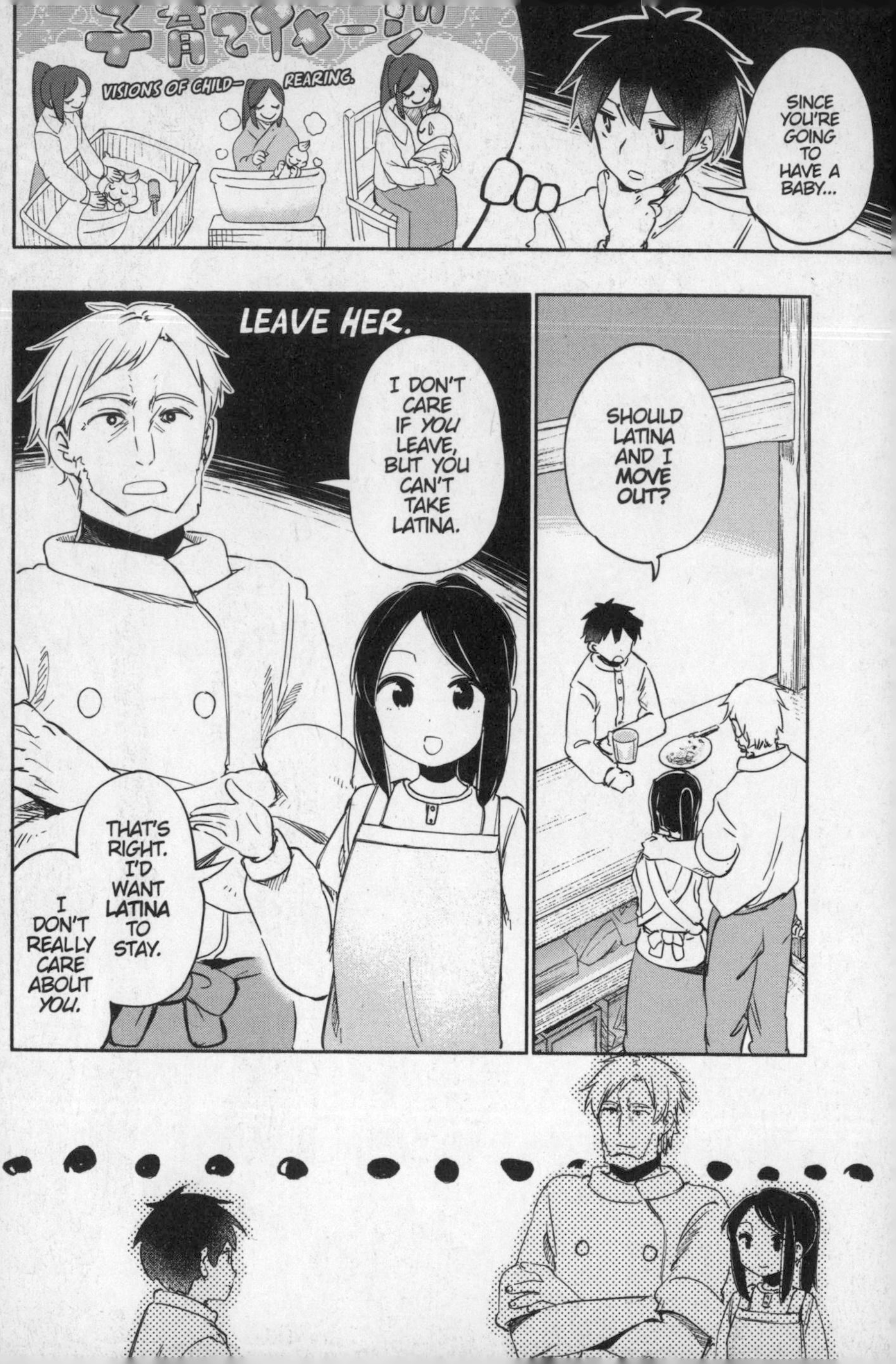
SINCE YOU'RE GOING TO HAVE A BABY...
子育てイメージ
VISIONS OF CHILD-REARING.
SHOULD LATINA AND I MOVE OUT?
LEAVE HER.
I DON'T CARE IF YOU LEAVE, BUT YOU CAN'T TAKE LATINA.
THAT'S RIGHT. I'D WANT LATINA TO STAY.
I DON'T REALLY CARE ABOUT YOU.

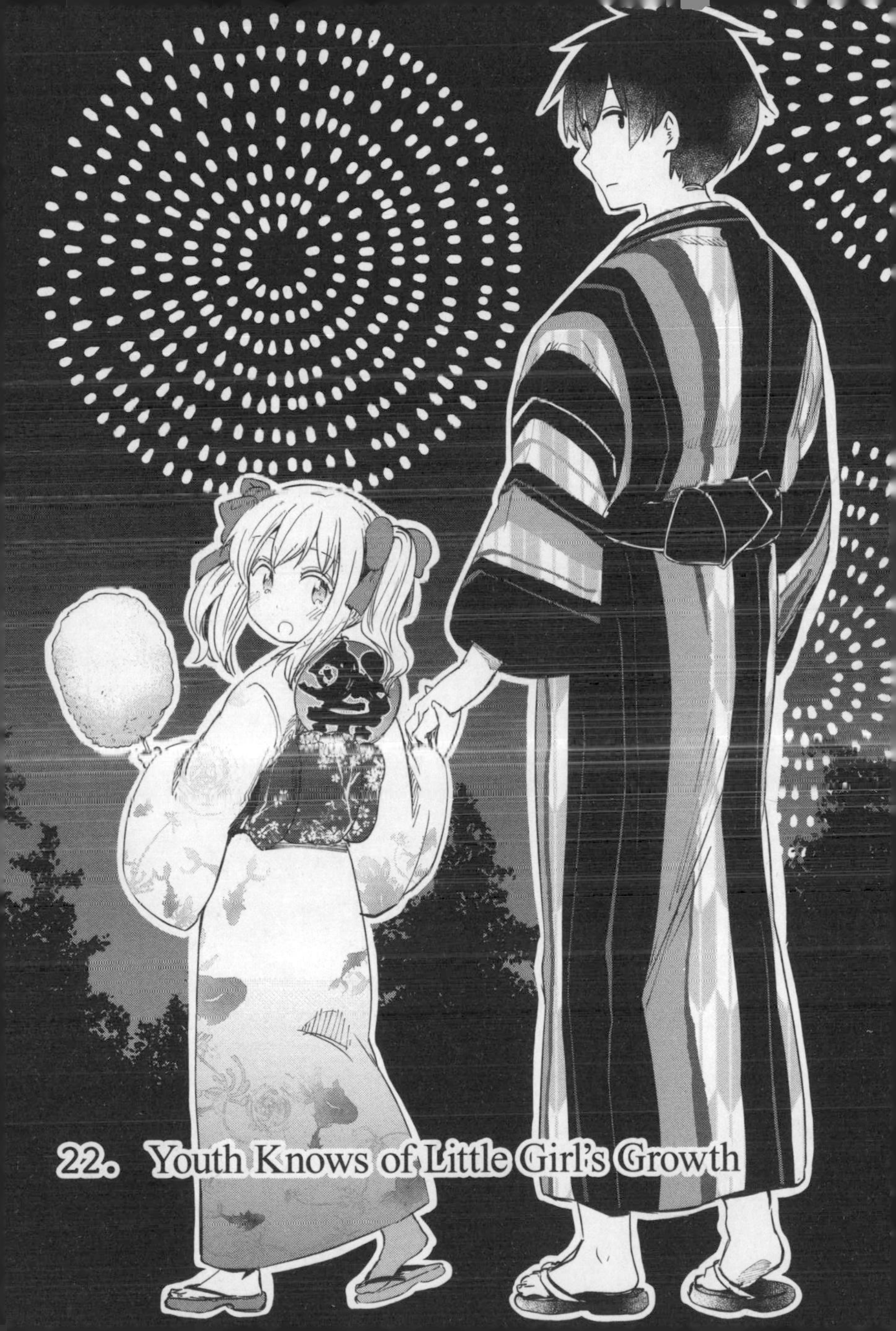
22. Youth Knows of Little Girl's Growth

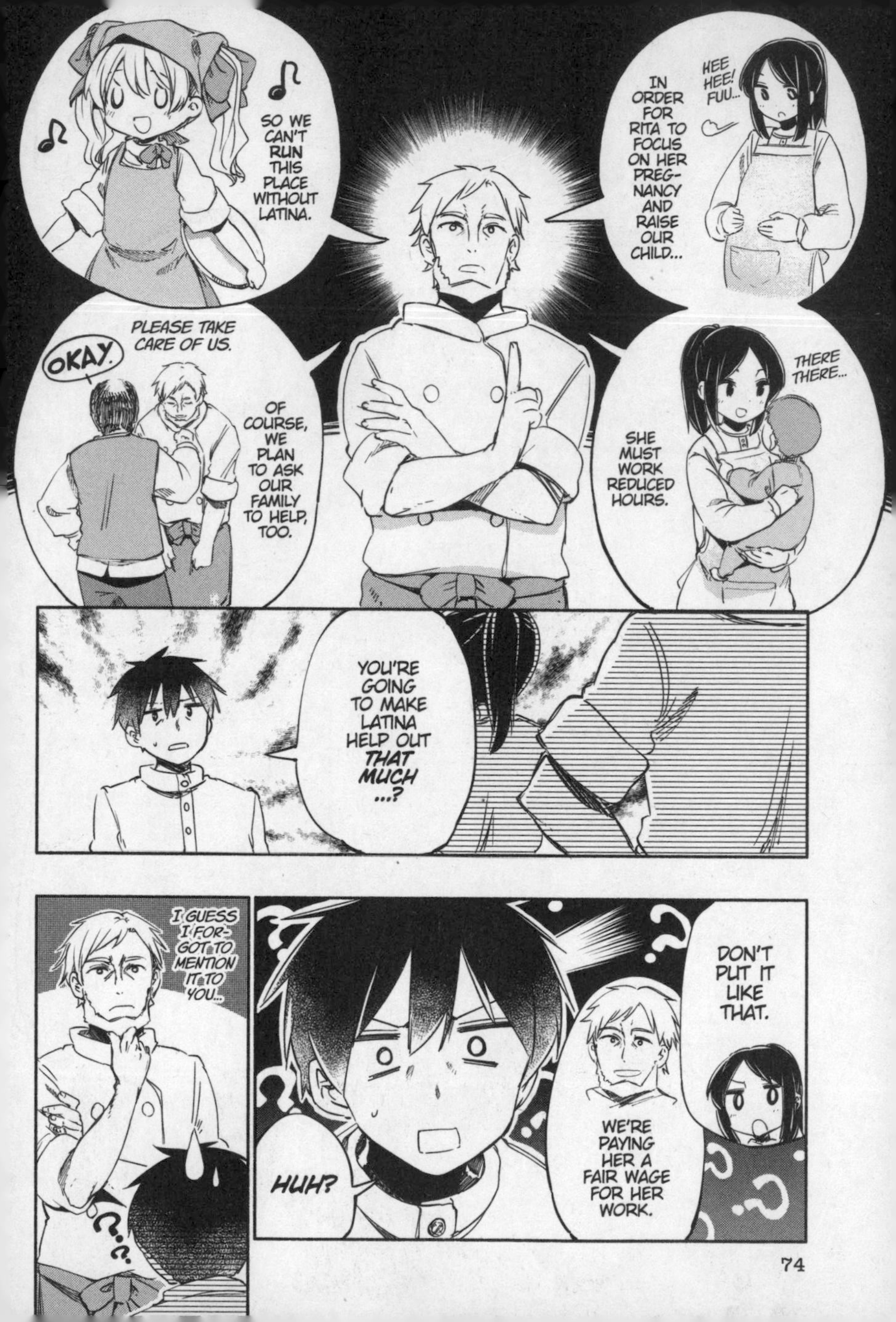
HEE HEE! FUU...
IN ORDER FOR RITA TO FOCUS ON HER PREGNANCY AND RAISE OUR CHILD...
THERE THERE...
SHE MUST WORK REDUCED HOURS.
SO WE CAN'T RUN THIS PLACE WITHOUT LATINA.
PLEASE TAKE CARE OF US.
OKAY.
OF COURSE, WE PLAN TO ASK OUR FAMILY TO HELP, TOO.
YOU'RE GOING TO MAKE LATINA HELP OUT *THAT MUCH*...?
DON'T PUT IT LIKE THAT.
WE'RE PAYING HER A FAIR WAGE FOR HER WORK.
HUH?
I GUESS I FORGOT TO MENTION IT TO YOU...

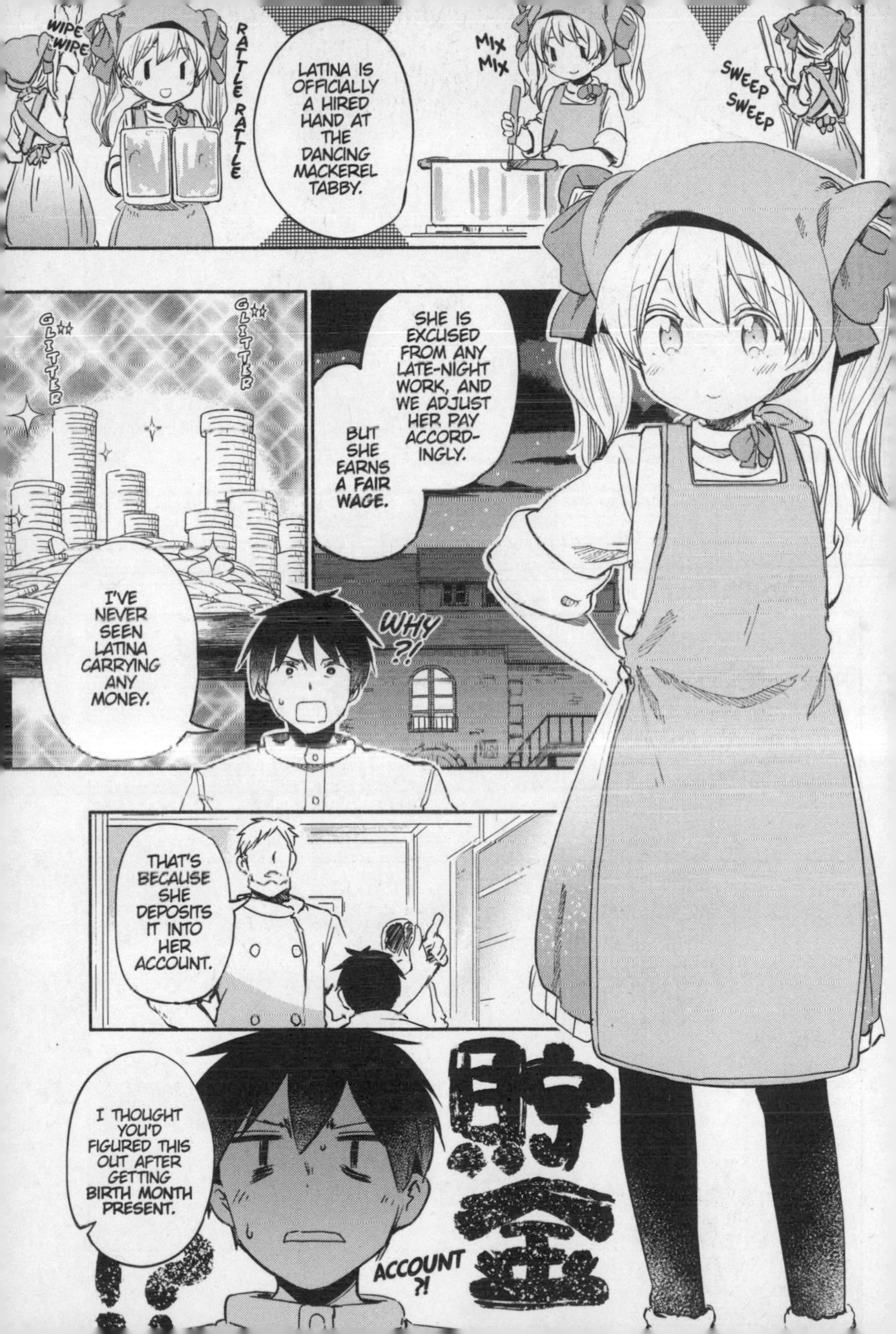
SWEEP SWEEP
MIX MIX
LATINA IS OFFICIALLY A HIRED HAND AT THE DANCING MACKEREL TABBY.
RATTLE RATTLE
WIPE WIPE
SHE IS EXCUSED FROM ANY LATE-NIGHT WORK, AND WE ADJUST HER PAY ACCORDINGLY.
BUT SHE EARNS A FAIR WAGE.
WHY ?!
GLITTER
GLITTER
I'VE NEVER SEEN LATINA CARRYING ANY MONEY.
THAT'S BECAUSE SHE DEPOSITS IT INTO HER ACCOUNT.
貯金
ACCOUNT ?!
I THOUGHT YOU'D FIGURED THIS OUT AFTER GETTING BIRTH MONTH PRESENT.

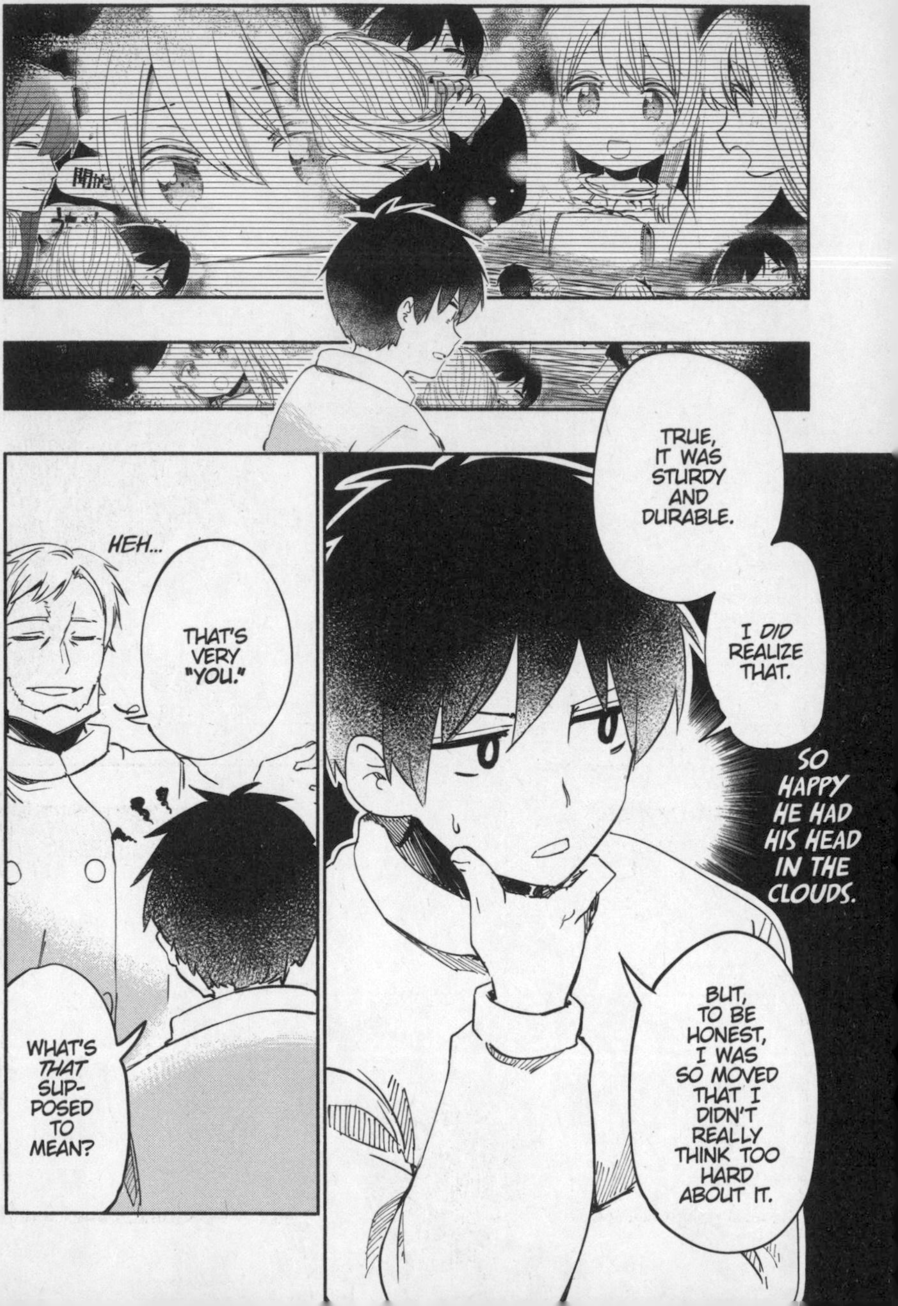
TRUE, IT WAS STURDY AND DURABLE.
I DID REALIZE THAT.
SO HAPPY HE HAD HIS HEAD IN THE CLOUDS.
BUT, TO BE HONEST, I WAS SO MOVED THAT I DIDN'T REALLY THINK TOO HARD ABOUT IT.
HEH...
THAT'S VERY "YOU."
WHAT'S THAT SUP-POSED TO MEAN?

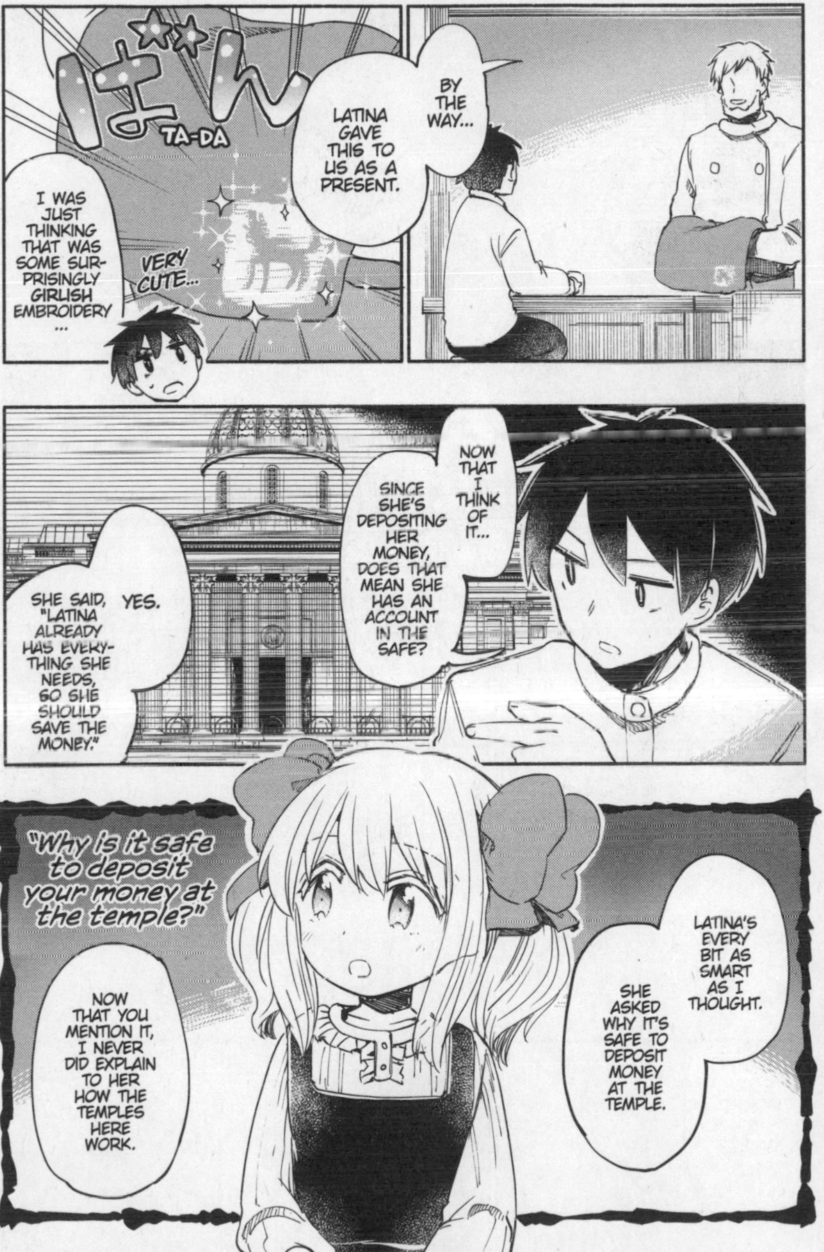
BY THE WAY...
LATINA GAVE THIS TO US AS A PRESENT.
TA-DA
VERY CUTE...
I WAS JUST THINKING THAT WAS SOME SUR-PRISINGLY GIRLISH EMBROIDERY...
NOW THAT I THINK OF IT...
SINCE SHE'S DEPOSITING HER MONEY, DOES THAT MEAN SHE HAS AN ACCOUNT IN THE SAFE?
YES.
SHE SAID, "LATINA ALREADY HAS EVERY-THING SHE NEEDS, SO SHE SHOULD SAVE THE MONEY."
LATINA'S EVERY BIT AS SMART AS I THOUGHT.
SHE ASKED WHY IT'S SAFE TO DEPOSIT MONEY AT THE TEMPLE.
"Why is it safe to deposit your money at the temple?"
NOW THAT YOU MENTION IT, I NEVER DID EXPLAIN TO HER HOW THE TEMPLES HERE WORK.

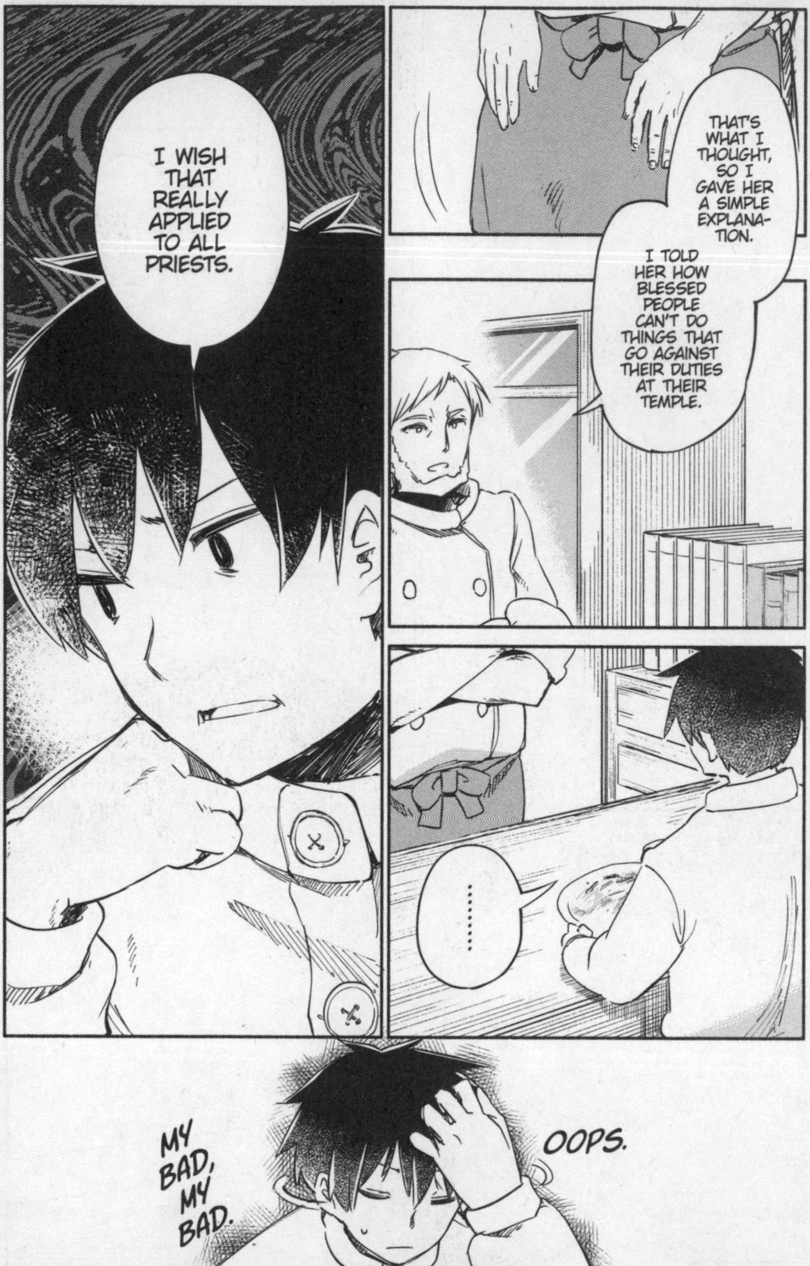
THAT'S WHAT I THOUGHT, SO I GAVE HER A SIMPLE EXPLANATION.
I TOLD HER HOW BLESSED PEOPLE CAN'T DO THINGS THAT GO AGAINST THEIR DUTIES AT THEIR TEMPLE.
......
I WISH THAT REALLY APPLIED TO ALL PRIESTS.
OOPS.
MY BAD, MY BAD.

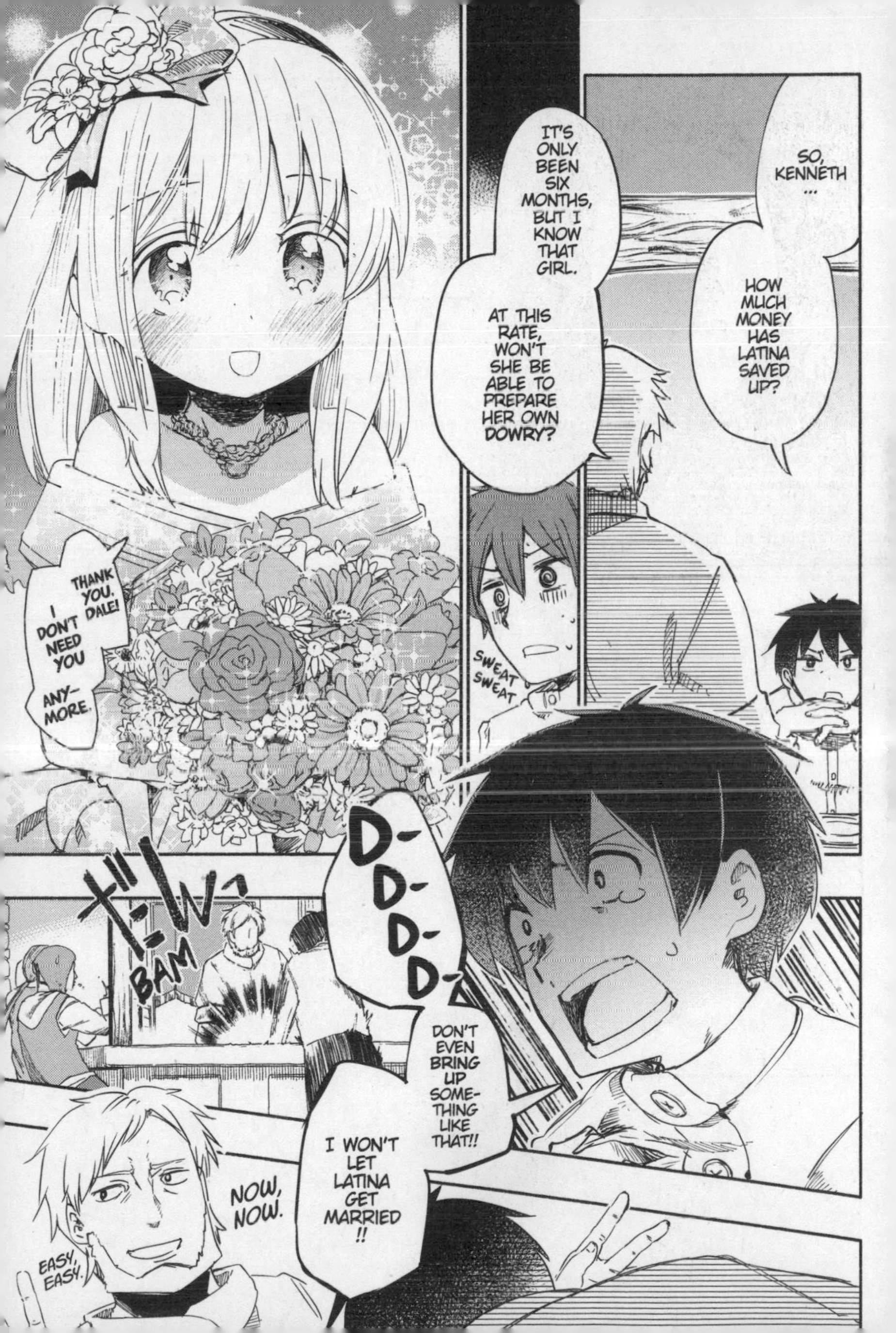
SO, KENNETH ...
HOW MUCH MONEY HAS LATINA SAVED UP?
IT'S ONLY BEEN SIX MONTHS, BUT I KNOW THAT GIRL.
AT THIS RATE, WON'T SHE BE ABLE TO PREPARE HER OWN DOWRY?
SWEAT SWEAT
THANK YOU, DALE!
I DON'T NEED YOU ANYMORE.
D-D-D-D-
DON'T EVEN BRING UP SOMETHING LIKE THAT!!
I WON'T LET LATINA GET MARRIED!!
BAM
NOW, NOW.
EASY, EASY.

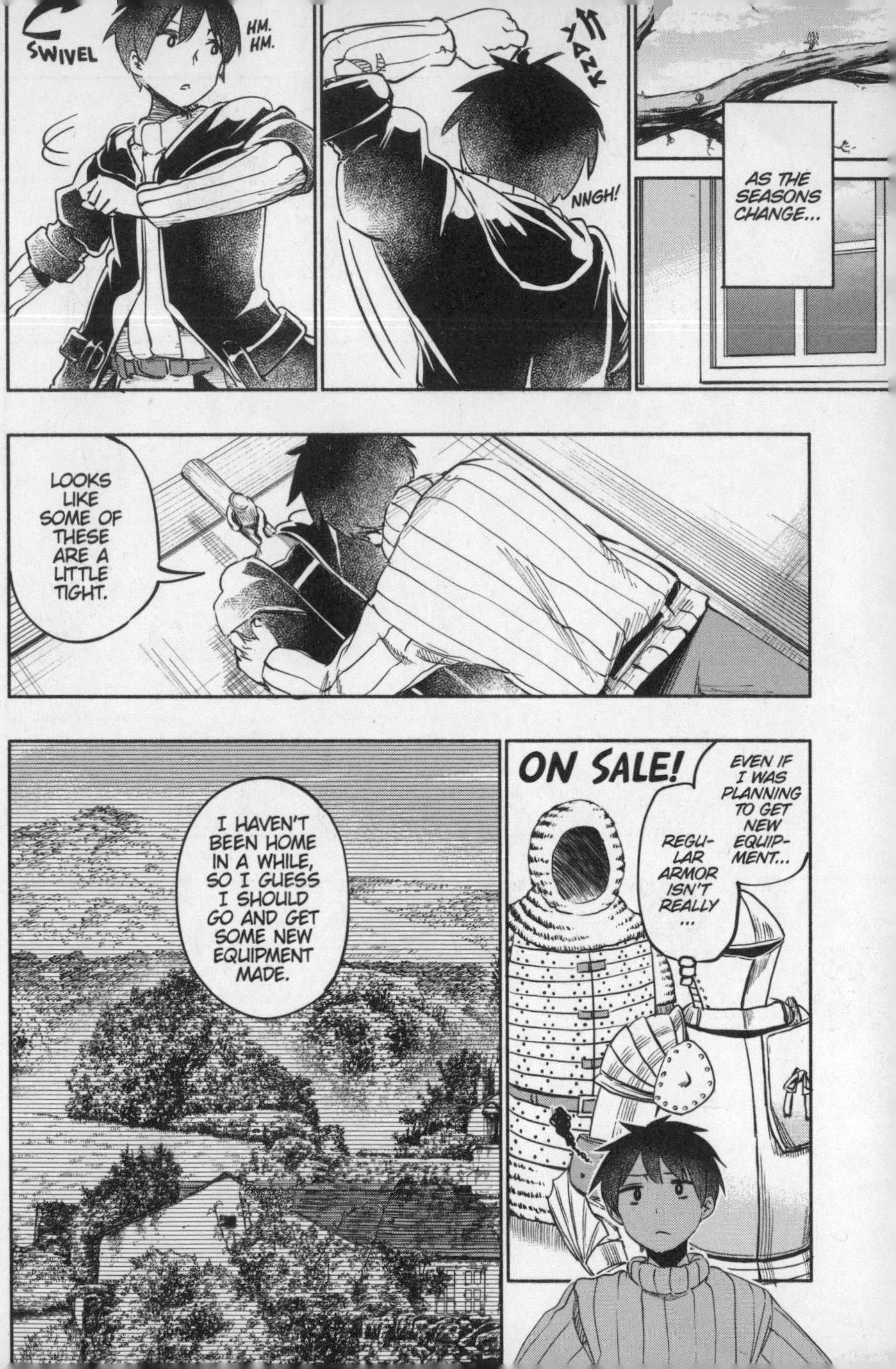
AS THE SEASONS CHANGE...
YANK
NNGH!
SWIVEL
HM. HM.
LOOKS LIKE SOME OF THESE ARE A LITTLE TIGHT.
EVEN IF I WAS PLANNING TO GET NEW EQUIPMENT...
REGULAR ARMOR ISN'T REALLY ...
ON SALE!
I HAVEN'T BEEN HOME IN A WHILE, SO I GUESS I SHOULD GO AND GET SOME NEW EQUIPMENT MADE.

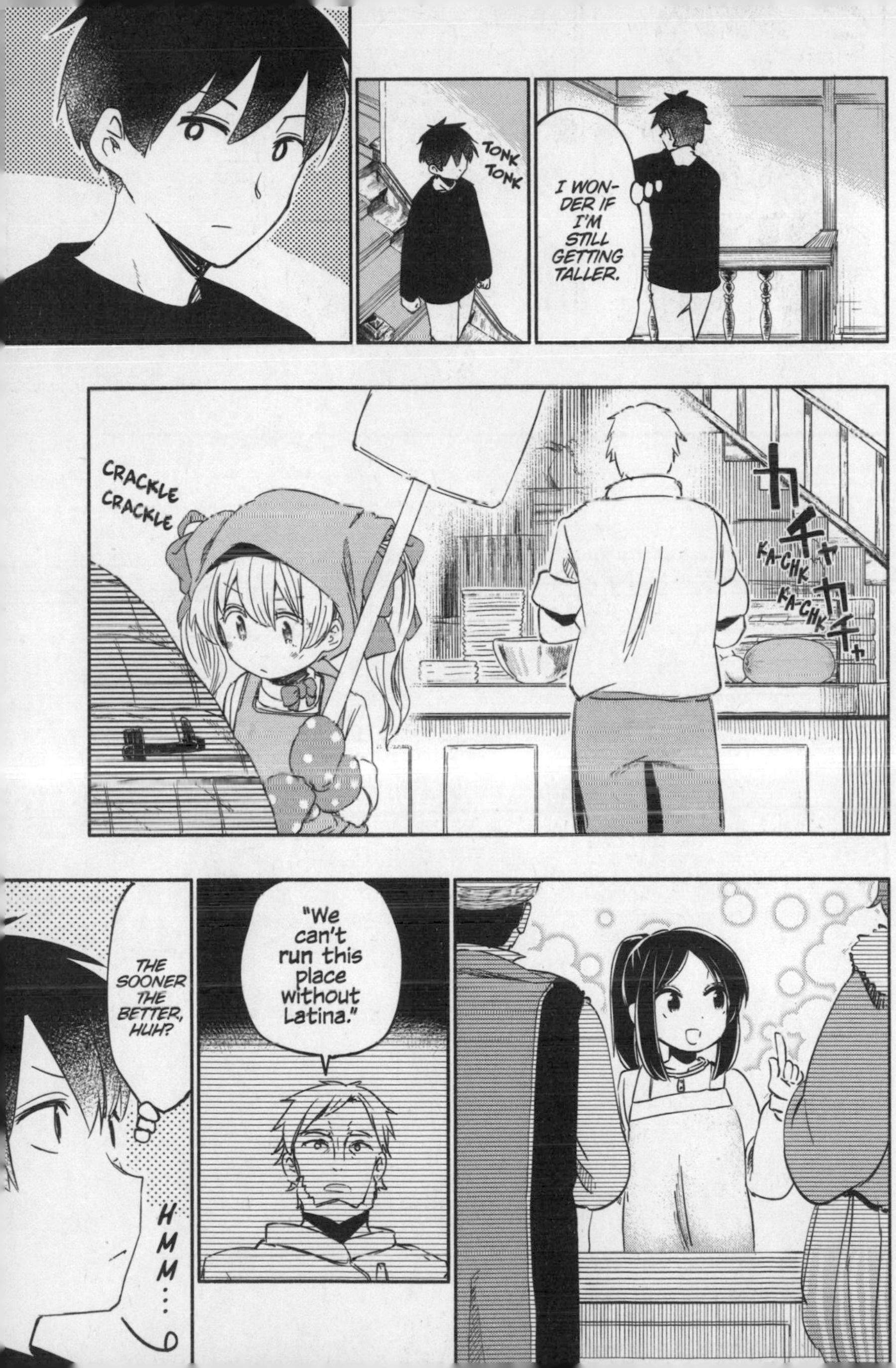
I WON-
DER IF
I'M
STILL
GETTING
TALLER.
TONK TONK
カチャ
KA-CHK
カチャ
KA-CHK
CRACKLE CRACKLE
"We can't run this place without Latina."
THE SOONER THE BETTER, HUH?
HMM...

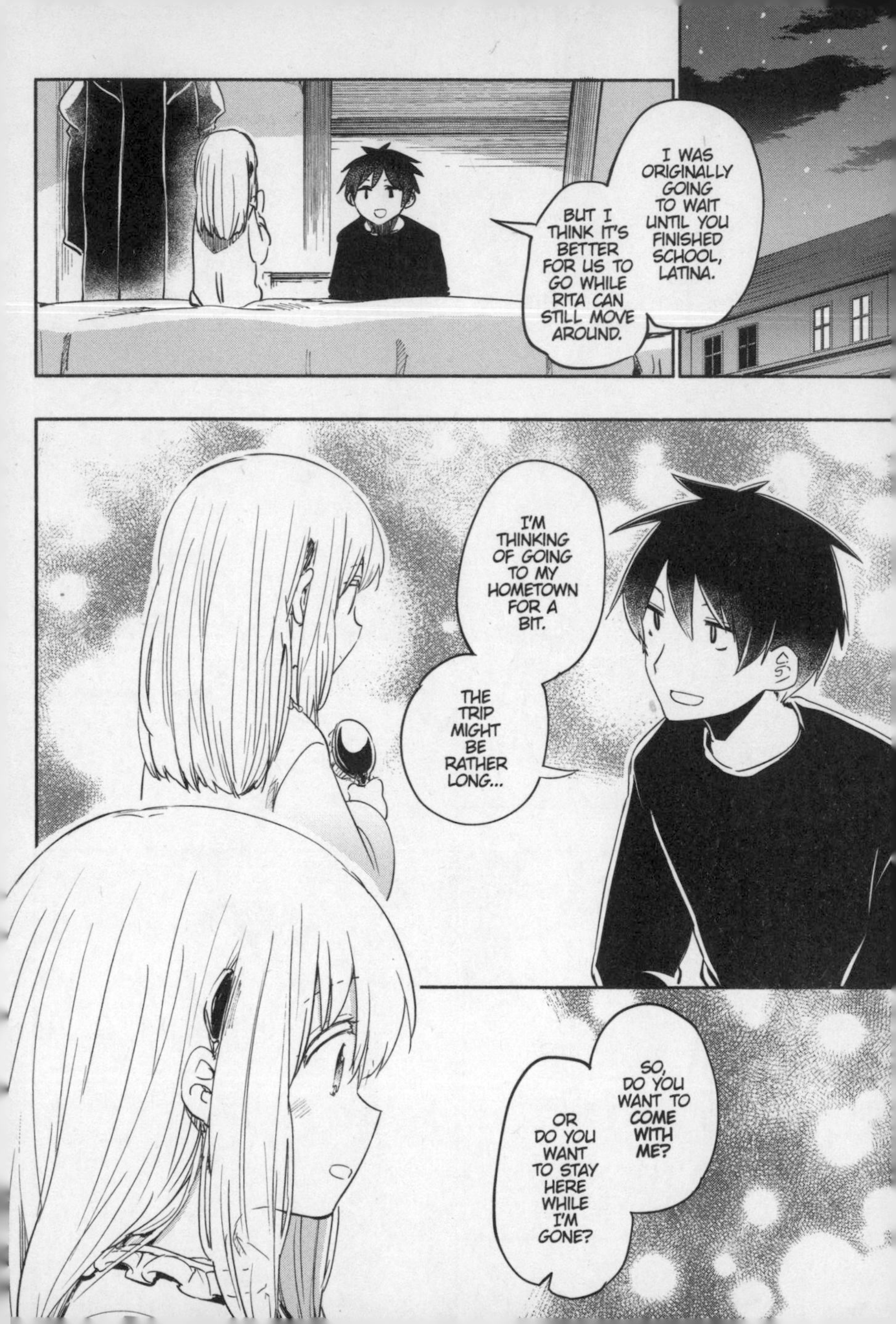
I WAS ORIGINALLY GOING TO WAIT UNTIL YOU FINISHED SCHOOL, LATINA.
BUT I THINK IT'S BETTER FOR US TO GO WHILE RITA CAN STILL MOVE AROUND.
I'M THINKING OF GOING TO MY HOMETOWN FOR A BIT.
THE TRIP MIGHT BE RATHER LONG...
SO, DO YOU WANT TO COME WITH ME?
OR DO YOU WANT TO STAY HERE WHILE I'M GONE?

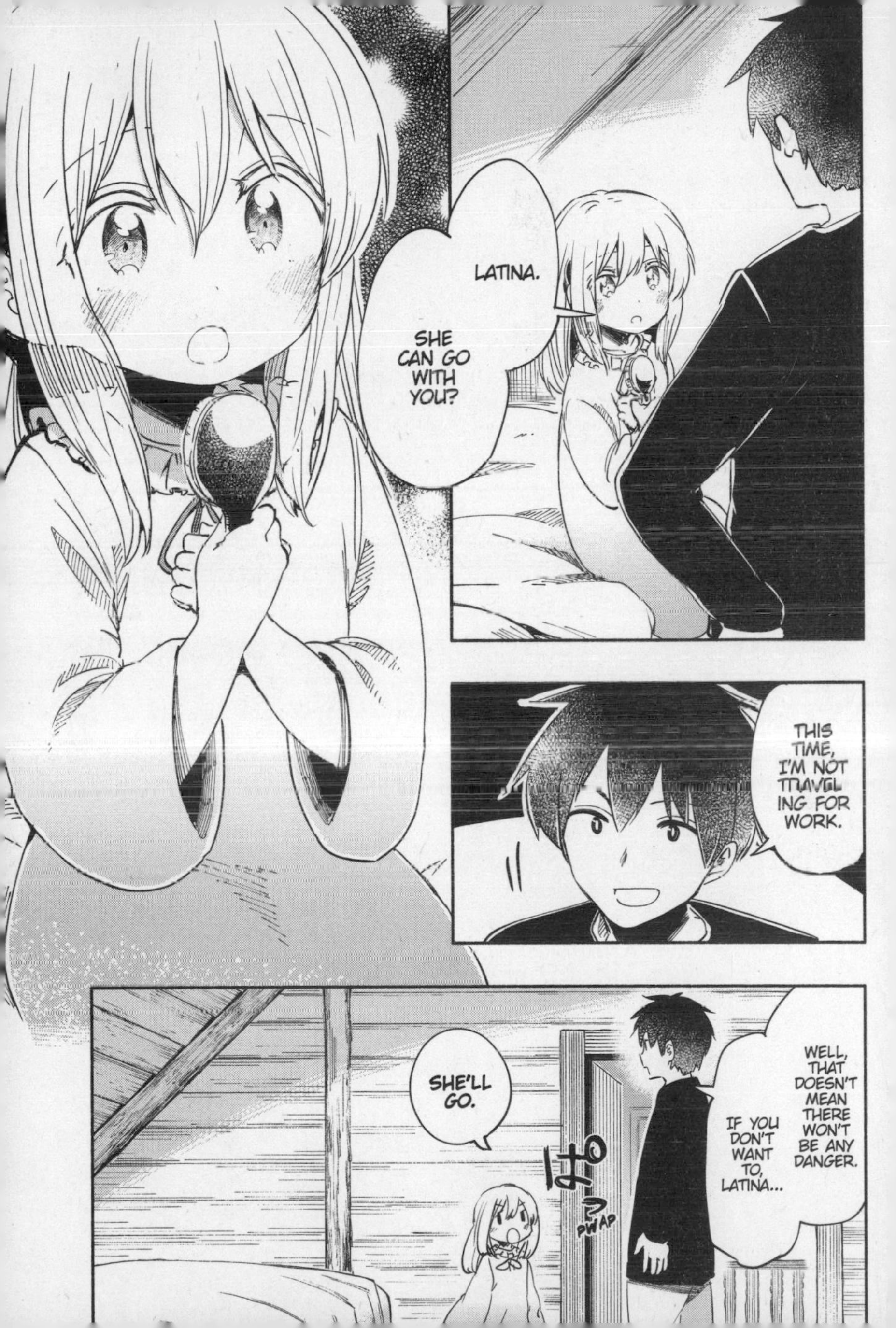
LATINA.
SHE CAN GO WITH YOU?
THIS TIME, I'M NOT TRAVEL-ING FOR WORK.
WELL, THAT DOESN'T MEAN THERE WON'T BE ANY DANGER.
IF YOU DON'T WANT TO, LATINA...
ぱっ
PWAP
SHE'LL GO.

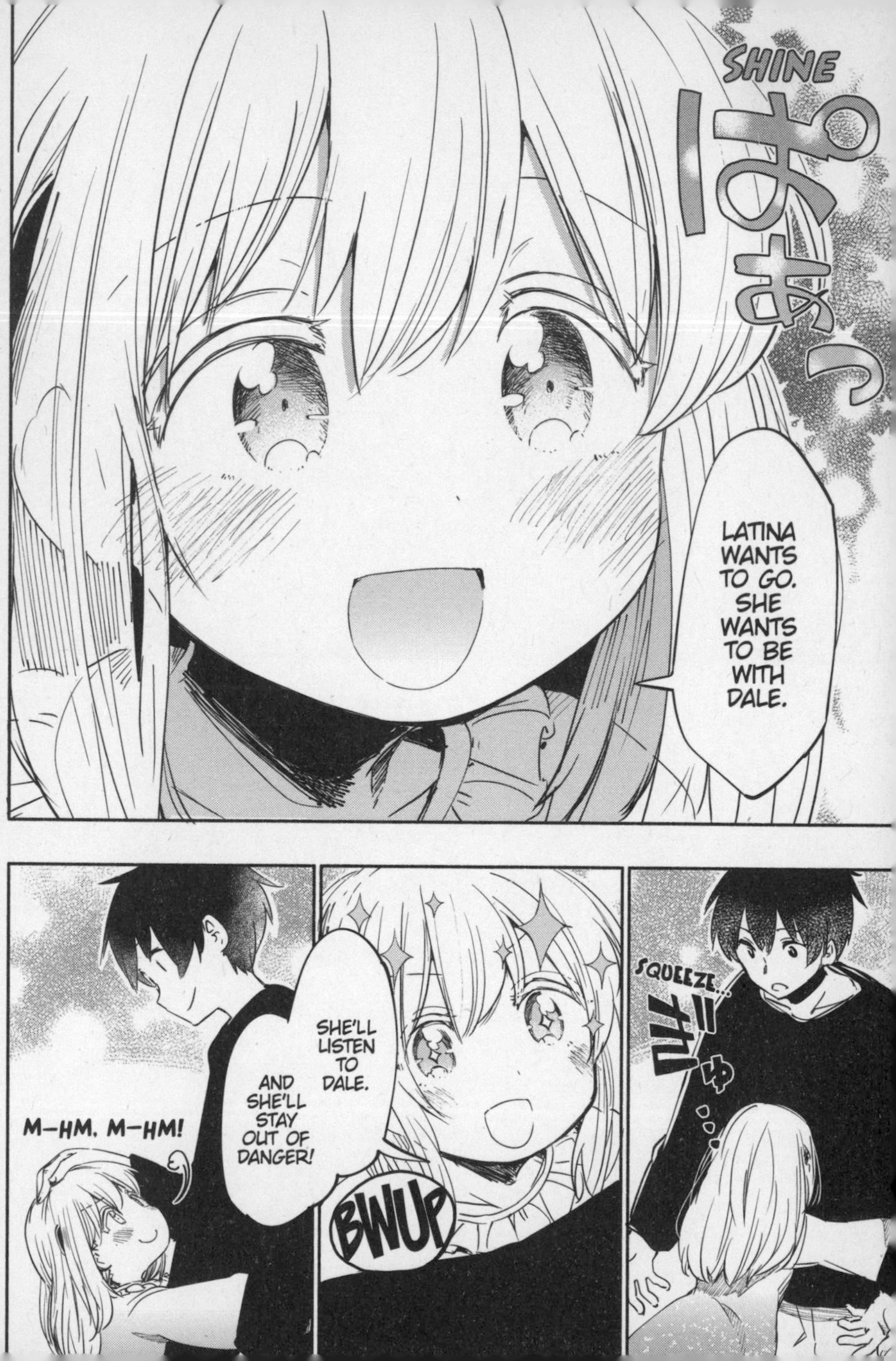
SHINE
ぱぁっ
LATINA WANTS TO GO. SHE WANTS TO BE WITH DALE.
SQUEEZE...
ぎゅ...
SHE'LL LISTEN TO DALE.
AND SHE'LL STAY OUT OF DANGER!
BWUP
M-HM. M-HM!

If It's For My Daughter I'd Even Defeat a Demon Lord

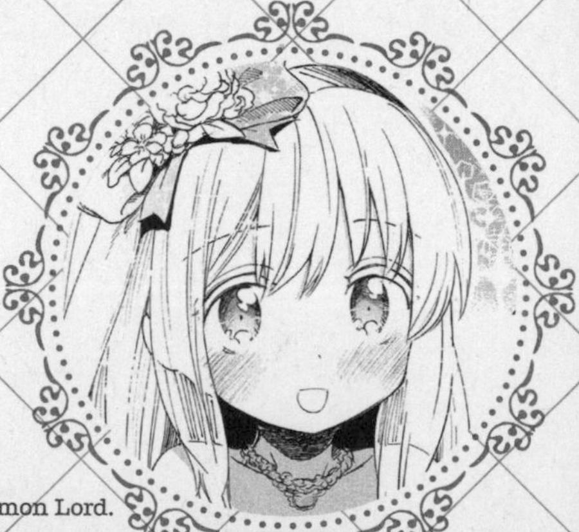

If It's For My Daughter, I'd Even Defeat a Demon Lord.

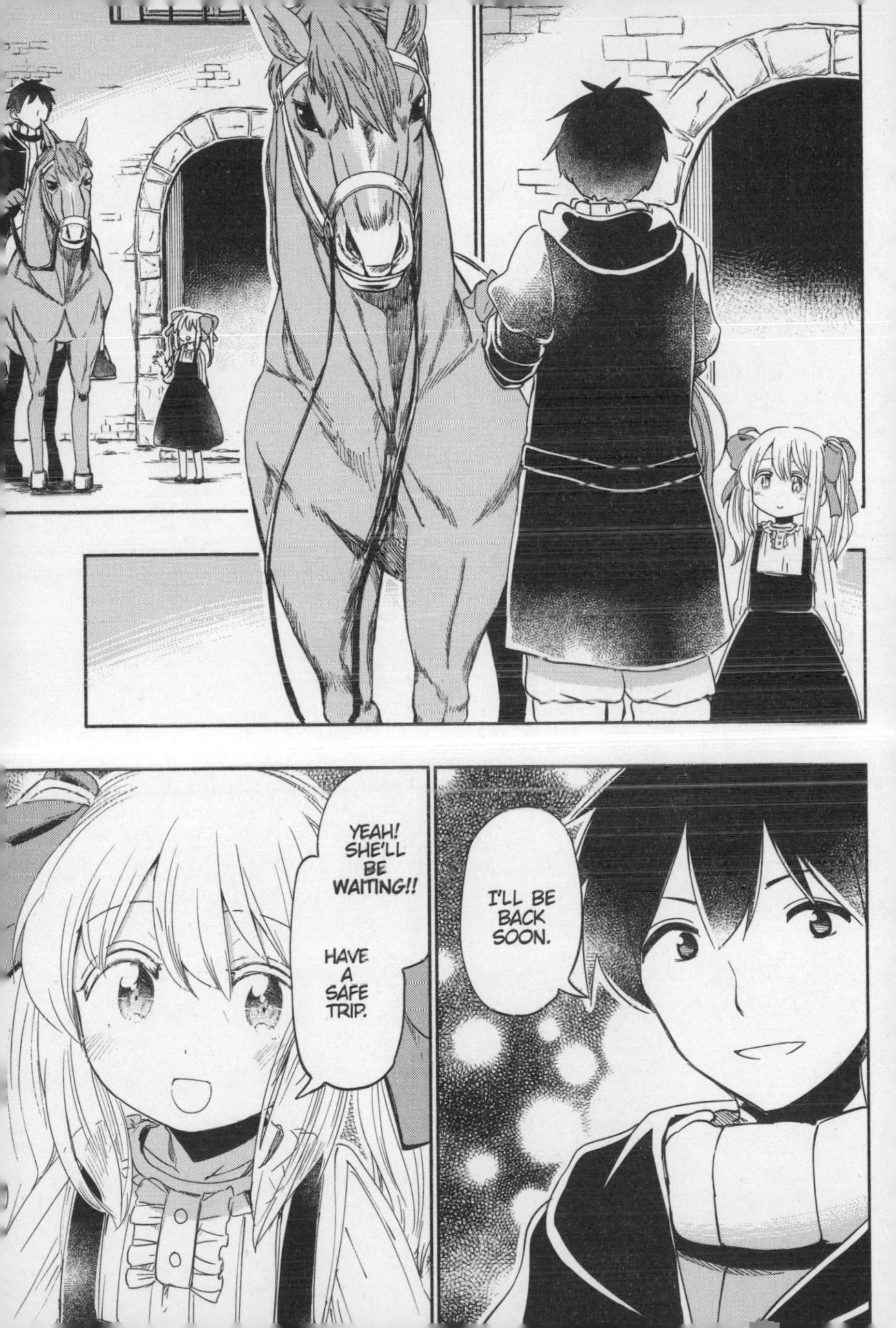
I'LL BE BACK SOON.
YEAH! SHE'LL BE WAITING!!
HAVE A SAFE TRIP.

23. Young Girl Prepares for a Journey

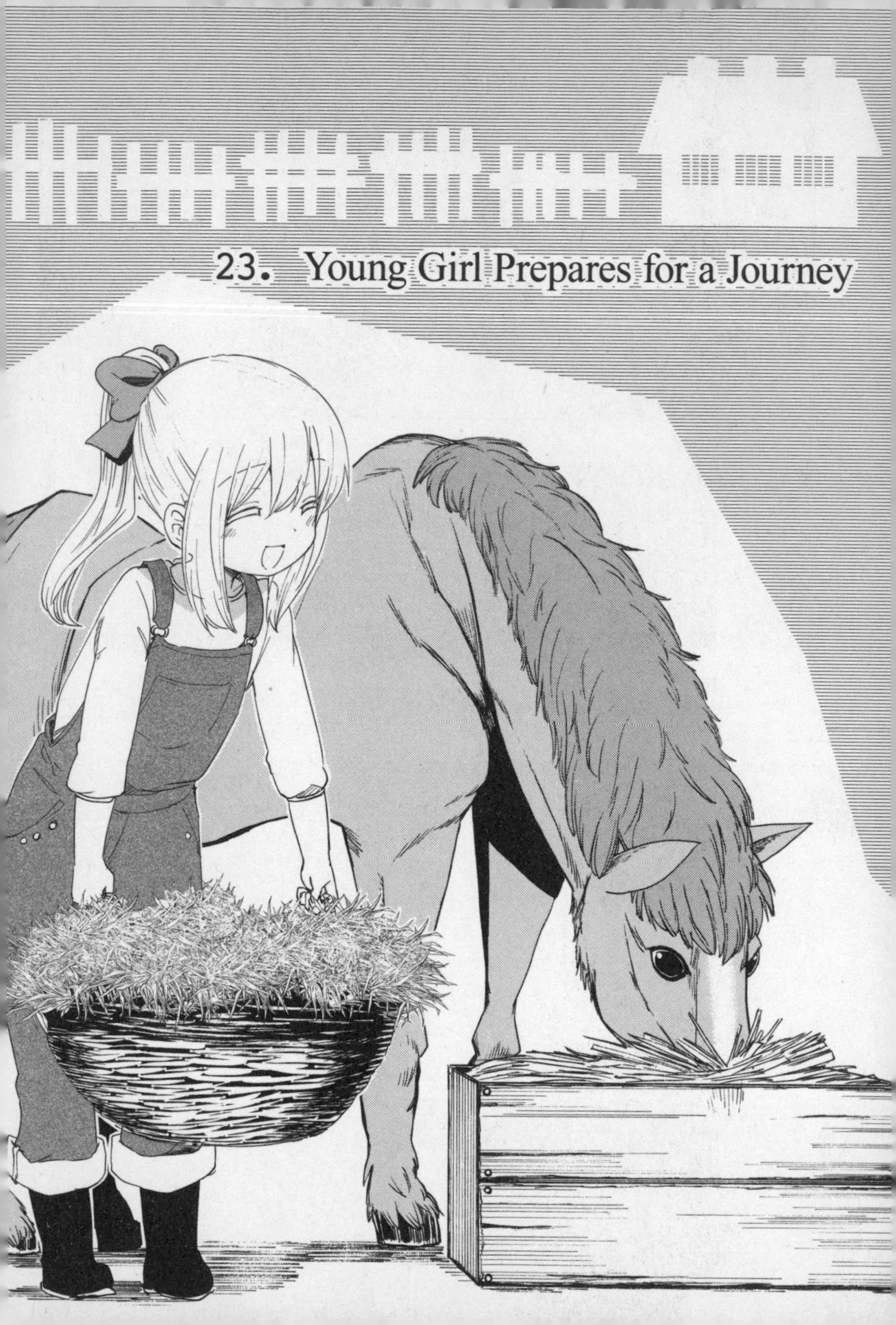

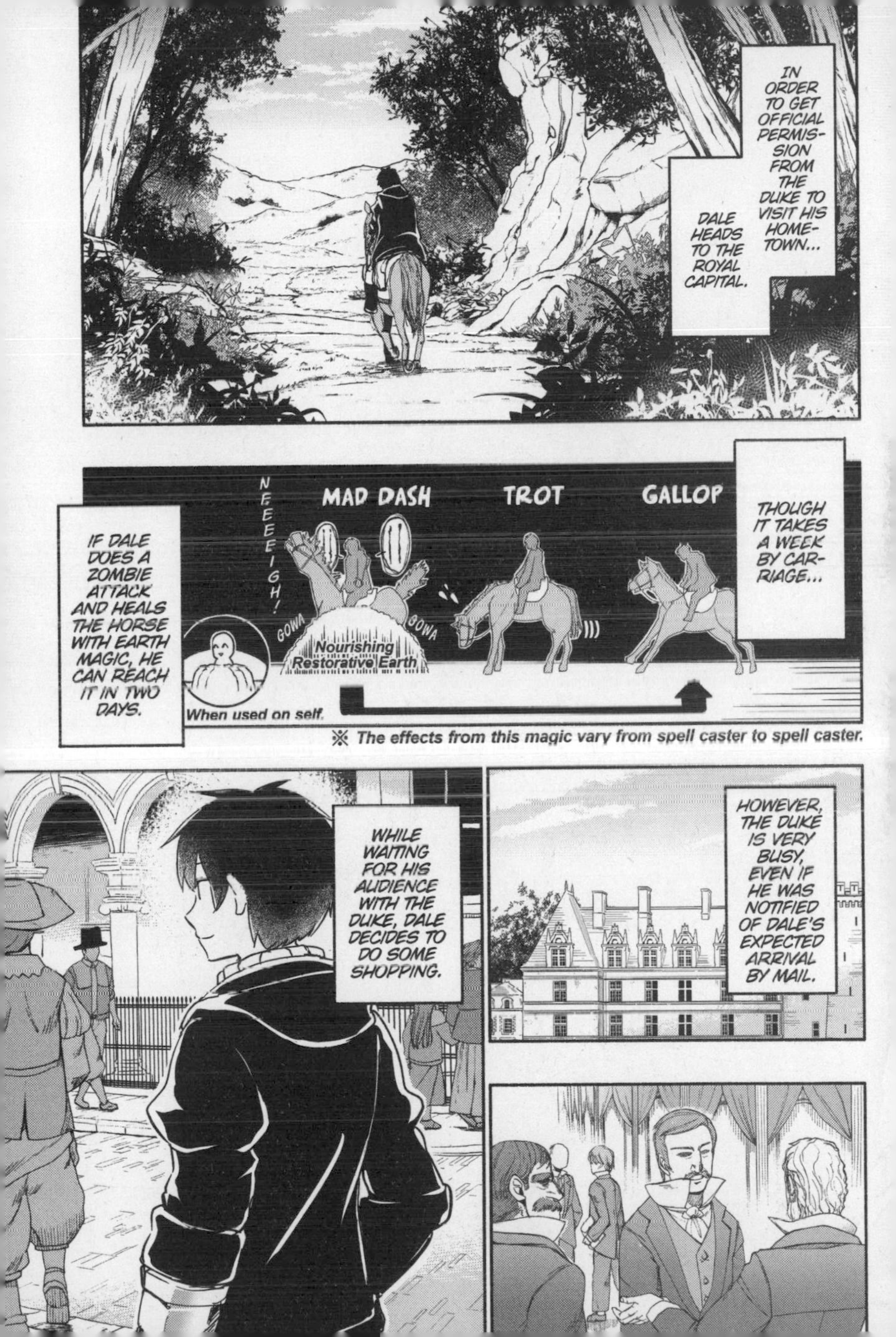
IN ORDER TO GET OFFICIAL PERMISSION FROM THE DUKE TO VISIT HIS HOMETOWN...
DALE HEADS TO THE ROYAL CAPITAL.
THOUGH IT TAKES A WEEK BY CARRIAGE...
GALLOP
TROT
MAD DASH
NEEEEIGH!
GOWA
GOWA
Nourishing Restorative Earth
When used on self.
IF DALE DOES A ZOMBIE ATTACK AND HEALS THE HORSE WITH EARTH MAGIC, HE CAN REACH IT IN TWO DAYS.
※ The effects from this magic vary from spell caster to spell caster.
HOWEVER, THE DUKE IS VERY BUSY, EVEN IF HE WAS NOTIFIED OF DALE'S EXPECTED ARRIVAL BY MAIL.
WHILE WAITING FOR HIS AUDIENCE WITH THE DUKE, DALE DECIDES TO DO SOME SHOPPING.

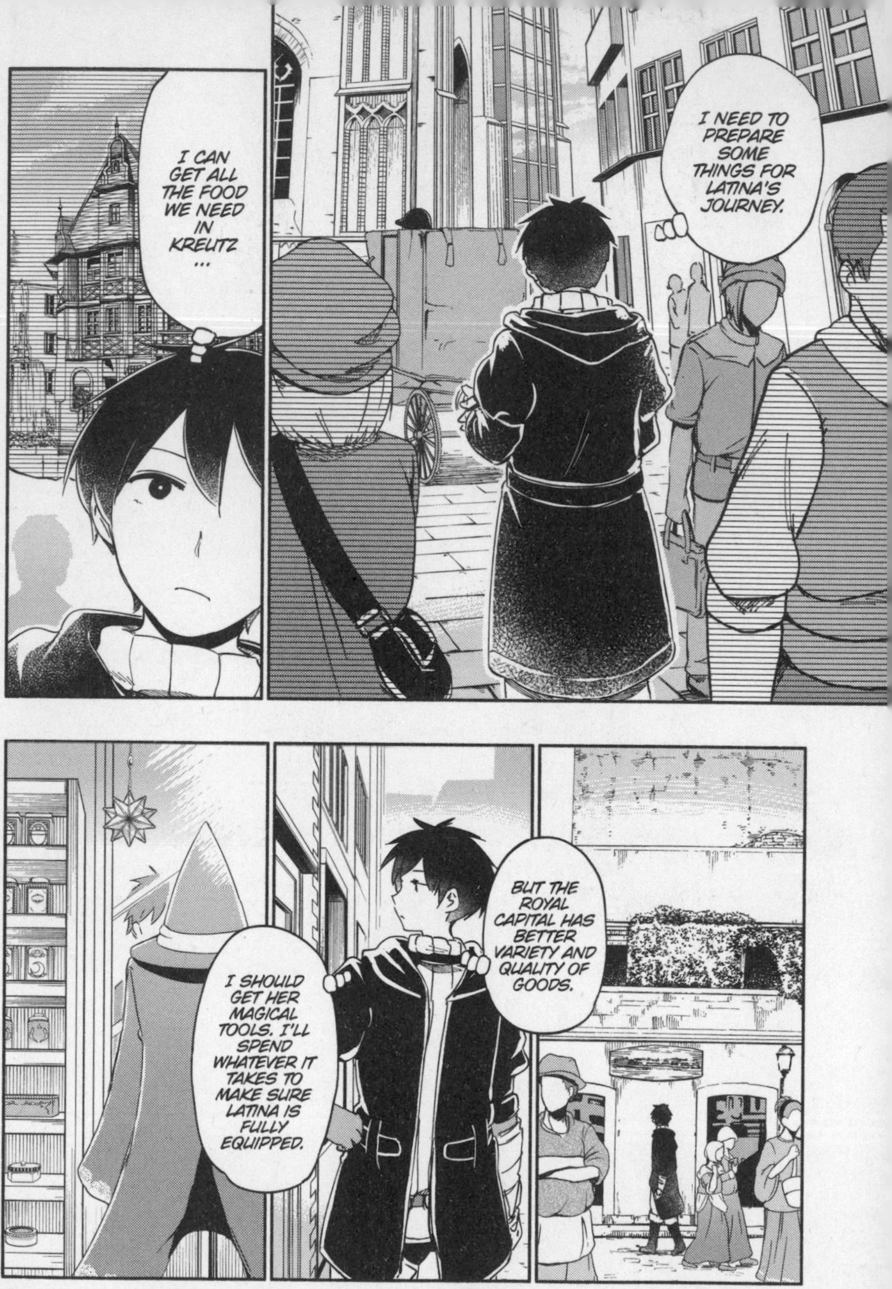
I NEED TO PREPARE SOME THINGS FOR LATINA'S JOURNEY.
I CAN GET ALL THE FOOD WE NEED IN KREUTZ...
BUT THE ROYAL CAPITAL HAS BETTER VARIETY AND QUALITY OF GOODS.
I SHOULD GET HER MAGICAL TOOLS. I'LL SPEND WHATEVER IT TAKES TO MAKE SURE LATINA IS FULLY EQUIPPED.

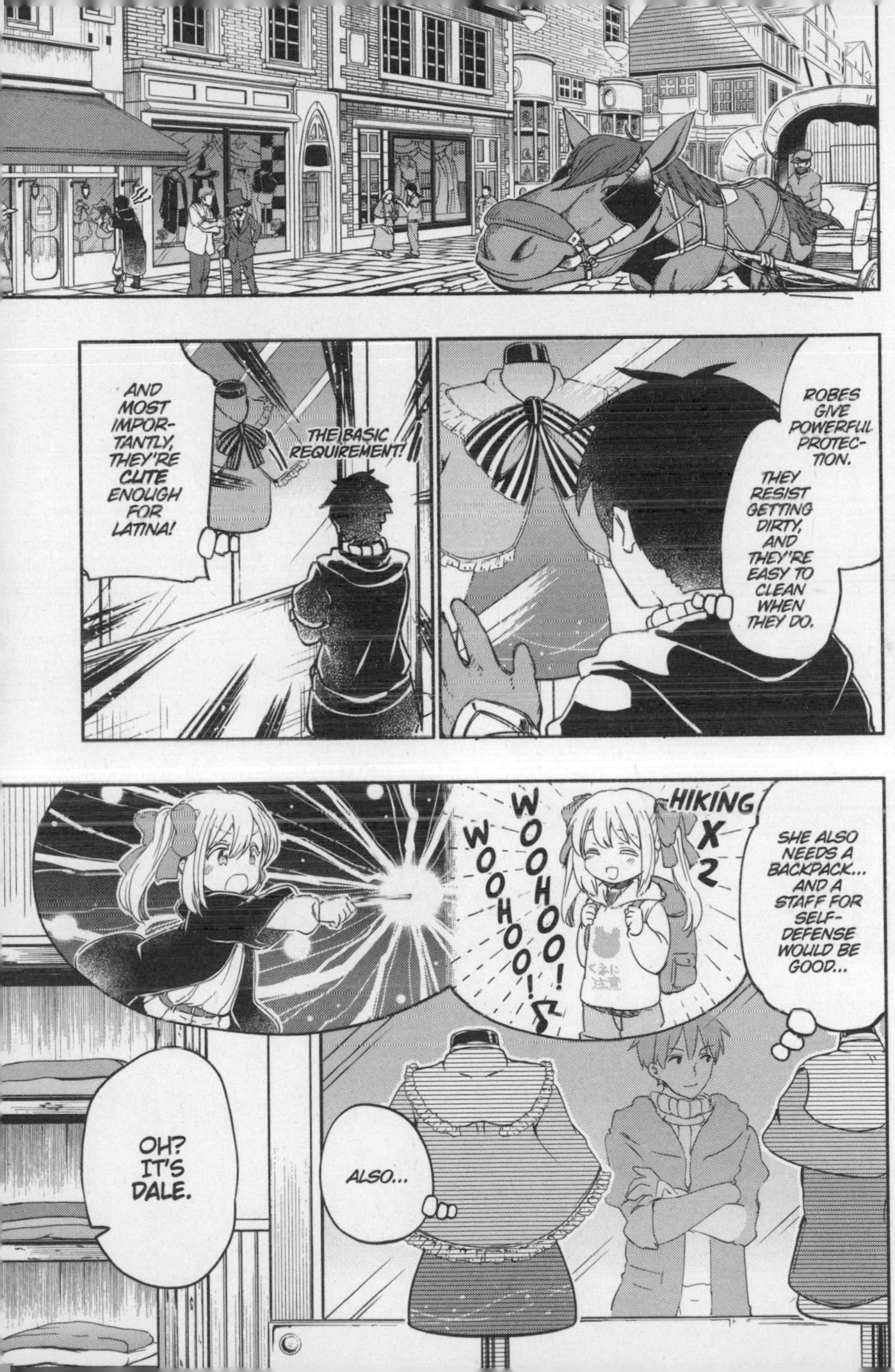
ROBES GIVE POWERFUL PROTECTION.
THEY RESIST GETTING DIRTY, AND THEY'RE EASY TO CLEAN WHEN THEY DO.
THE BASIC REQUIREMENT!
AND MOST IMPORTANTLY, THEY'RE CUTE ENOUGH FOR LATINA!
SHE ALSO NEEDS A BACKPACK... AND A STAFF FOR SELF-DEFENSE WOULD BE GOOD...
HIKING X2
WOOHOOO!
WOOHOO!
ALSO...
OH? IT'S DALE.

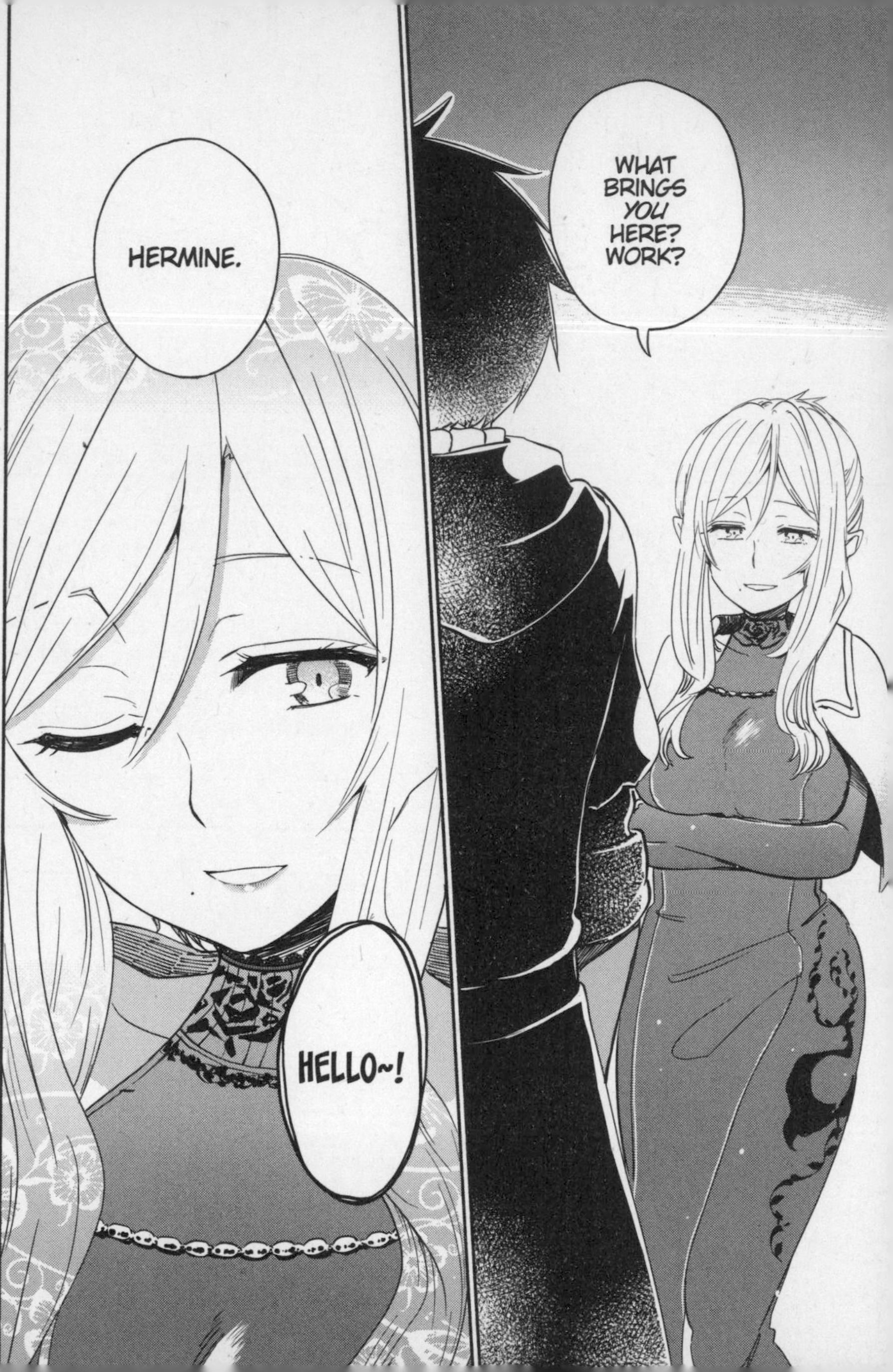
WHAT BRINGS YOU HERE? WORK?
HERMINE.
HELLO~!

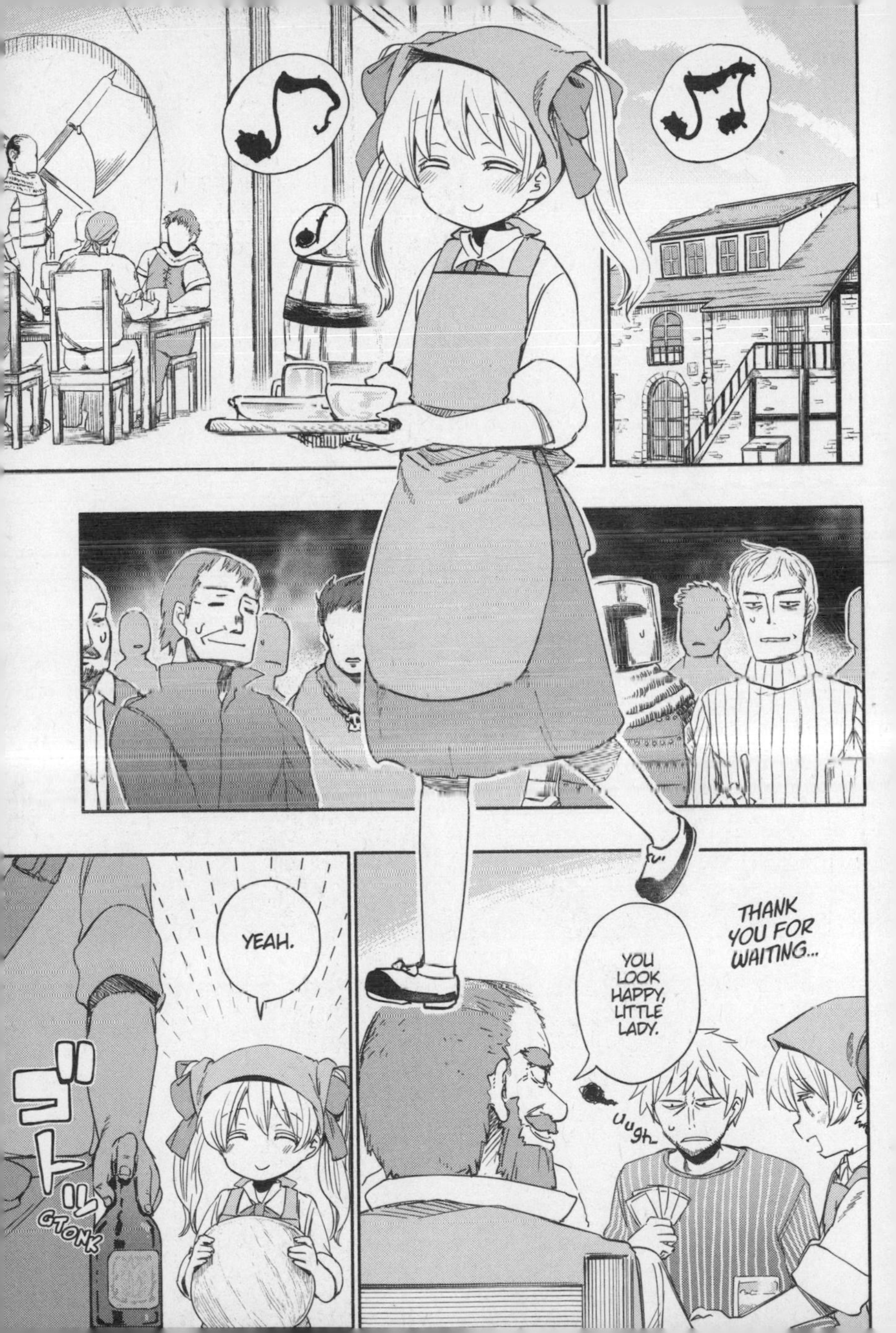
THANK YOU FOR WAITING...
YOU LOOK HAPPY, LITTLE LADY.
Uugh
YEAH.
ゴトッ
GTONK

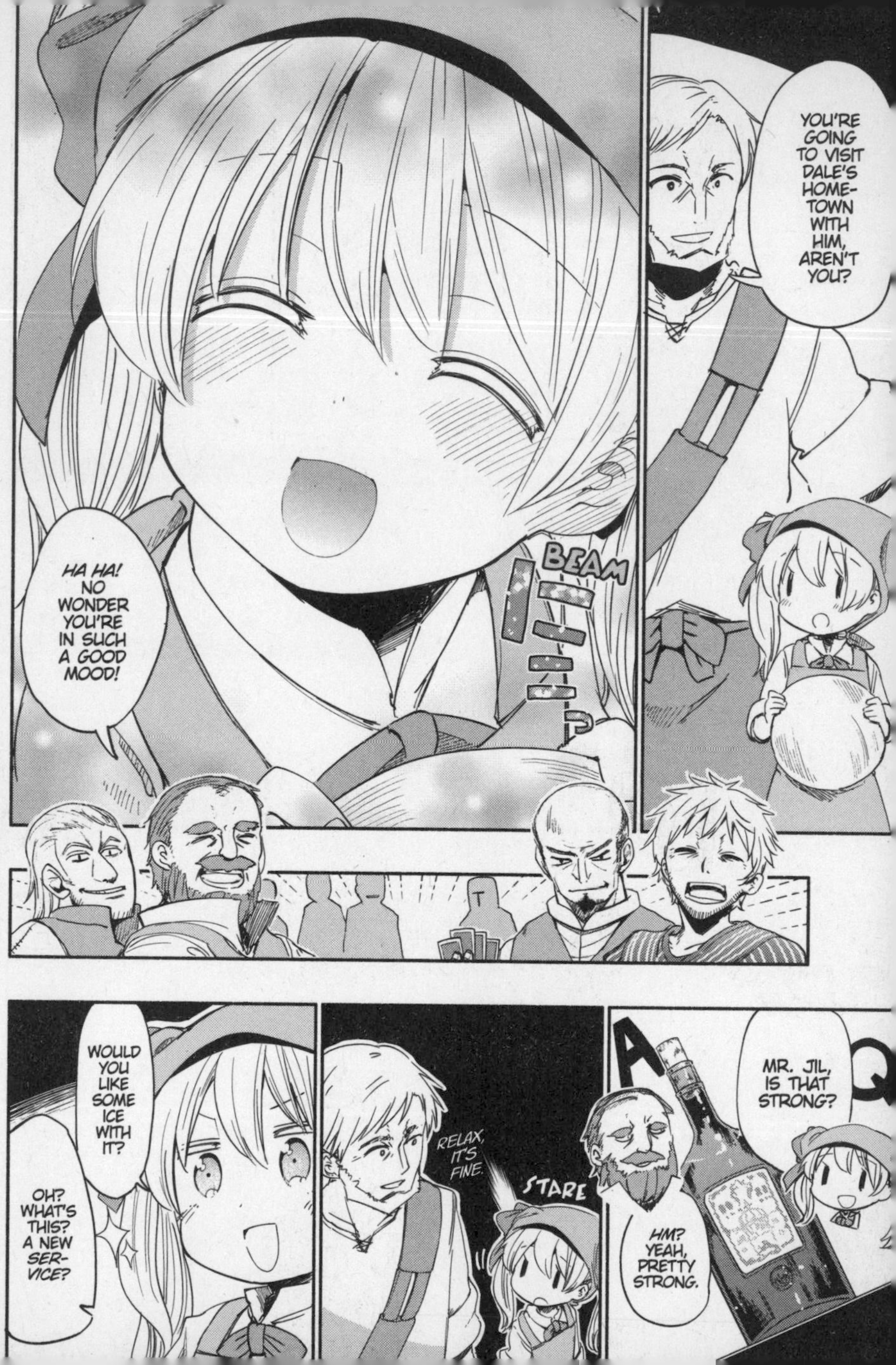
YOU'RE GOING TO VISIT DALE'S HOME-TOWN WITH HIM, AREN'T YOU?
BEAM
HA HA! NO WONDER YOU'RE IN SUCH A GOOD MOOD!
MR. JIL, IS THAT STRONG?
HM? YEAH, PRETTY STRONG.
STARE
RELAX, IT'S FINE.
WOULD YOU LIKE SOME ICE WITH IT?
OH? WHAT'S THIS? A NEW SER-VICE?

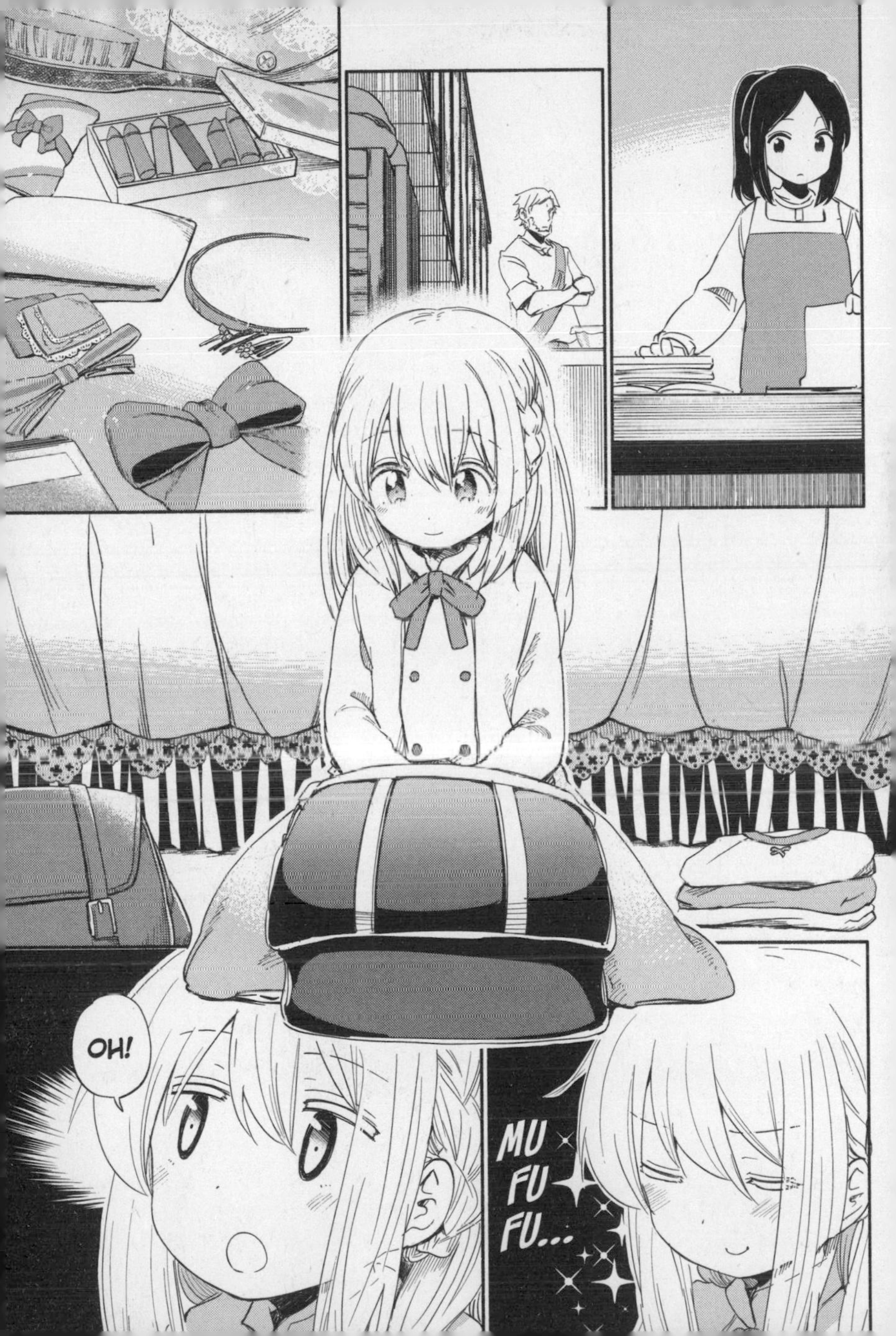
MU FU FU...
OH!

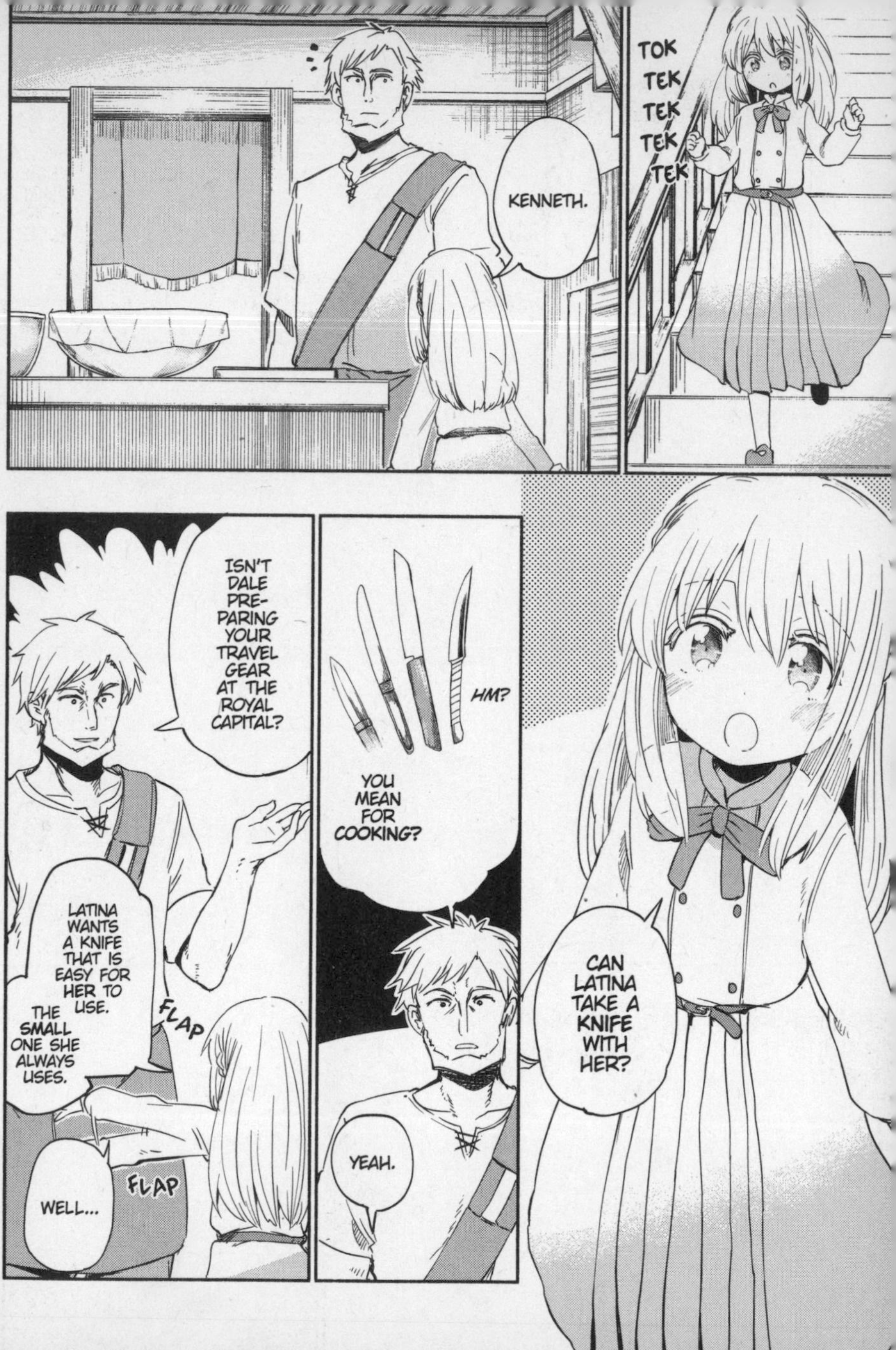
TOK
TEK
TEK
TEK
TEK
KENNETH.
CAN LATINA TAKE A KNIFE WITH HER?
HM?
YOU MEAN FOR COOKING?
YEAH.
ISN'T DALE PRE-PARING YOUR TRAVEL GEAR AT THE ROYAL CAPITAL?
LATINA WANTS A KNIFE THAT IS EASY FOR HER TO USE.
THE SMALL ONE SHE ALWAYS USES.
FLAP
FLAP
WELL...

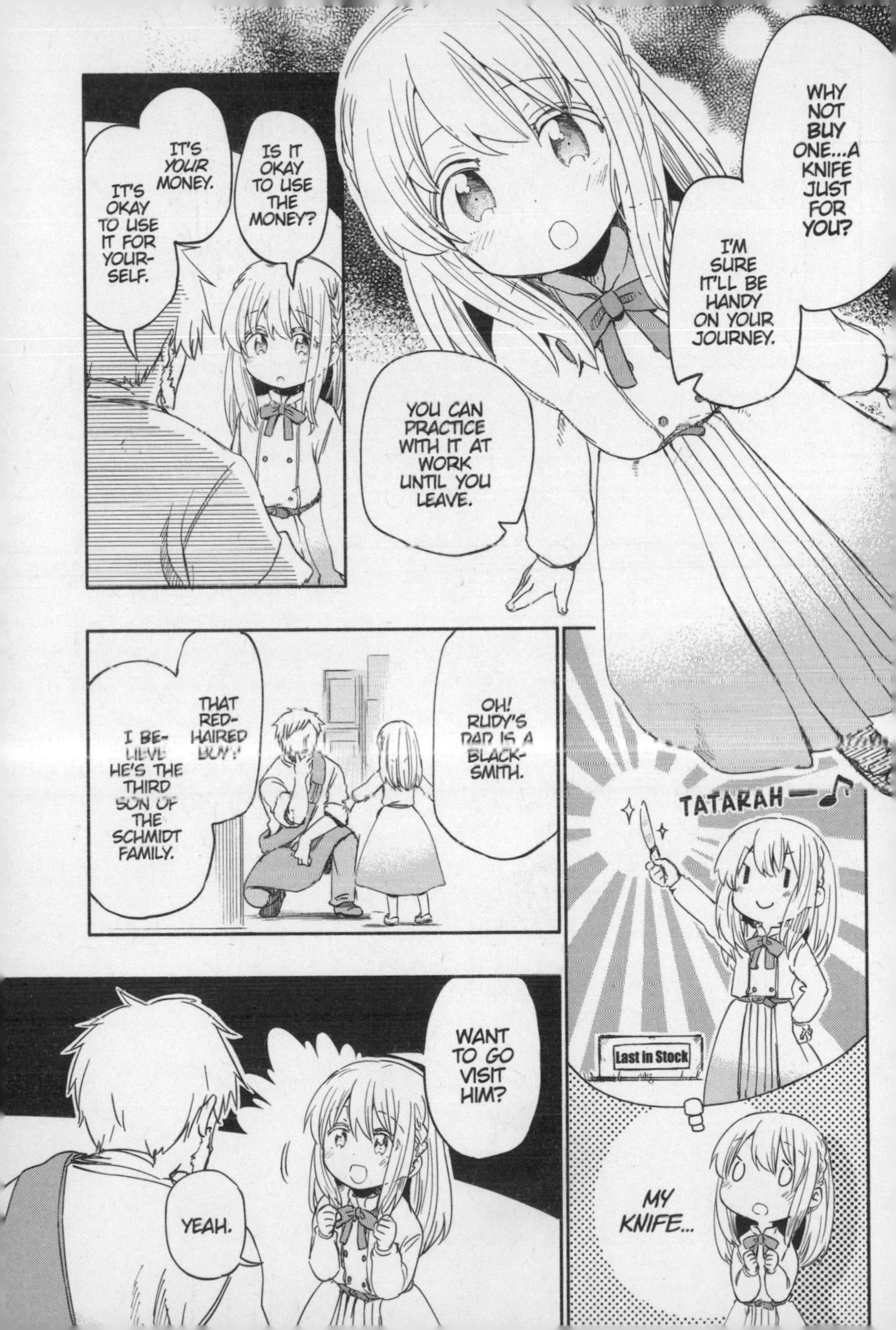
WHY NOT BUY ONE...A KNIFE JUST FOR YOU?
I'M SURE IT'LL BE HANDY ON YOUR JOURNEY.
YOU CAN PRACTICE WITH IT AT WORK UNTIL YOU LEAVE.
IS IT OKAY TO USE THE MONEY?
IT'S *YOUR* MONEY.
IT'S OKAY TO USE IT FOR YOURSELF.
TATARAH—♪
Last in Stock
MY KNIFE...
OH! RUDY'S DAD IS A BLACKSMITH.
THAT RED-HAIRED BOY?
I BELIEVE HE'S THE THIRD SON OF THE SCHMIDT FAMILY.
WANT TO GO VISIT HIM?
YEAH.

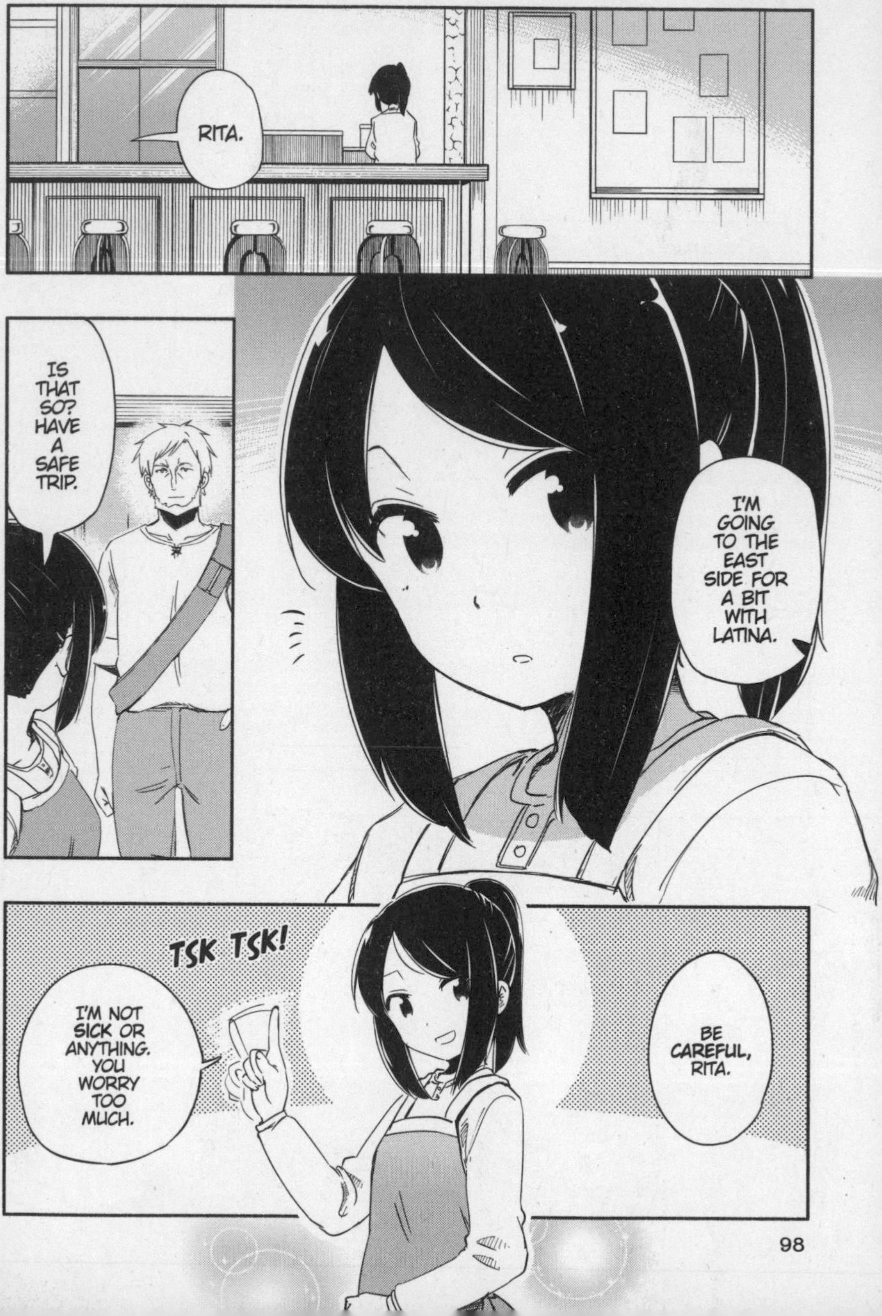
RITA.
I'M GOING TO THE EAST SIDE FOR A BIT WITH LATINA.
IS THAT SO? HAVE A SAFE TRIP.
BE CAREFUL, RITA.
TSK TSK!
I'M NOT SICK OR ANYTHING. YOU WORRY TOO MUCH.

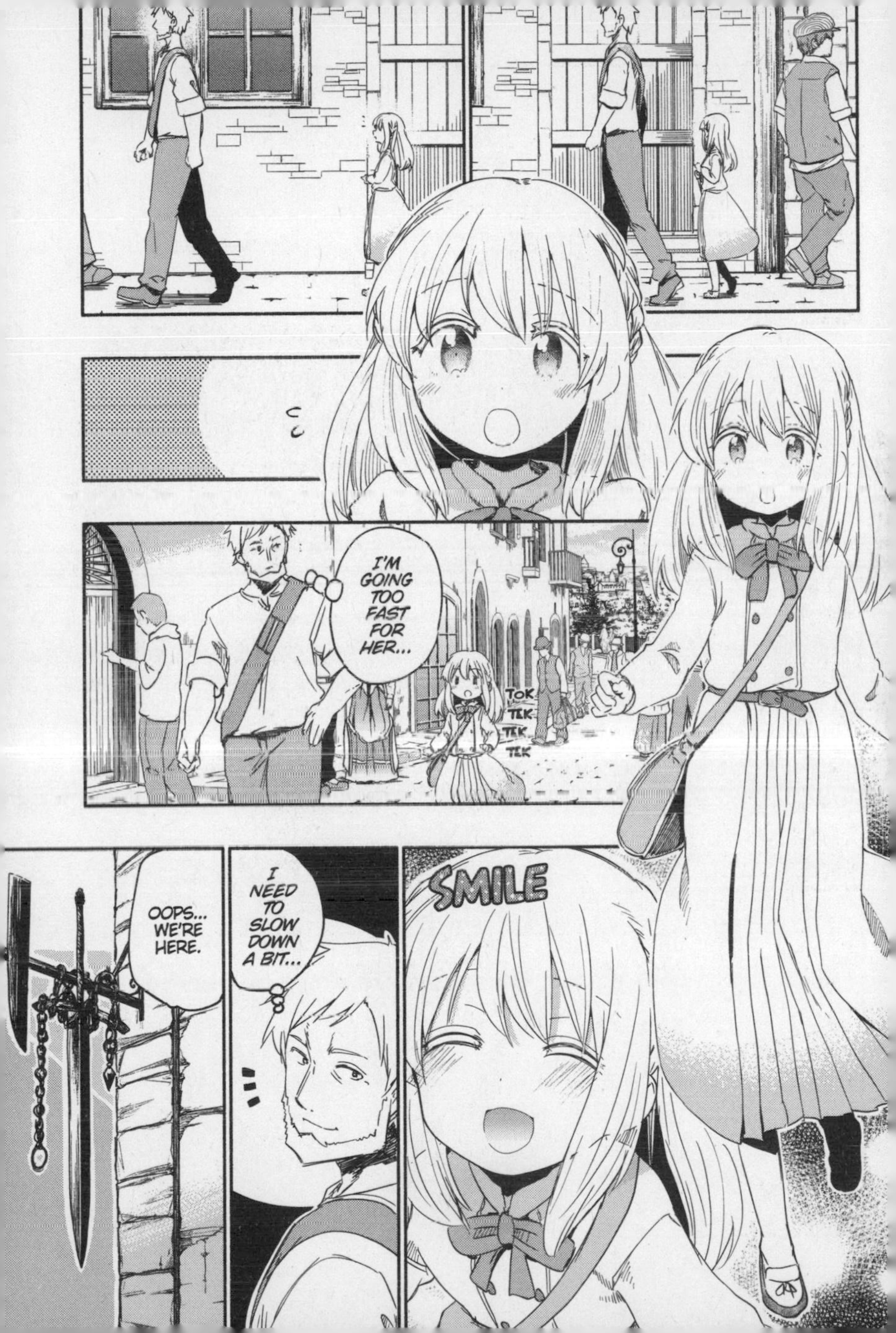
I'M GOING TOO FAST FOR HER...
TOK TEK TEK TEK
SMILE
I NEED TO SLOW DOWN A BIT...
OOPS... WE'RE HERE.

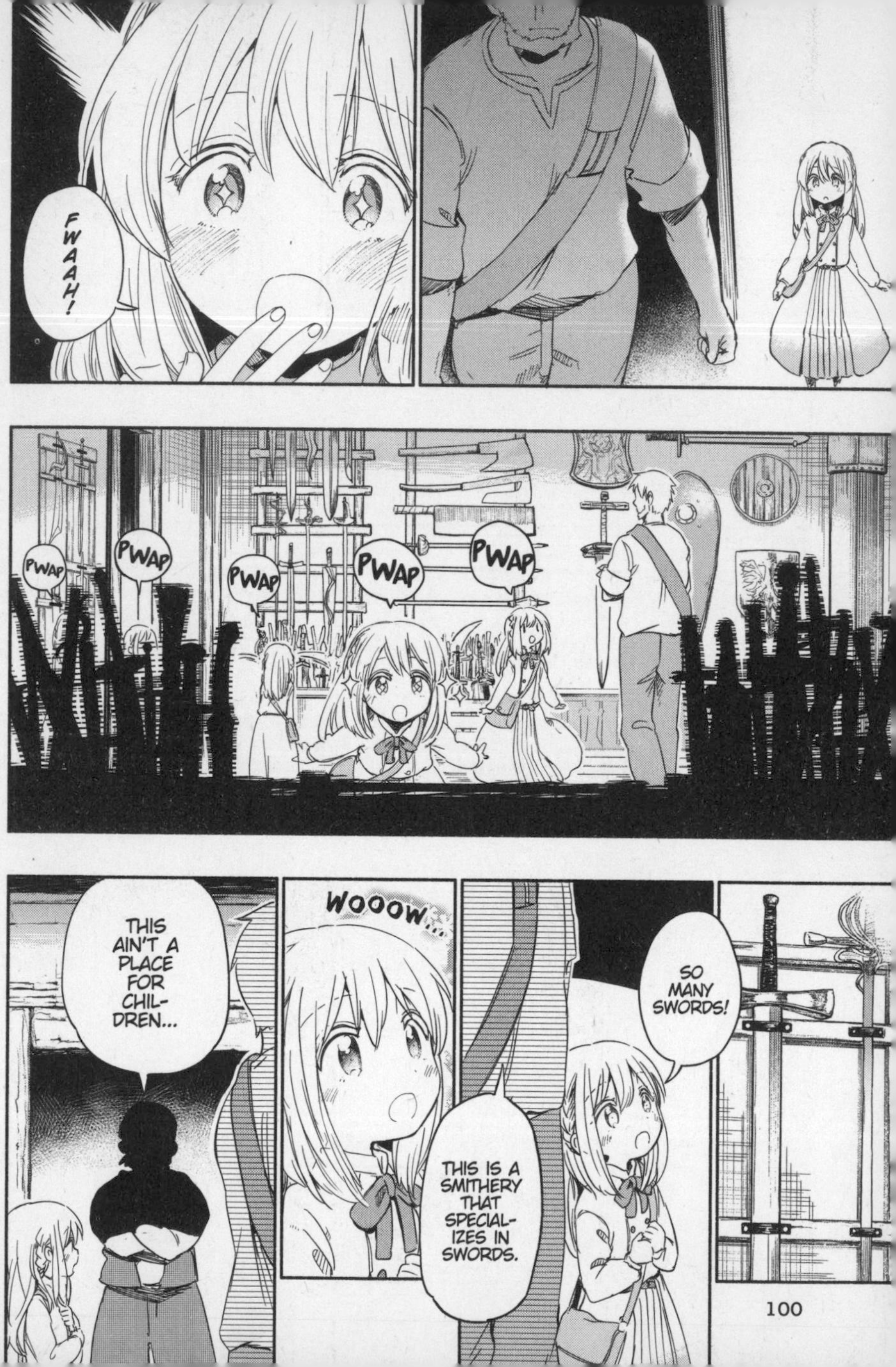
FWAAH!
PWAP
PWAP
PWAP
PWAP
PWAP
SO MANY SWORDS!
WOOOW...
THIS IS A SMITHERY THAT SPECIALIZES IN SWORDS.
THIS AIN'T A PLACE FOR CHILDREN...

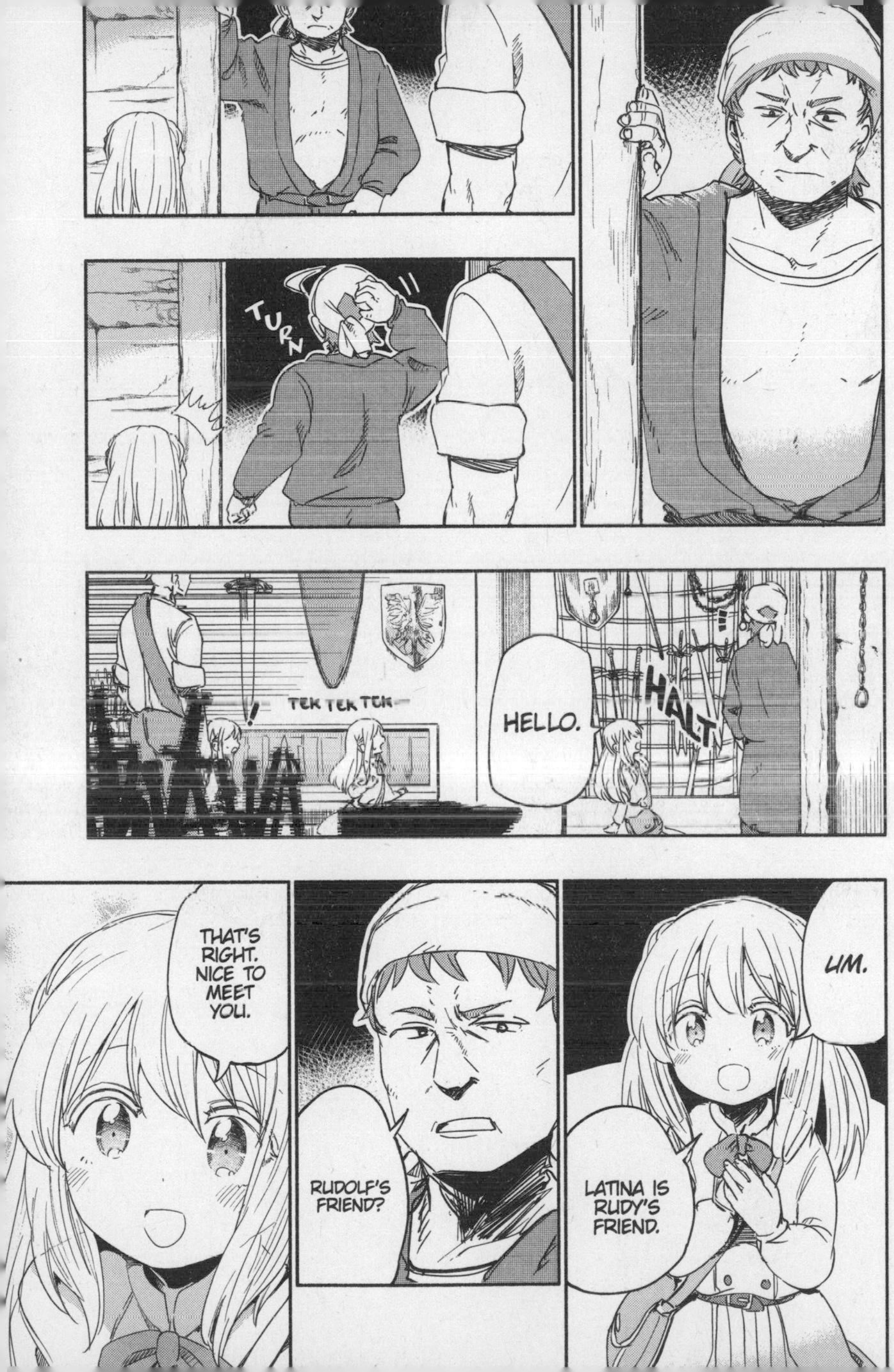
TURN
HALT
HELLO.
TEK TEK TEK
UM.
LATINA IS RUDY'S FRIEND.
RUDOLF'S FRIEND?
THAT'S RIGHT. NICE TO MEET YOU.

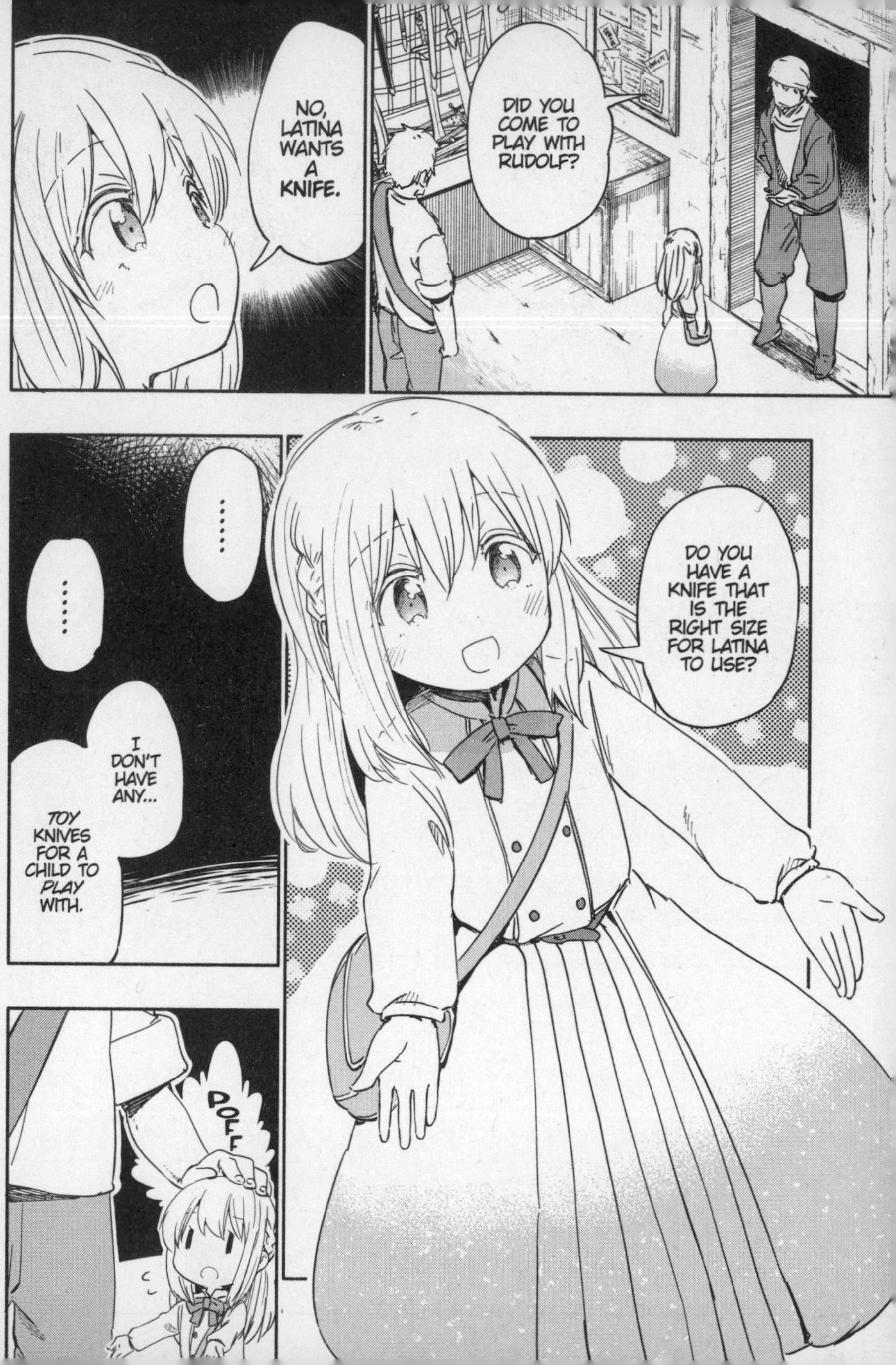
DID YOU COME TO PLAY WITH RUDOLF?
NO, LATINA WANTS A KNIFE.
DO YOU HAVE A KNIFE THAT IS THE RIGHT SIZE FOR LATINA TO USE?
......
......
I DON'T HAVE ANY...
TOY KNIVES FOR A CHILD TO *PLAY* WITH.
DOFF

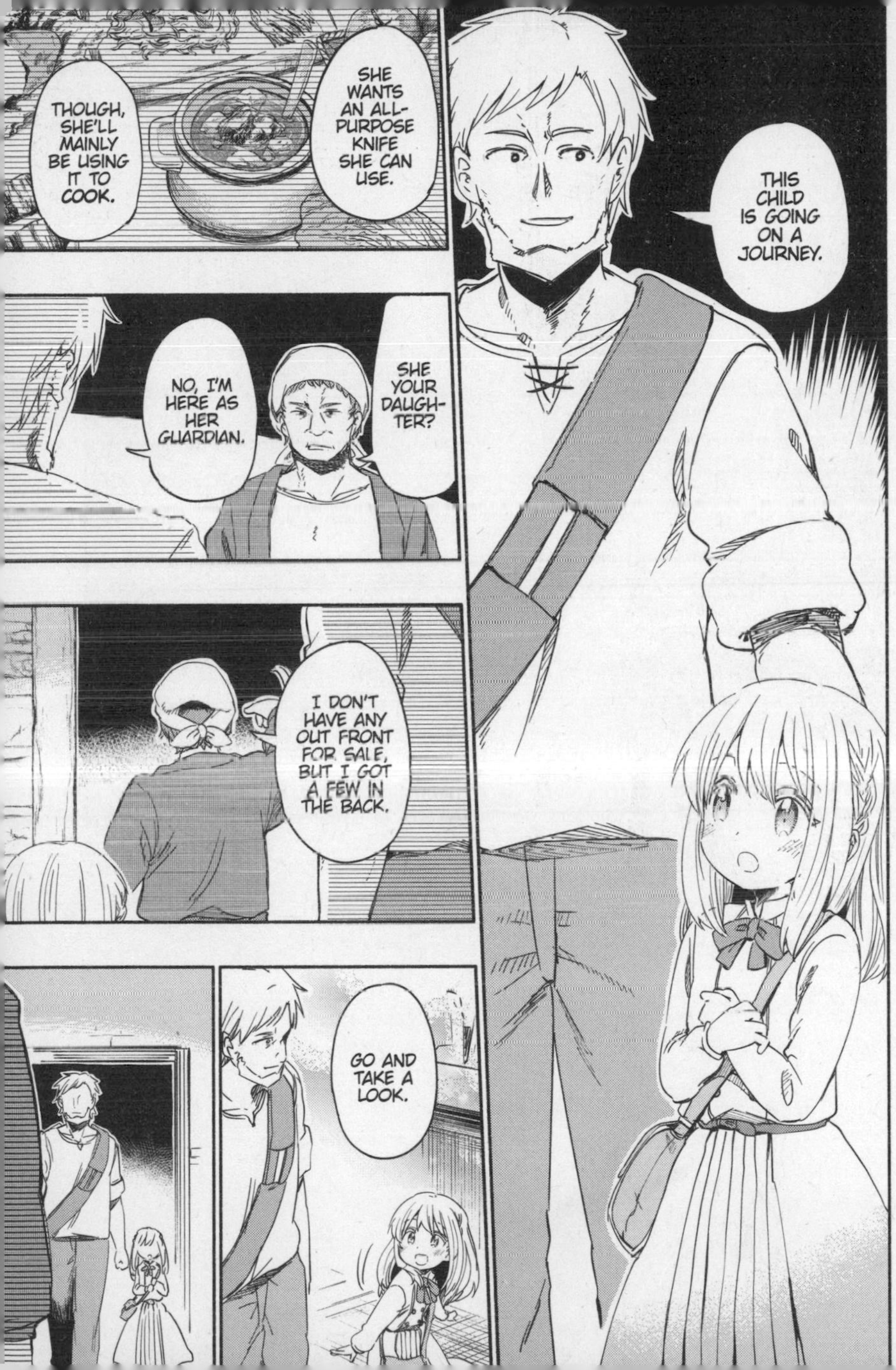
THIS CHILD IS GOING ON A JOURNEY.
SHE WANTS AN ALL-PURPOSE KNIFE SHE CAN USE.
THOUGH, SHE'LL MAINLY BE USING IT TO COOK.
SHE YOUR DAUGHTER?
NO, I'M HERE AS HER GUARDIAN.
I DON'T HAVE ANY OUT FRONT FOR SALE, BUT I GOT A FEW IN THE BACK.
GO AND TAKE A LOOK.

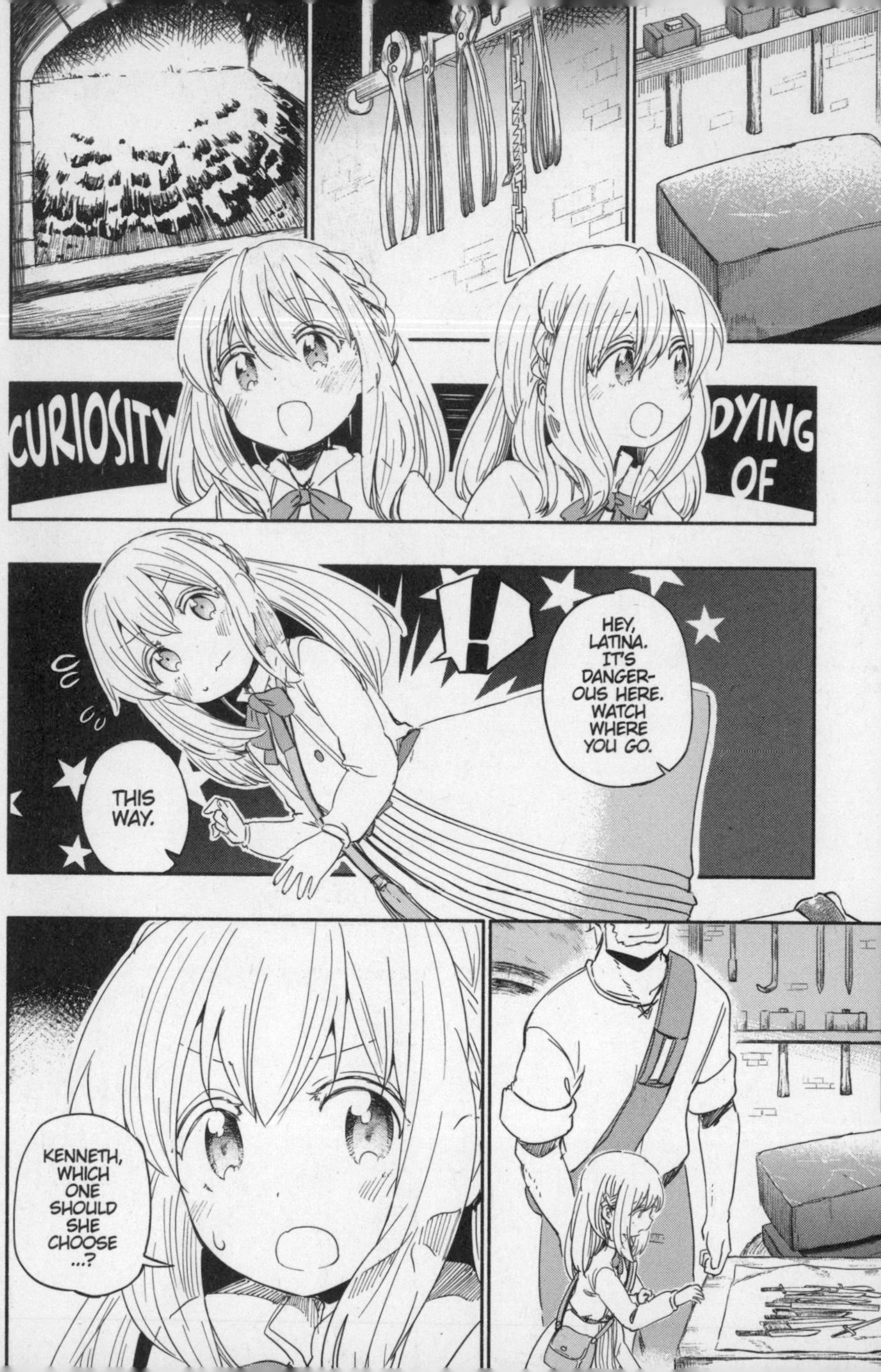
DYING OF
CURIOSITY
!
HEY, LATINA. IT'S DANGER-OUS HERE. WATCH WHERE YOU GO.
THIS WAY.
KENNETH, WHICH ONE SHOULD SHE CHOOSE ...?

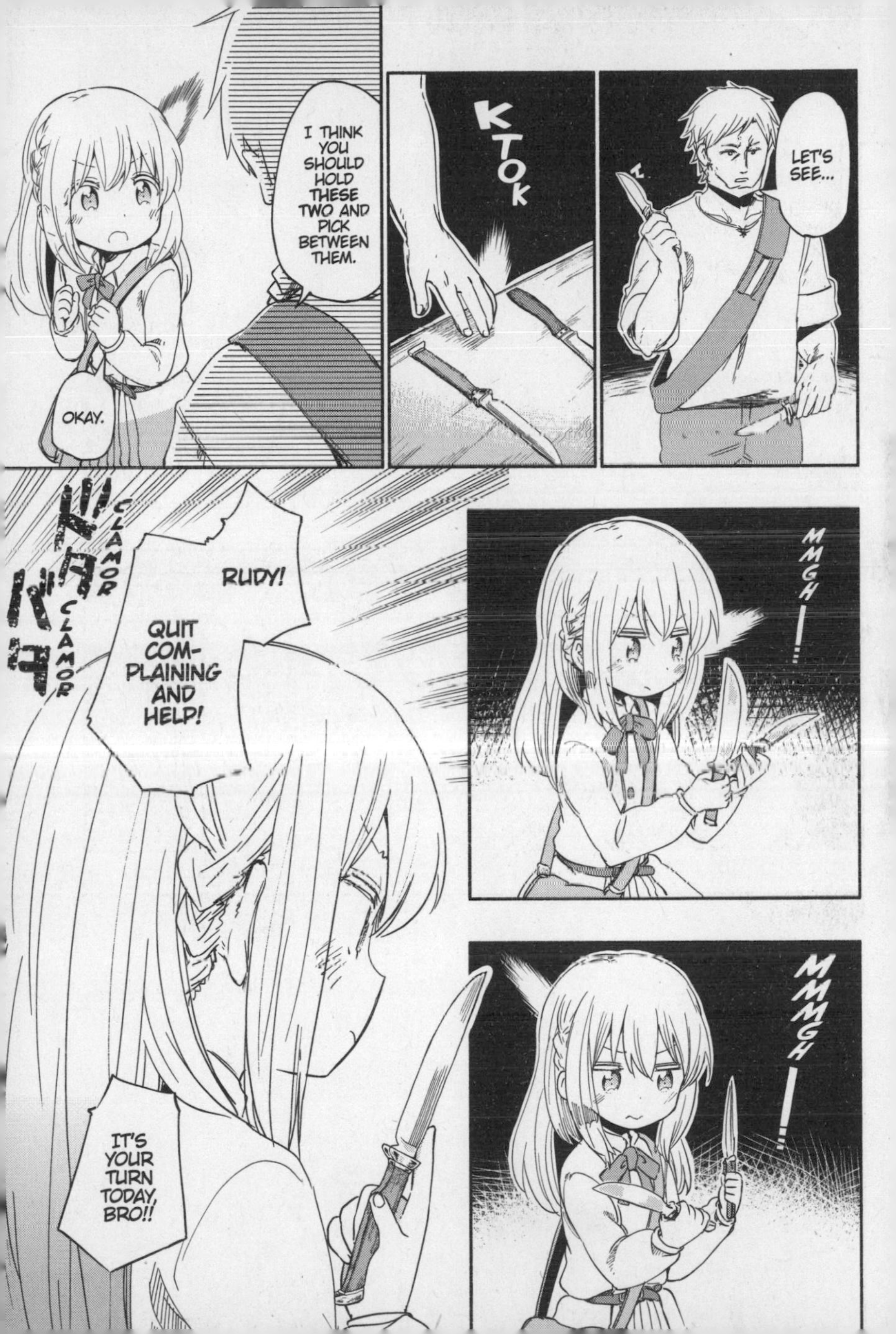
LET'S SEE...
KTOK
I THINK YOU SHOULD HOLD THESE TWO AND PICK BETWEEN THEM.
OKAY.
MMGH!!
MMMGH!!
CLAMOR CLAMOR
RUDY!
QUIT COM-PLAINING AND HELP!
IT'S YOUR TURN TODAY, BRO!!

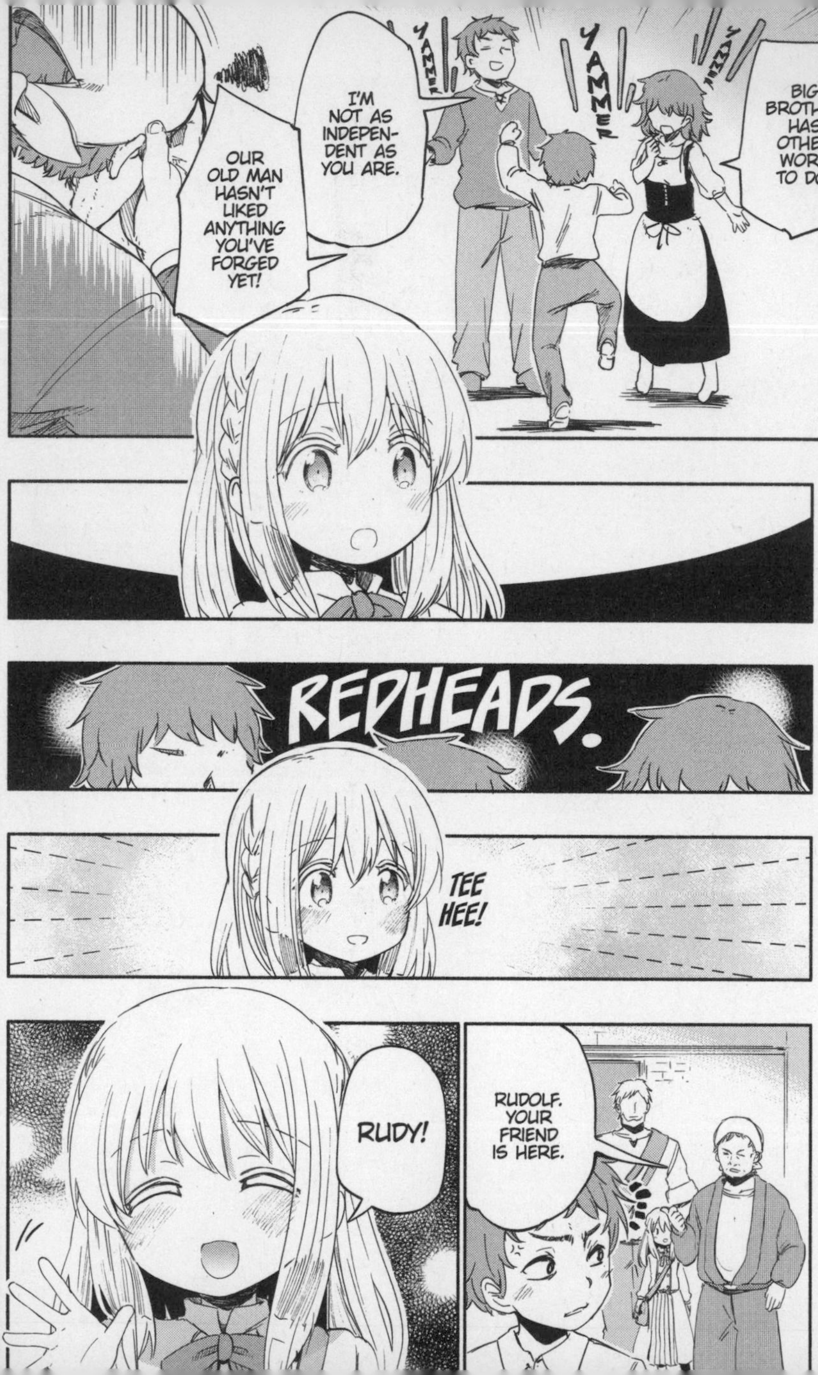
YAMMER
BIG BROTHER HAS OTHER WORK TO DO!
YAMMER
YAMMER
I'M NOT AS INDEPEN-DENT AS YOU ARE.
OUR OLD MAN HASN'T LIKED ANYTHING YOU'VE FORGED YET!
REDHEADS.
TEE HEE!
RUDOLF. YOUR FRIEND IS HERE.
RUDY!

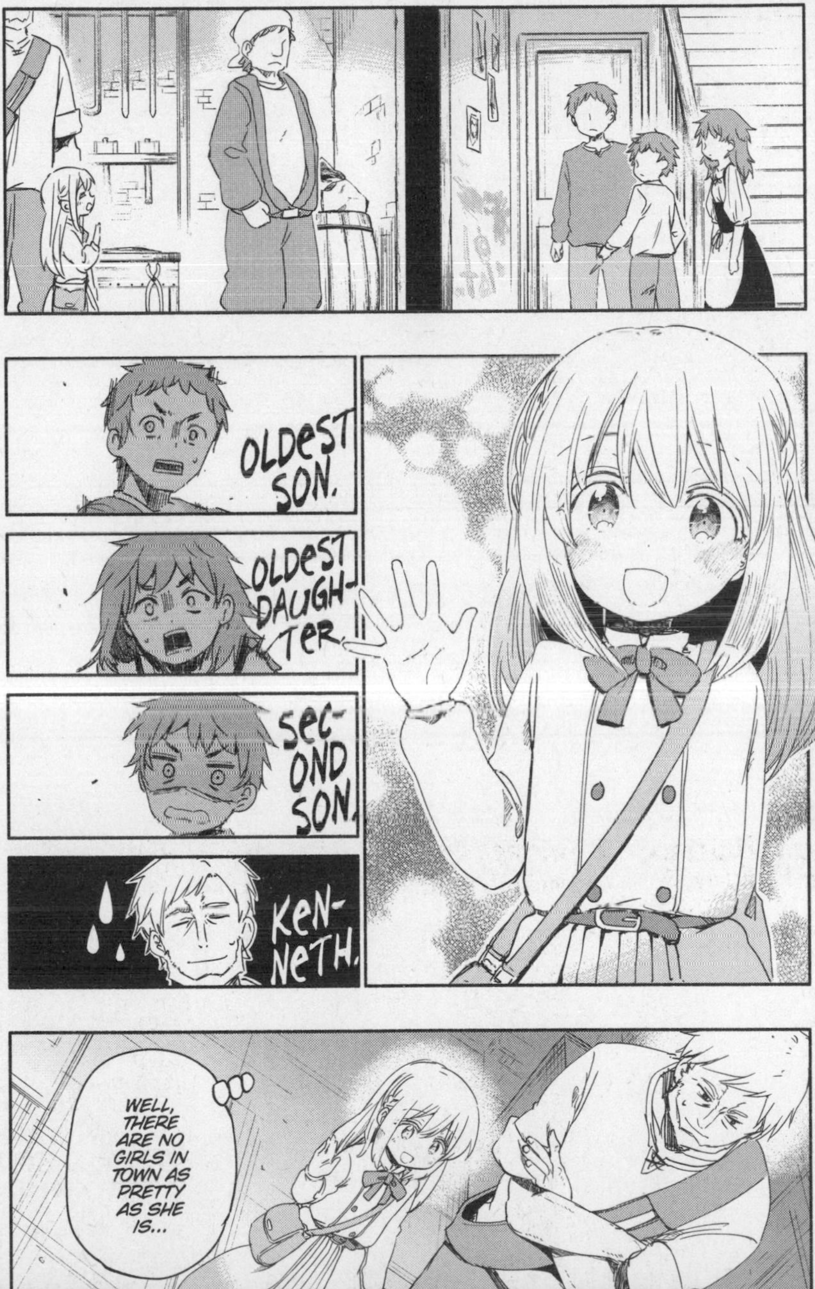
OLDEST SON.
OLDEST DAUGH-TER.
SEC-OND SON.
KEN-NETH.
WELL, THERE ARE NO GIRLS IN TOWN AS PRETTY AS SHE IS...

If It's For My Daughter, I'd Even Defeat a Demon Lord.

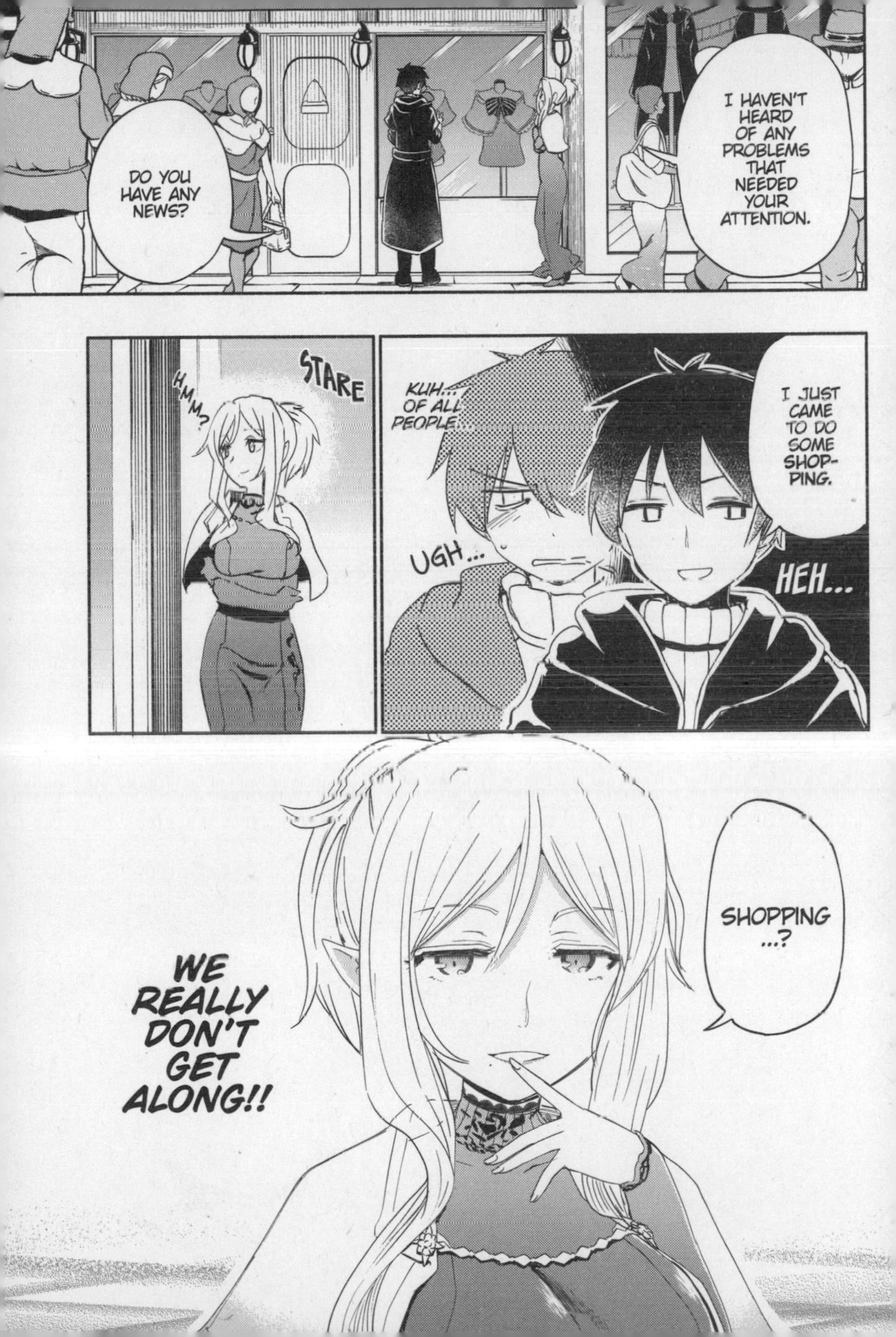
I HAVEN'T HEARD OF ANY PROBLEMS THAT NEEDED YOUR ATTENTION.
DO YOU HAVE ANY NEWS?
I JUST CAME TO DO SOME SHOP-PING.
HEH...
KUH... OF ALL PEOPLE...
UGH...
STARE
HMM?
SHOPPING ...?
WE REALLY DON'T GET ALONG!!

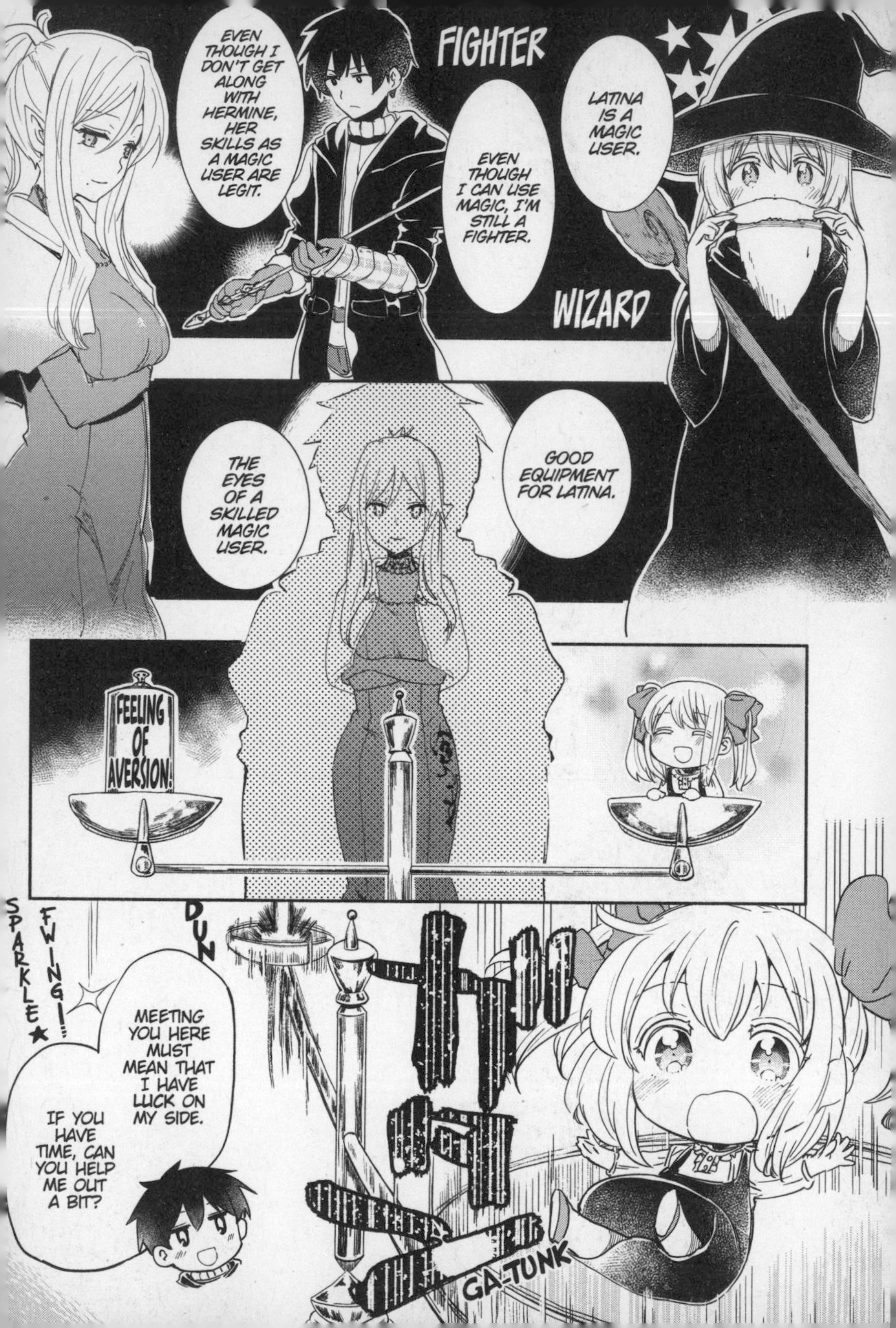
LATINA IS A MAGIC USER.
WIZARD
EVEN THOUGH I CAN USE MAGIC, I'M STILL A FIGHTER.
FIGHTER
EVEN THOUGH I DON'T GET ALONG WITH HERMINE, HER SKILLS AS A MAGIC USER ARE LEGIT.
GOOD EQUIPMENT FOR LATINA.
THE EYES OF A SKILLED MAGIC USER.
FEELING OF AVERSION!
GA-TUNK
DUN
FWING!!
SPARKLE★
MEETING YOU HERE MUST MEAN THAT I HAVE LUCK ON MY SIDE.
IF YOU HAVE TIME, CAN YOU HELP ME OUT A BIT?

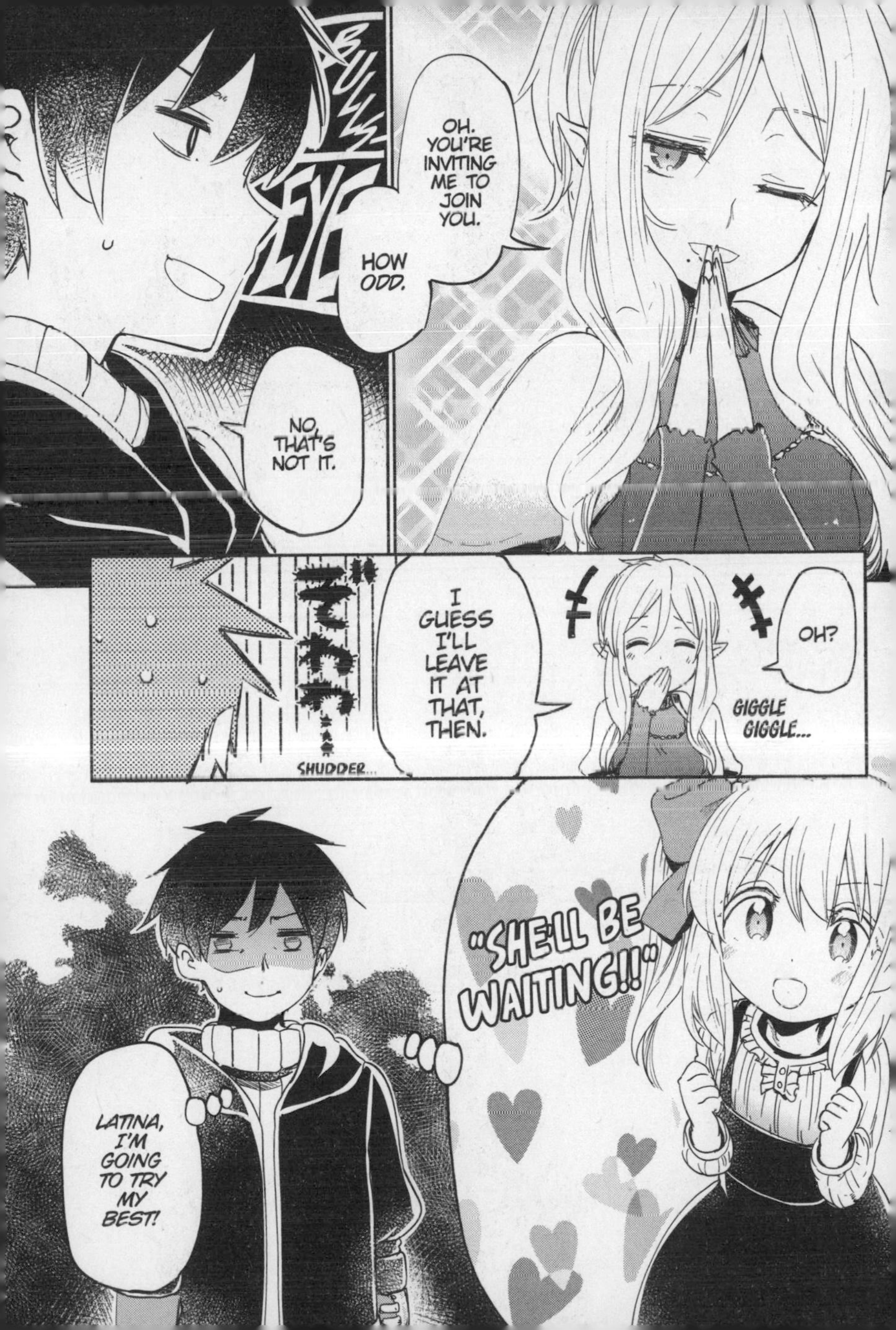
OH. YOU'RE INVITING ME TO JOIN YOU.
HOW ODD.
NO, THAT'S NOT IT.
OH?
GIGGLE GIGGLE...
I GUESS I'LL LEAVE IT AT THAT, THEN.
SHUDDER...
"SHE'LL BE WAITING!!"
LATINA, I'M GOING TO TRY MY BEST!

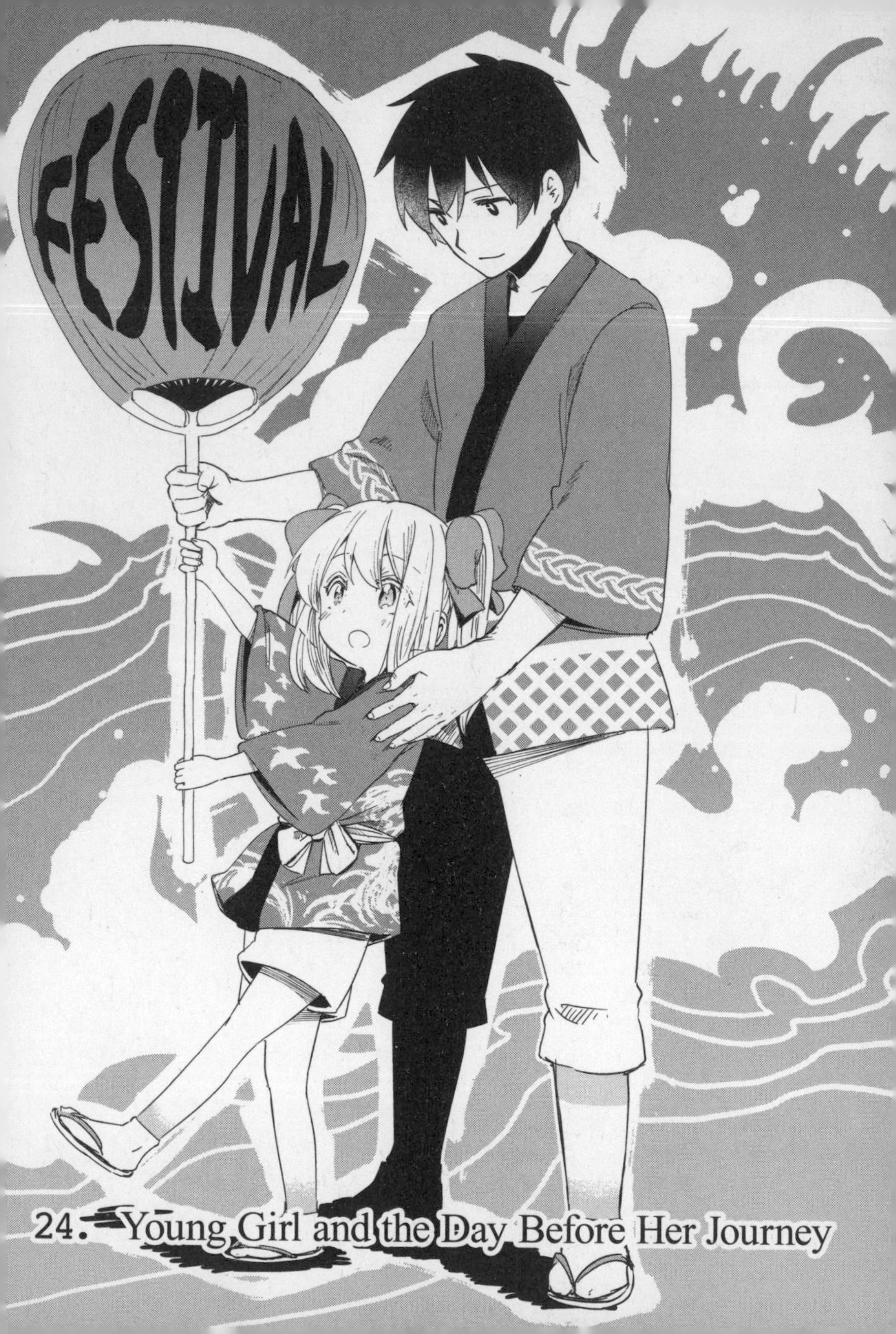
FESTIVAL

24. Young Girl and the Day Before Her Journey

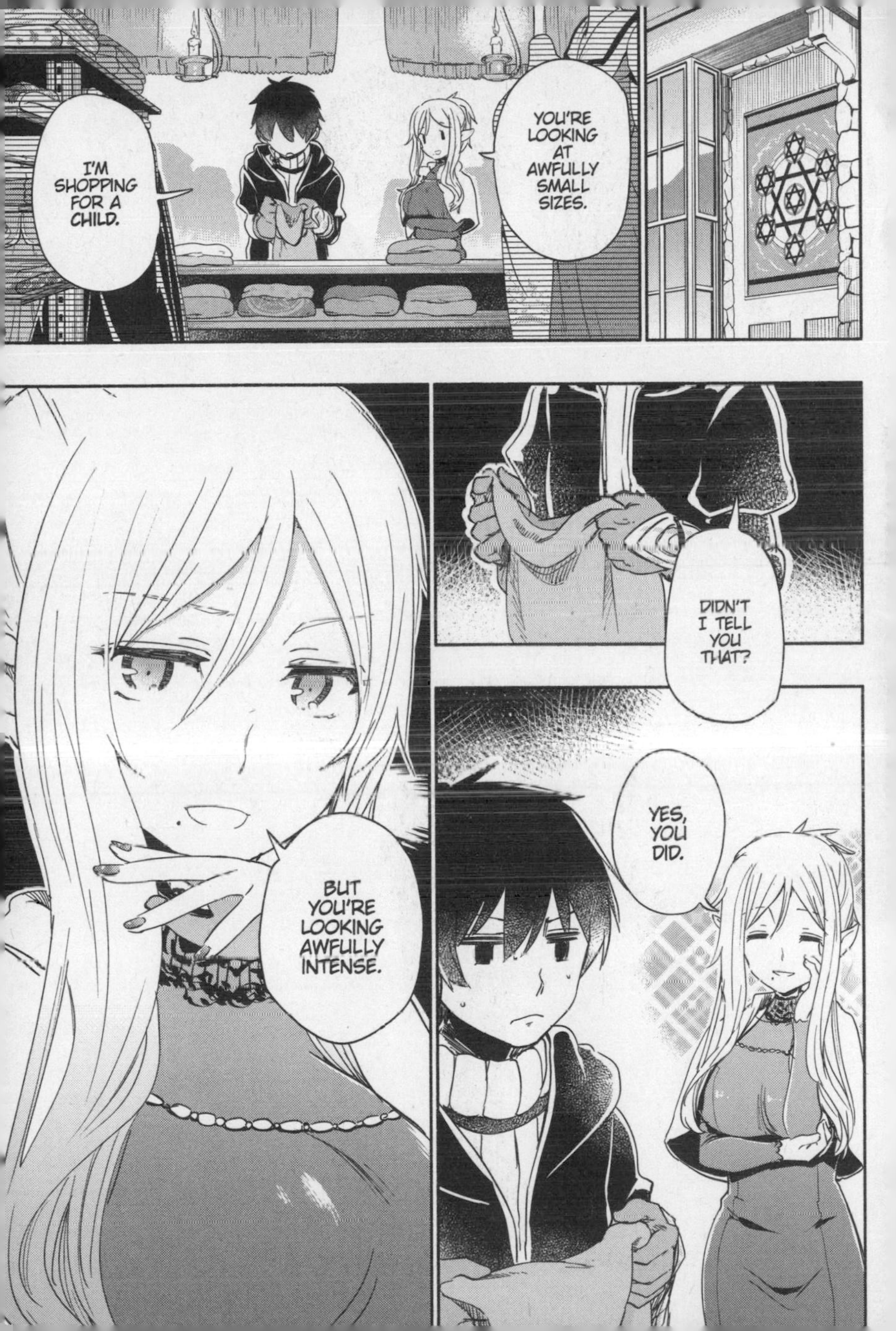
YOU'RE LOOKING AT AWFULLY SMALL SIZES.
I'M SHOPPING FOR A CHILD.
DIDN'T I TELL YOU THAT?
YES, YOU DID.
BUT YOU'RE LOOKING AWFULLY INTENSE.

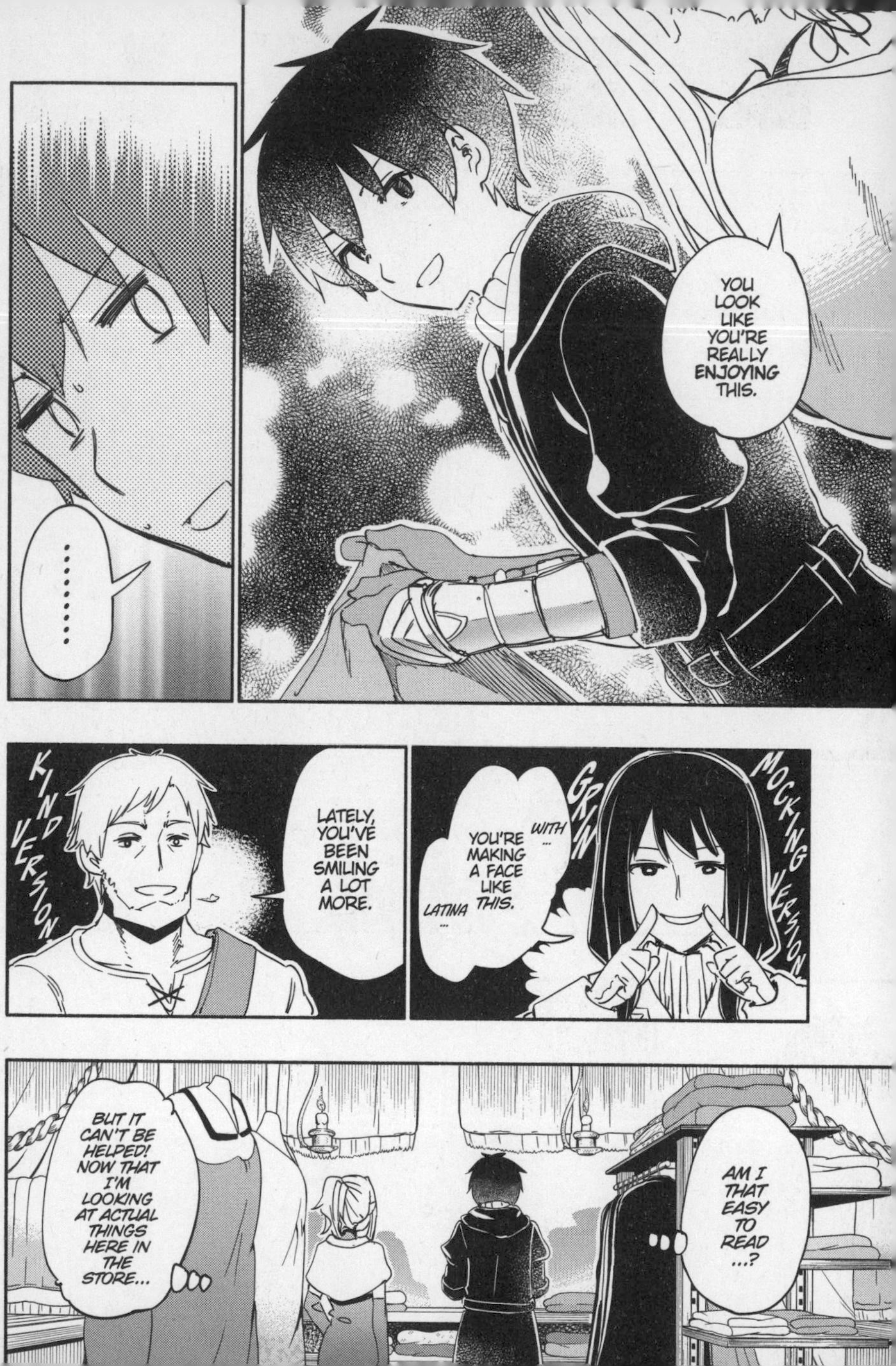
YOU LOOK LIKE YOU'RE REALLY ENJOYING THIS.
....
MOCKING VERSION
GRIN
WITH ...
YOU'RE MAKING A FACE LIKE THIS.
LATINA ...
KIND VERSION
LATELY, YOU'VE BEEN SMILING A LOT MORE.
AM I THAT EASY TO READ ...?
BUT IT CAN'T BE HELPED! NOW THAT I'M LOOKING AT ACTUAL THINGS HERE IN THE STORE...

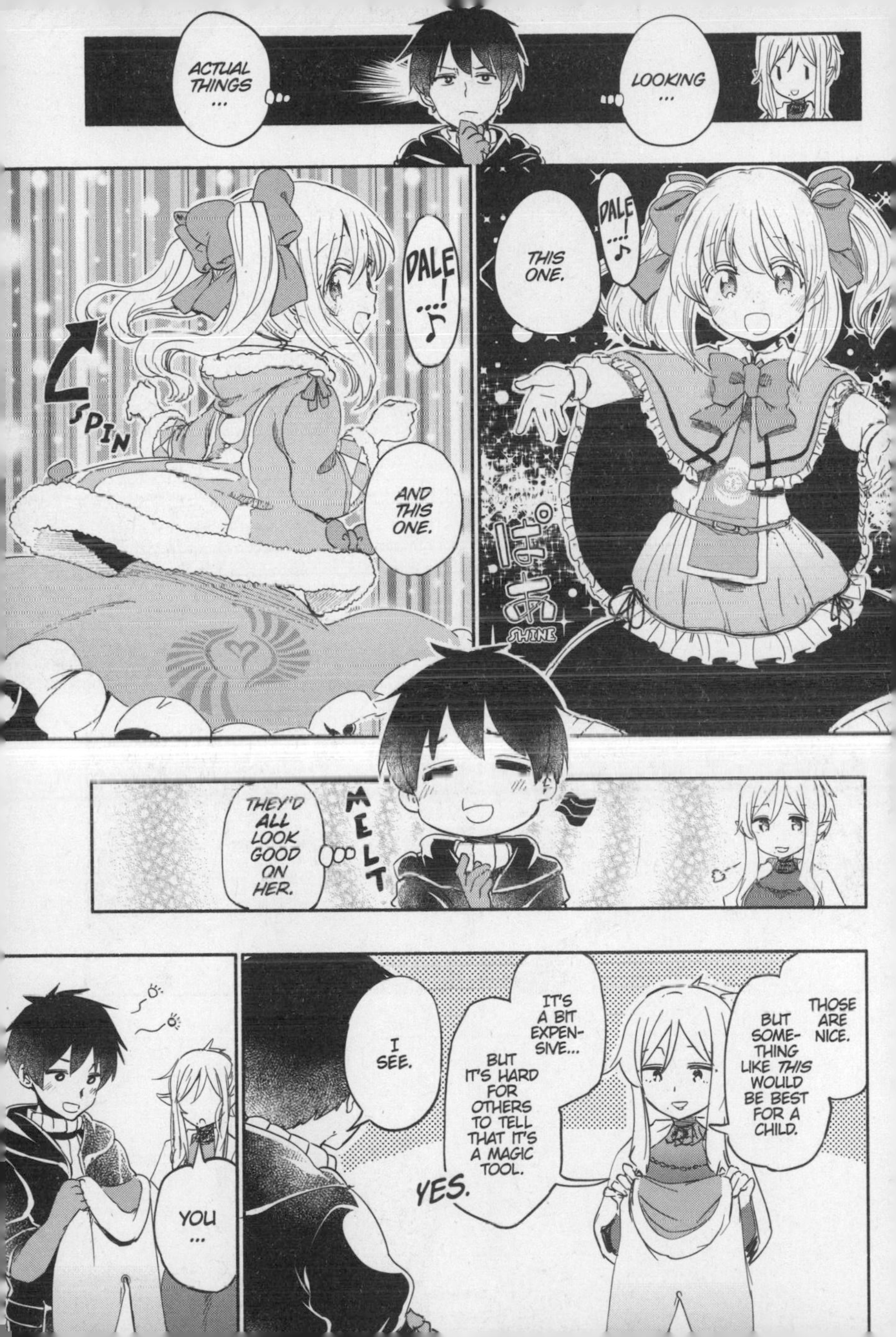
LOOKING ...
ACTUAL THINGS ...
DALE...!♪
THIS ONE.
ぱあ
SHINE
DALE...!♪
AND THIS ONE.
SPIN
THEY'D ALL LOOK GOOD ON HER.
MELT
THOSE ARE NICE. BUT SOMETHING LIKE *THIS* WOULD BE BEST FOR A CHILD.
IT'S A BIT EXPENSIVE... BUT IT'S HARD FOR OTHERS TO TELL THAT IT'S A MAGIC TOOL.
I SEE.
YES.
YOU ...

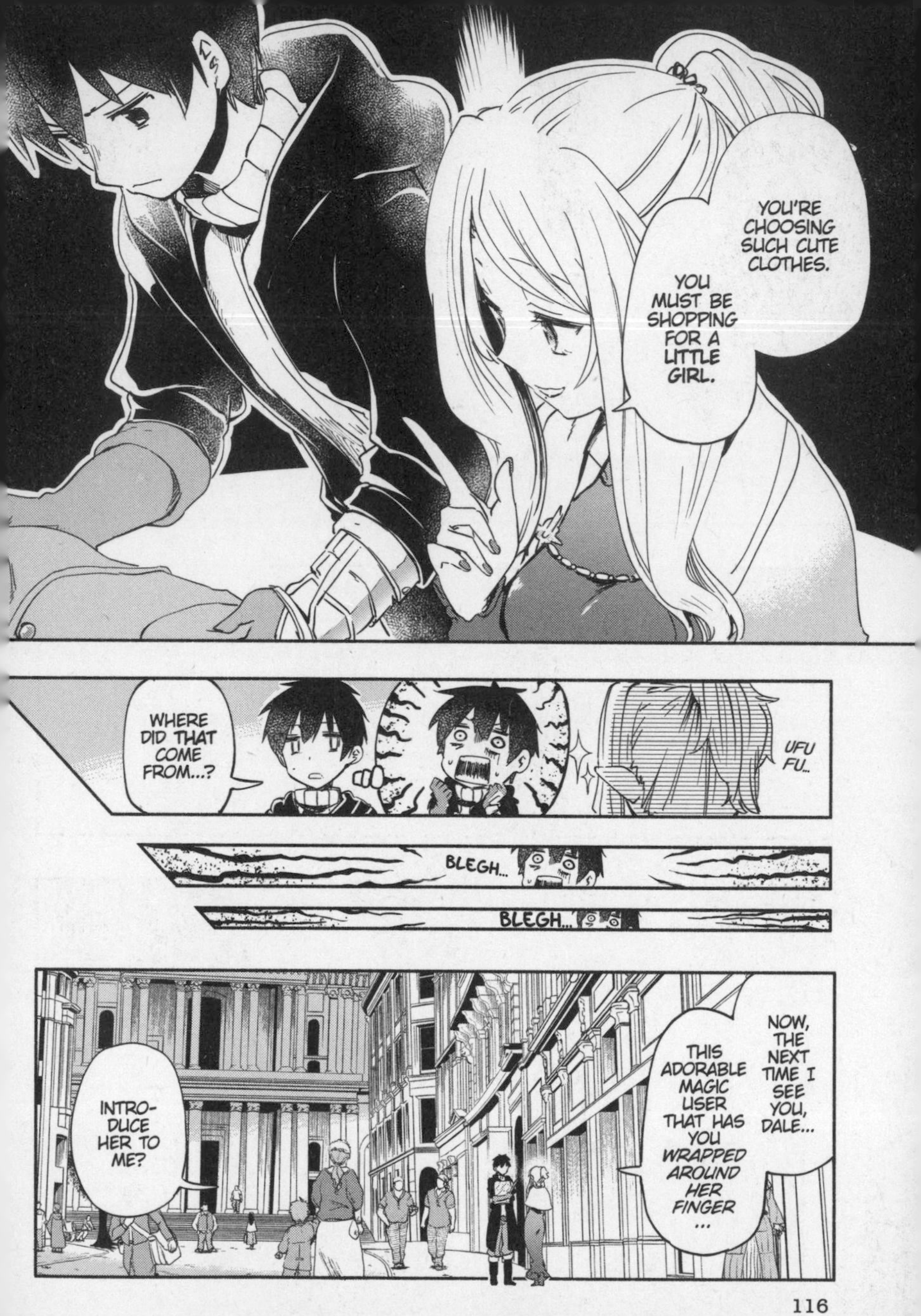
YOU'RE CHOOSING SUCH CUTE CLOTHES.
YOU MUST BE SHOPPING FOR A LITTLE GIRL.
UFU FU...
WHERE DID THAT COME FROM...?
BLEGH...
BLEGH...
NOW, THE NEXT TIME I SEE YOU, DALE...
THIS ADORABLE MAGIC USER THAT HAS YOU *WRAPPED AROUND HER FINGER*...
INTRO-DUCE HER TO ME?

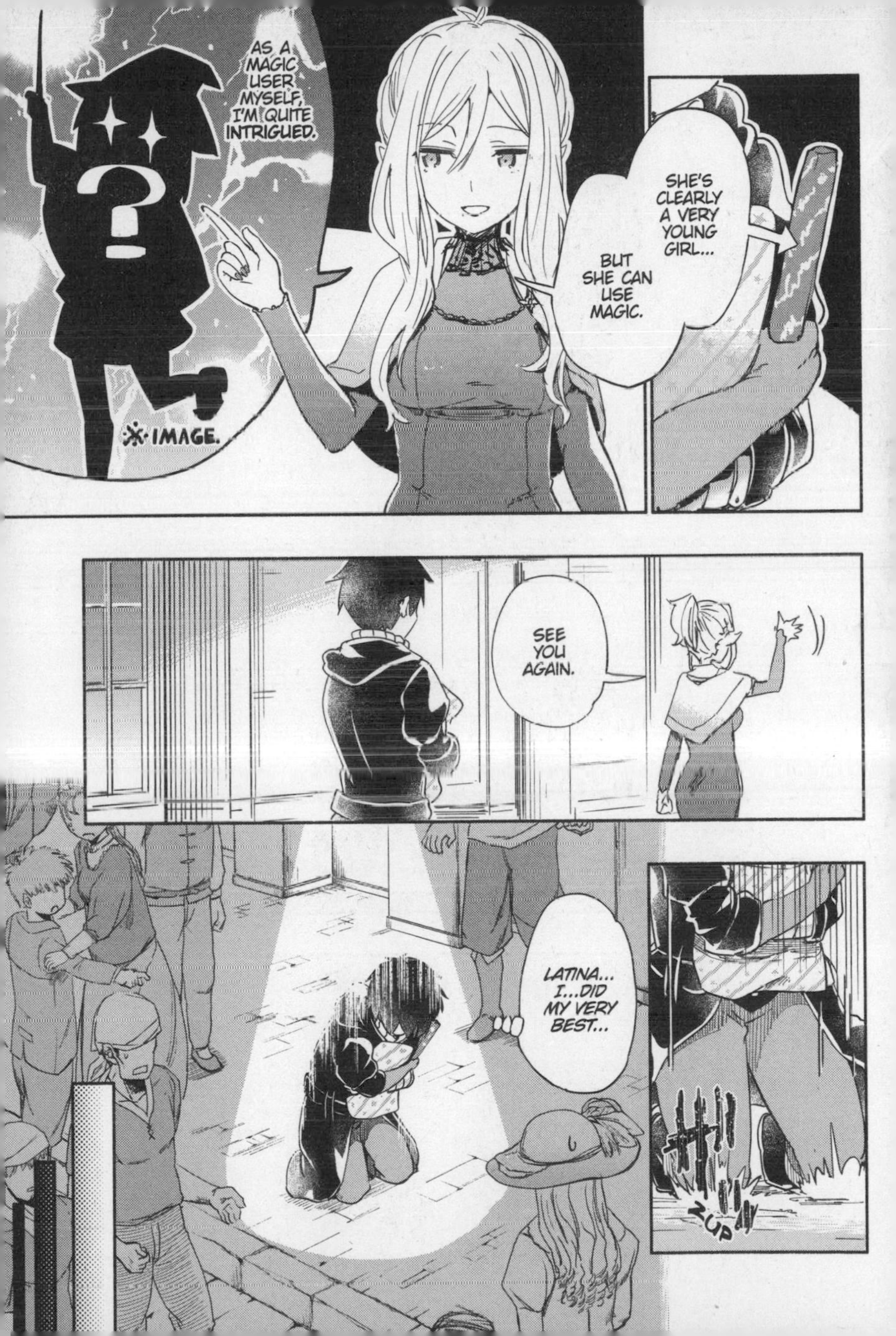
SHE'S CLEARLY A VERY YOUNG GIRL...
BUT SHE CAN USE MAGIC.
AS A MAGIC USER MYSELF, I'M QUITE INTRIGUED.
※IMAGE.
SEE YOU AGAIN.
ZUP
LATINA... I...DID MY VERY BEST...

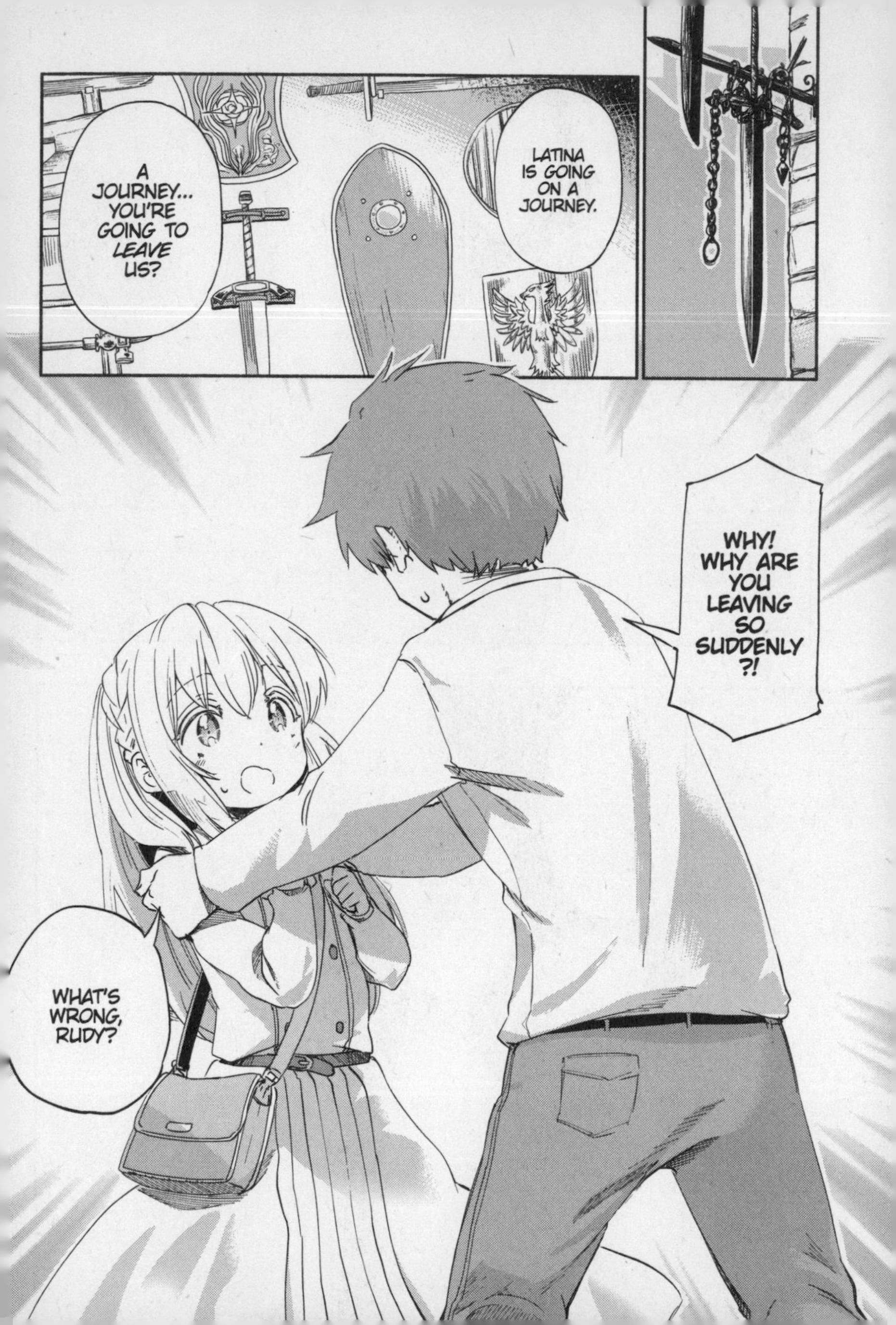
LATINA IS GOING ON A JOURNEY.
A JOURNEY... YOU'RE GOING TO *LEAVE* US?
WHY! WHY ARE YOU LEAVING SO SUDDENLY?!
WHAT'S WRONG, RUDY?

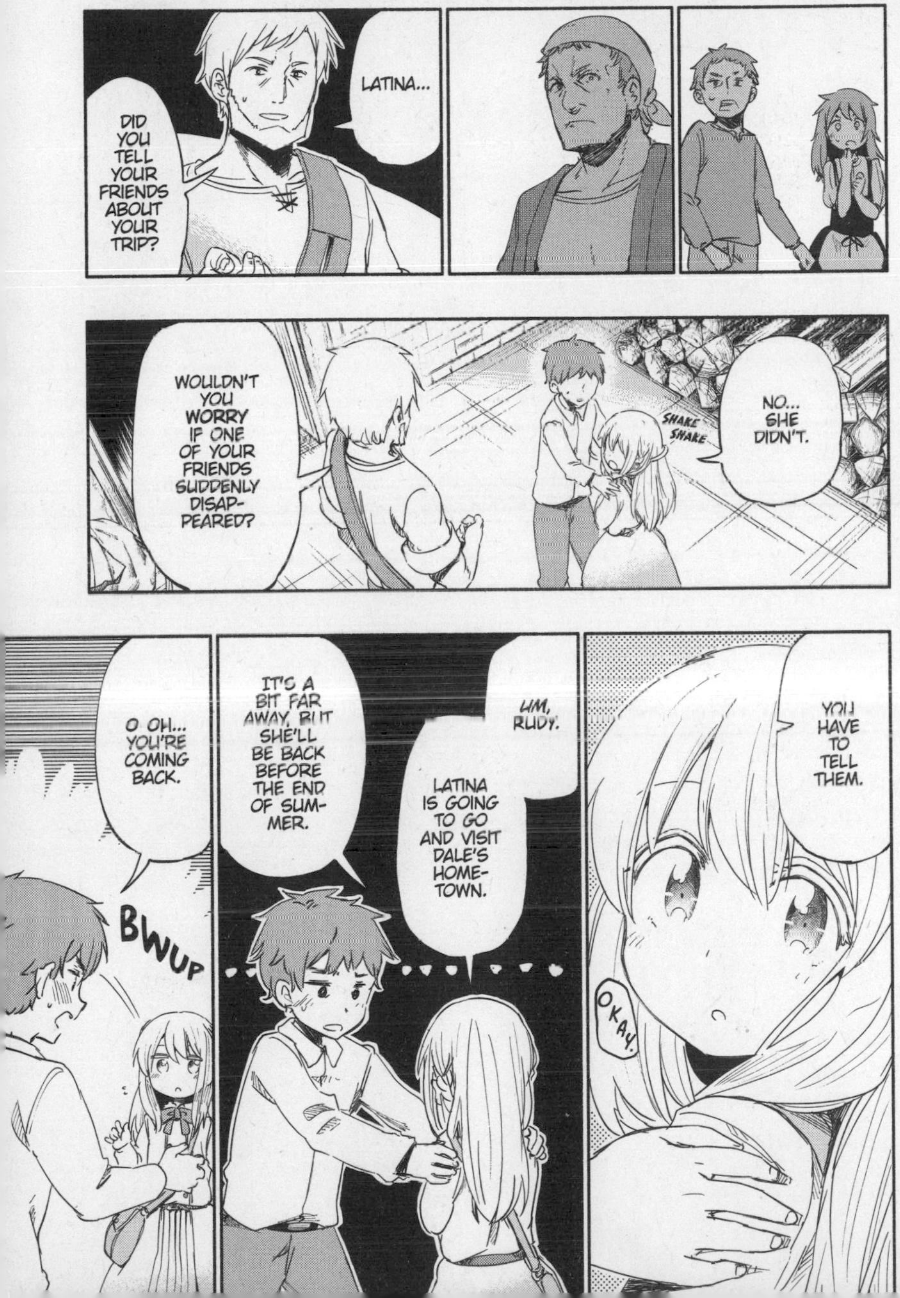
LATINA...
DID YOU TELL YOUR FRIENDS ABOUT YOUR TRIP?
NO... SHE DIDN'T.
SHAKE SHAKE
WOULDN'T YOU WORRY IF ONE OF YOUR FRIENDS SUDDENLY DISAP-PEARED?
YOU HAVE TO TELL THEM.
OKAY.
UM, RUDY.
LATINA IS GOING TO GO AND VISIT DALE'S HOME-TOWN.
IT'S A BIT FAR AWAY, BUT SHE'LL BE BACK BEFORE THE END OF SUM-MER.
O OH... YOU'RE COMING BACK.
BWUP

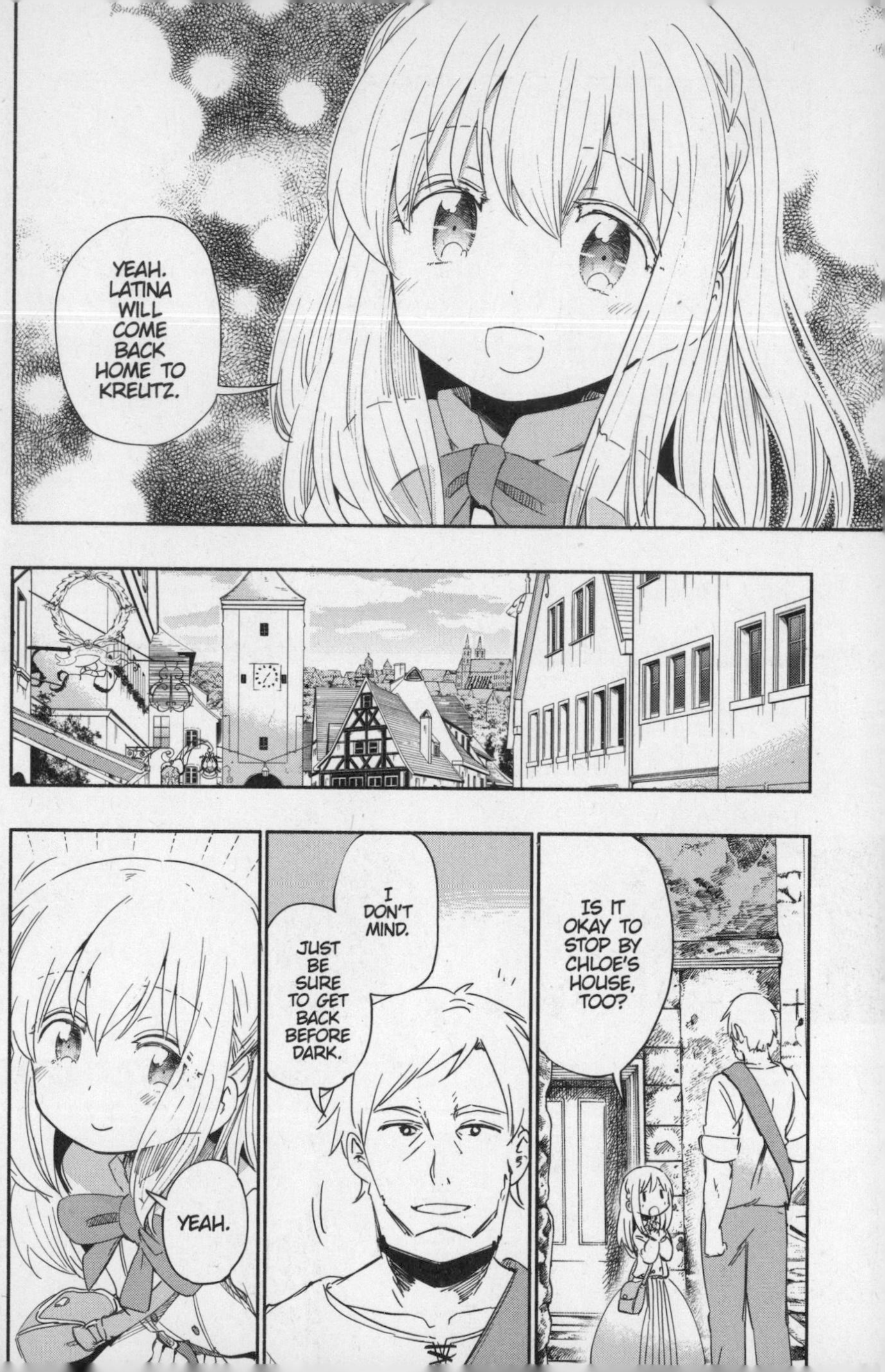
YEAH. LATINA WILL COME BACK HOME TO KREUTZ.
IS IT OKAY TO STOP BY CHLOE'S HOUSE, TOO?
I DON'T MIND.
JUST BE SURE TO GET BACK BEFORE DARK.
YEAH.

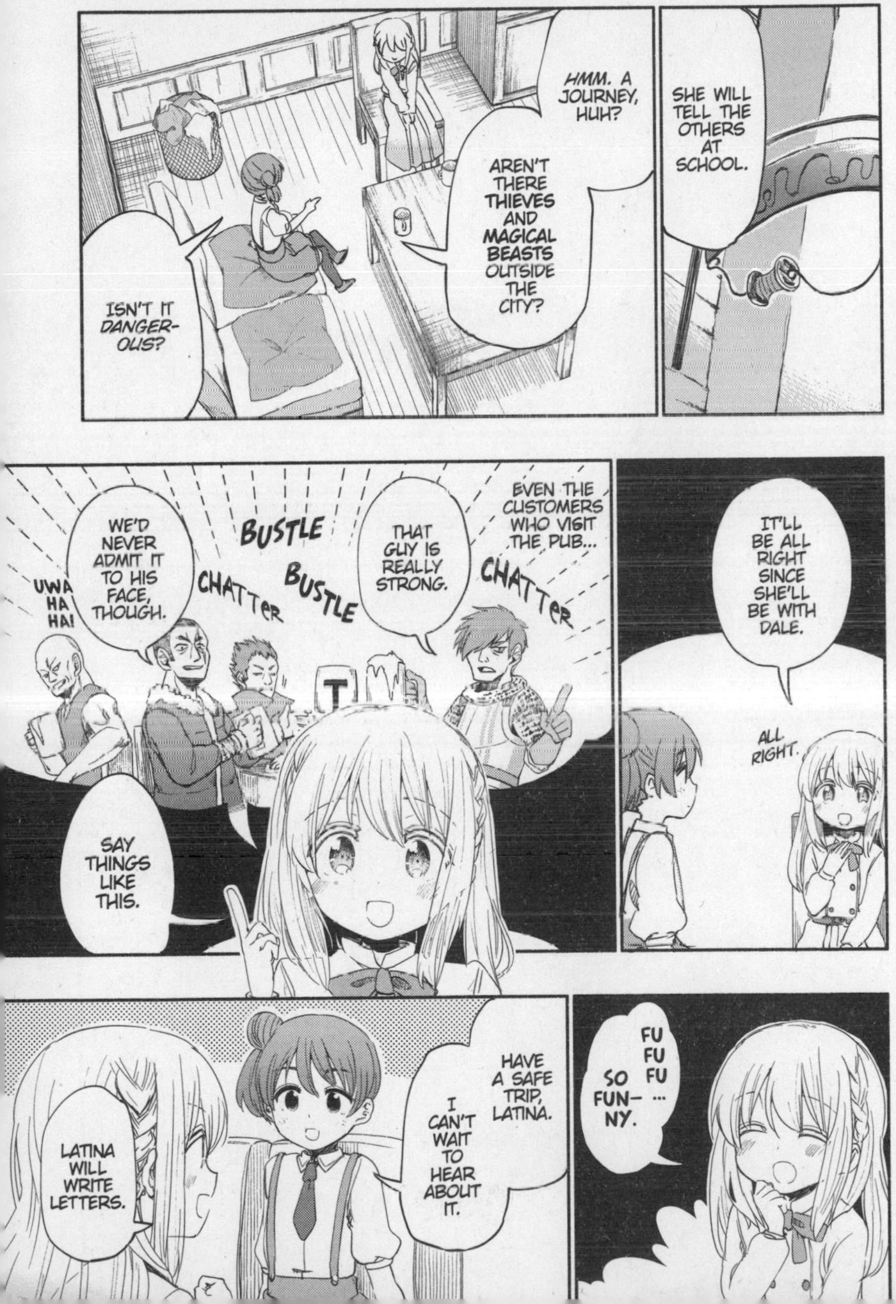
SHE WILL TELL THE OTHERS AT SCHOOL.
HMM. A JOURNEY, HUH?
AREN'T THERE THIEVES AND MAGICAL BEASTS OUTSIDE THE CITY?
ISN'T IT DANGER-OUS?
IT'LL BE ALL RIGHT SINCE SHE'LL BE WITH DALE.
ALL RIGHT.
EVEN THE CUSTOMERS WHO VISIT THE PUB...
CHATTER
THAT GUY IS REALLY STRONG.
BUSTLE
BUSTLE
WE'D NEVER ADMIT IT TO HIS FACE, THOUGH.
CHATTER
UWA HA HA!
SAY THINGS LIKE THIS.
FU FU FU...
SO FUN-NY.
HAVE A SAFE TRIP, LATINA.
I CAN'T WAIT TO HEAR ABOUT IT.
LATINA WILL WRITE LETTERS.

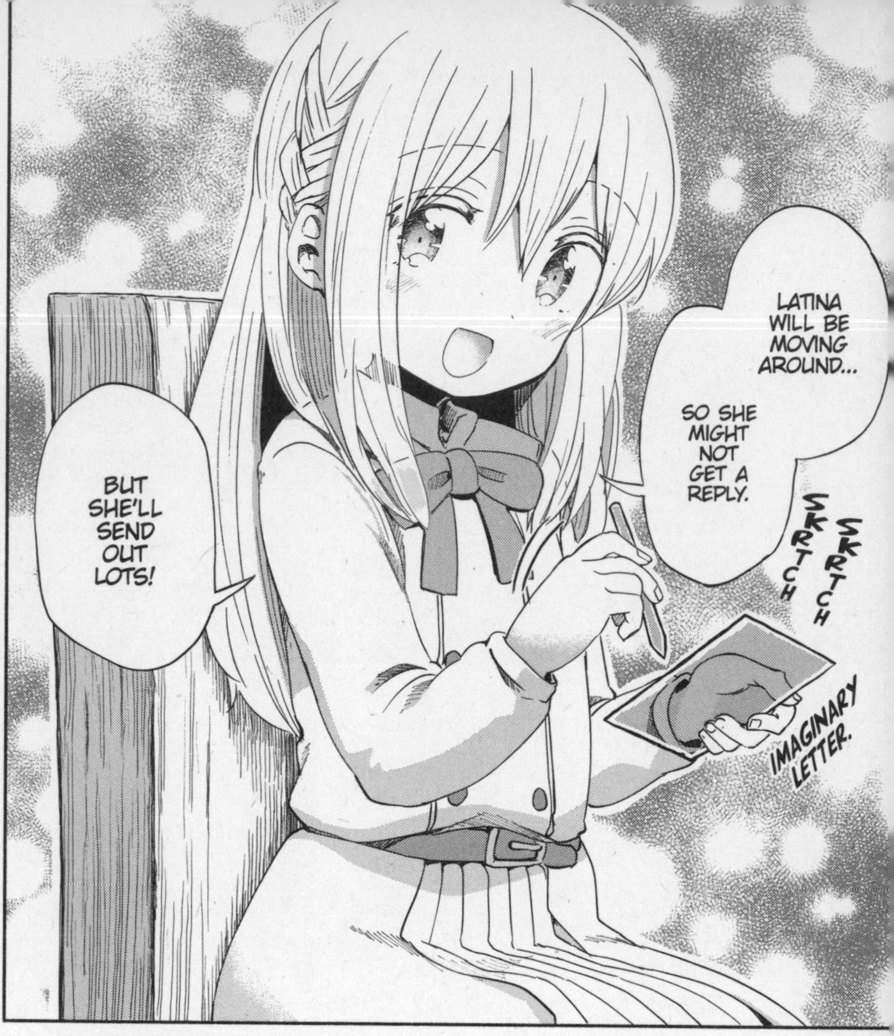
LATINA WILL BE MOVING AROUND...
SO SHE MIGHT NOT GET A REPLY.
SKRTCH SKRTCH
IMAGINARY LETTER.
BUT SHE'LL SEND OUT LOTS!
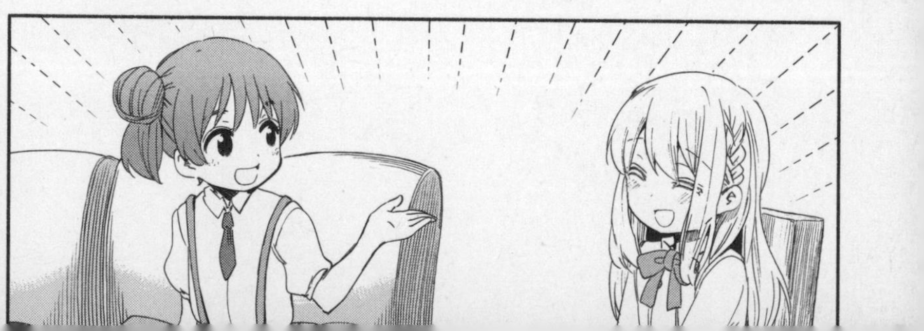

IF It's
For My
Daughter
I'd Even DeFeat
a **Demon**
Lord

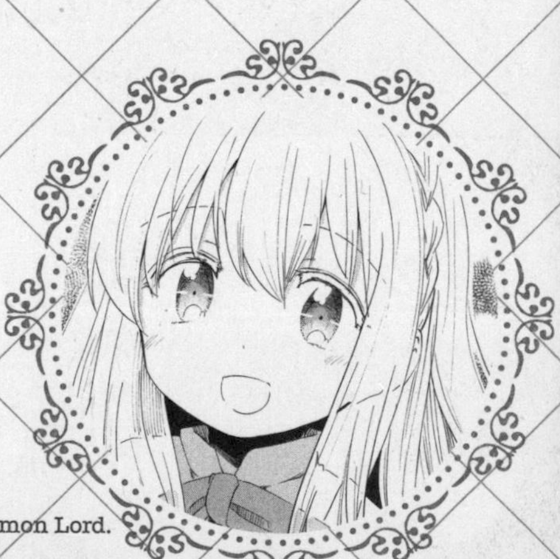

If It's For My Daughter, I'd Even Defeat a Demon Lord.

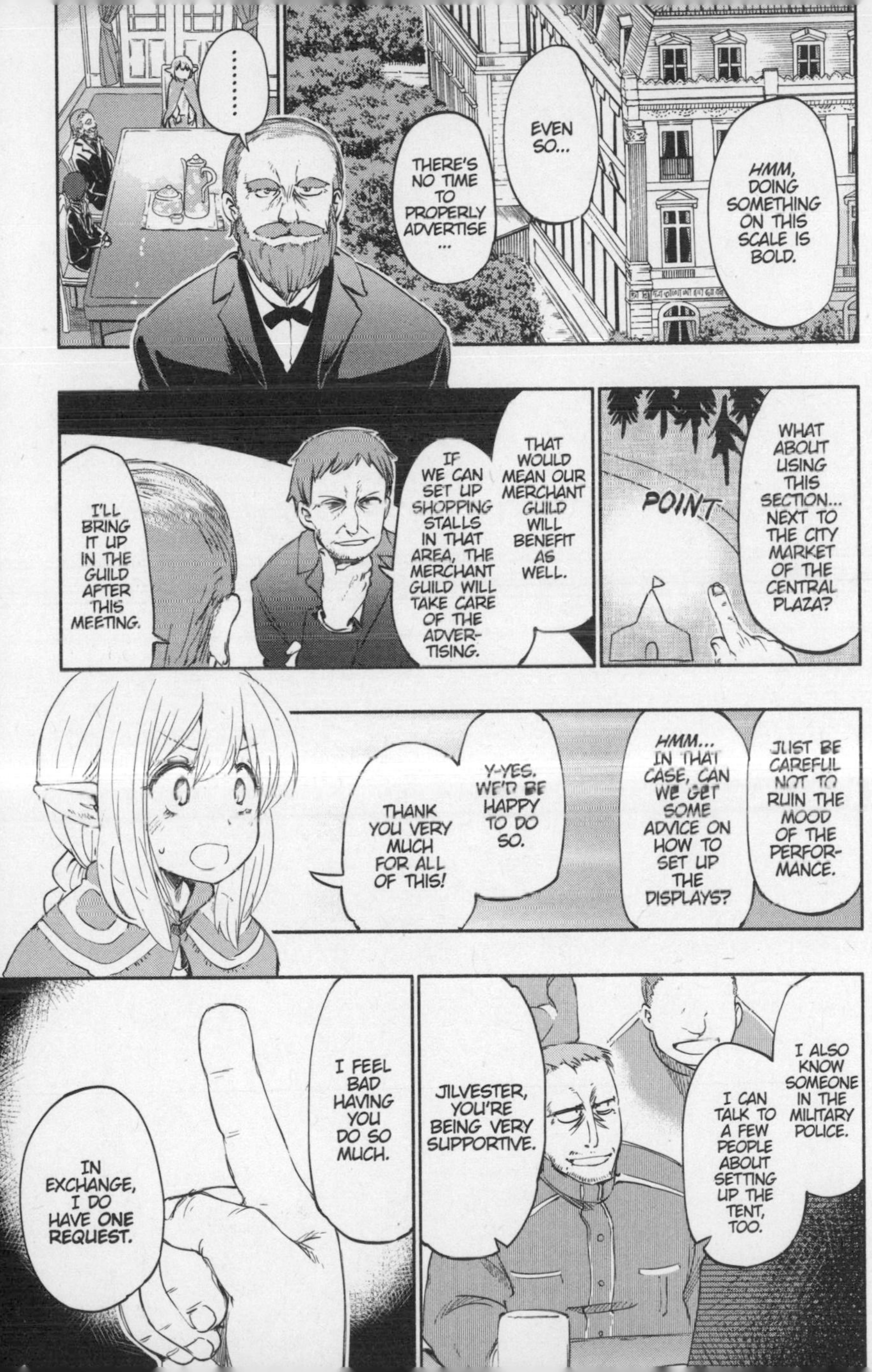
HMM, DOING SOMETHING ON THIS SCALE IS BOLD.
EVEN SO...
THERE'S NO TIME TO PROPERLY ADVERTISE ...
......
WHAT ABOUT USING THIS SECTION... NEXT TO THE CITY MARKET OF THE CENTRAL PLAZA?
POINT
THAT WOULD MEAN OUR MERCHANT GUILD WILL BENEFIT AS WELL.
IF WE CAN SET UP SHOPPING STALLS IN THAT AREA, THE MERCHANT GUILD WILL TAKE CARE OF THE ADVERTISING.
I'LL BRING IT UP IN THE GUILD AFTER THIS MEETING.
JUST BE CAREFUL NOT TO RUIN THE MOOD OF THE PERFORMANCE.
HMM... IN THAT CASE, CAN WE GET SOME ADVICE ON HOW TO SET UP THE DISPLAYS?
Y-YES. WE'D BE HAPPY TO DO SO.
THANK YOU VERY MUCH FOR ALL OF THIS!
I ALSO KNOW SOMEONE IN THE MILITARY POLICE.
I CAN TALK TO A FEW PEOPLE ABOUT SETTING UP THE TENT, TOO.
JILVESTER, YOU'RE BEING VERY SUPPORTIVE.
I FEEL BAD HAVING YOU DO SO MUCH.
IN EXCHANGE, I DO HAVE ONE REQUEST.

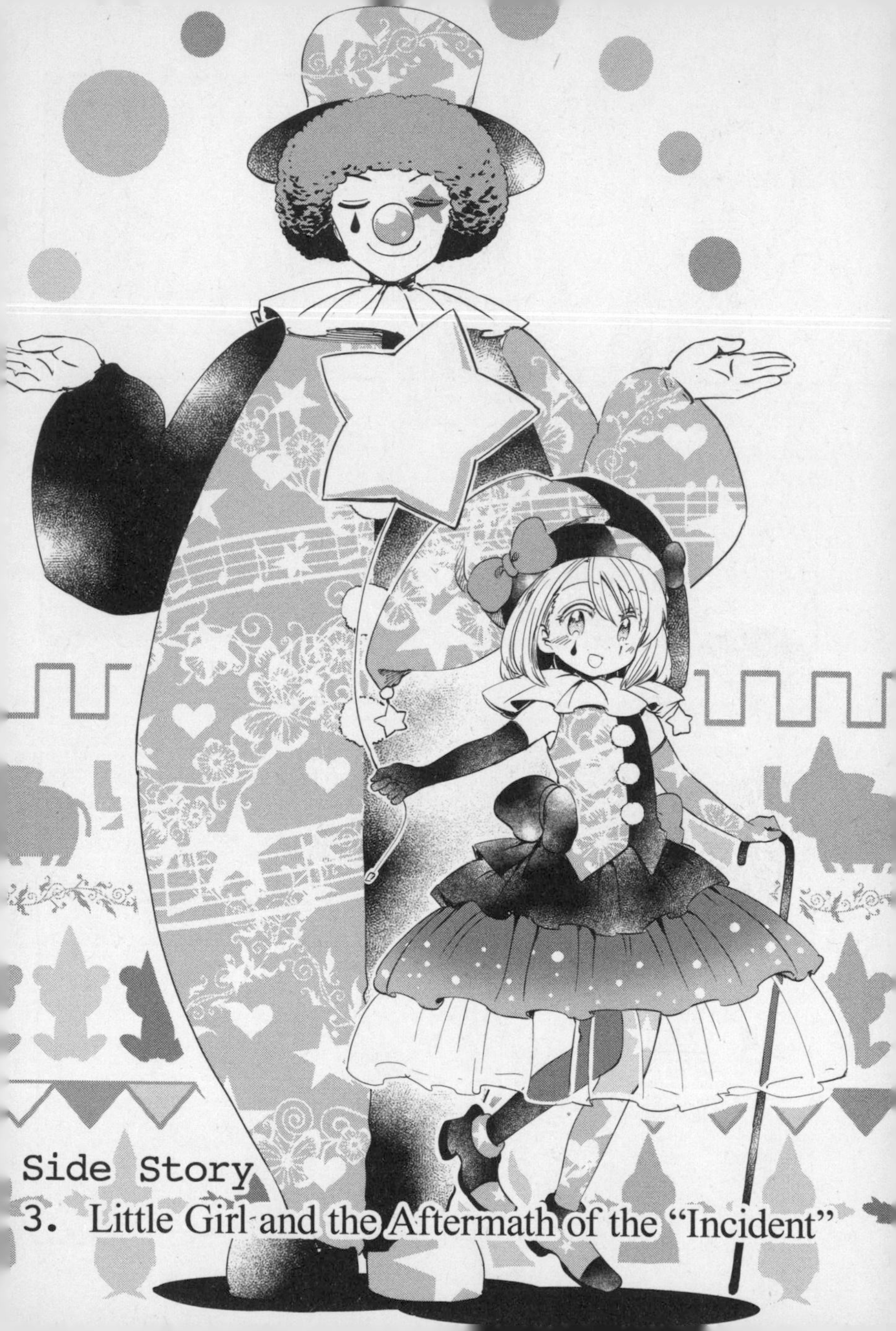

Side Story
3. Little Girl and the Aftermath of the "Incident"

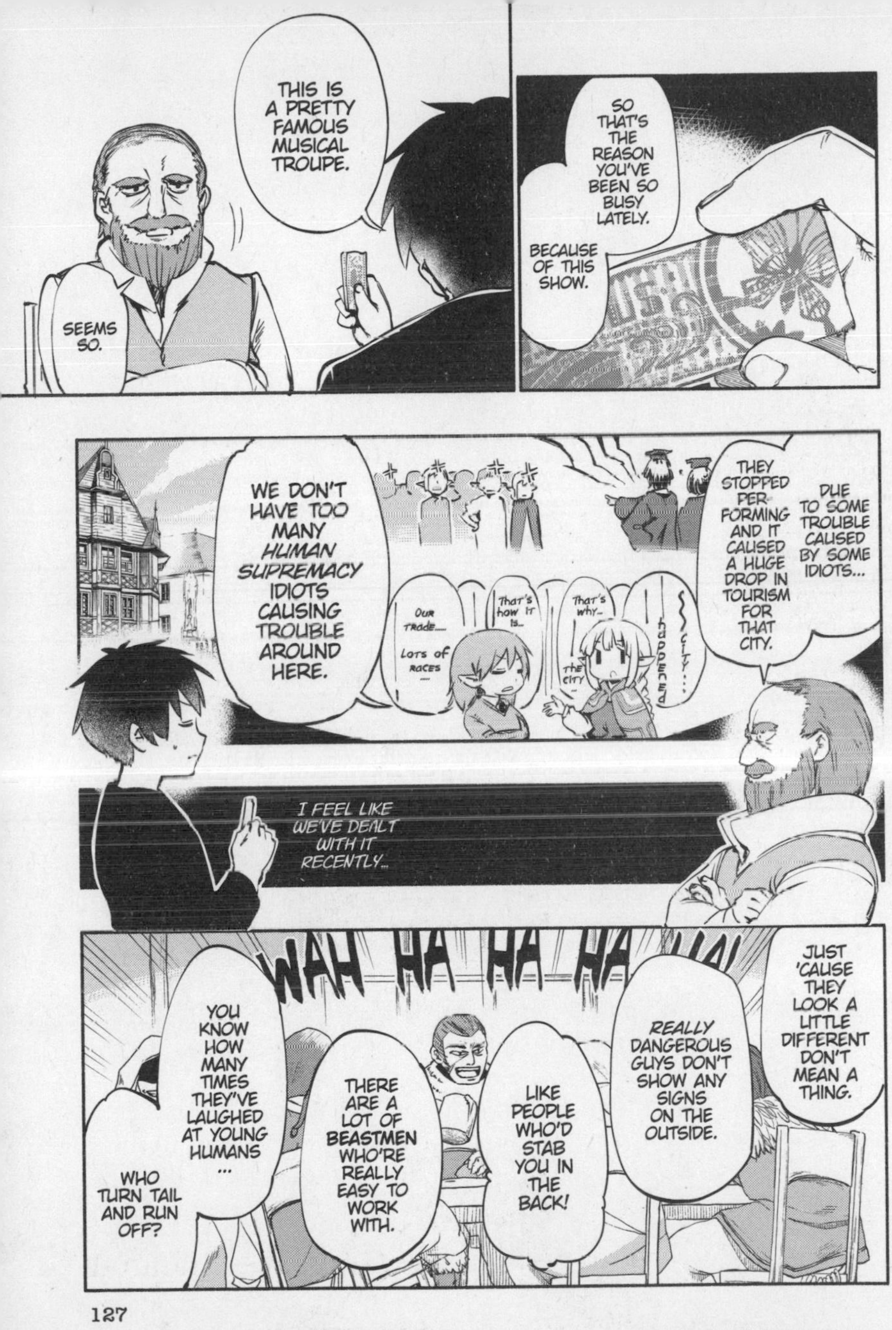
SO THAT'S THE REASON YOU'VE BEEN SO BUSY LATELY.
BECAUSE OF THIS SHOW.
THIS IS A PRETTY FAMOUS MUSICAL TROUPE.
SEEMS SO.
DUE TO SOME TROUBLE CAUSED BY SOME IDIOTS...
THEY STOPPED PER-FORMING AND IT CAUSED A HUGE DROP IN TOURISM FOR THAT CITY.
~City... happened
That's why... the city...
That's how it is...
Our trade..... Lots of races....
WE DON'T HAVE TOO MANY *HUMAN SUPREMACY* IDIOTS CAUSING TROUBLE AROUND HERE.
I FEEL LIKE WE'VE DEALT WITH IT RECENTLY...
WAH HA HA HA HA!
JUST 'CAUSE THEY LOOK A LITTLE DIFFERENT DON'T MEAN A THING.
REALLY DANGEROUS GUYS DON'T SHOW ANY SIGNS ON THE OUTSIDE.
LIKE PEOPLE WHO'D STAB YOU IN THE BACK!
THERE ARE A LOT OF BEASTMEN WHO'RE REALLY EASY TO WORK WITH.
YOU KNOW HOW MANY TIMES THEY'VE LAUGHED AT YOUNG HUMANS ...
WHO TURN TAIL AND RUN OFF?

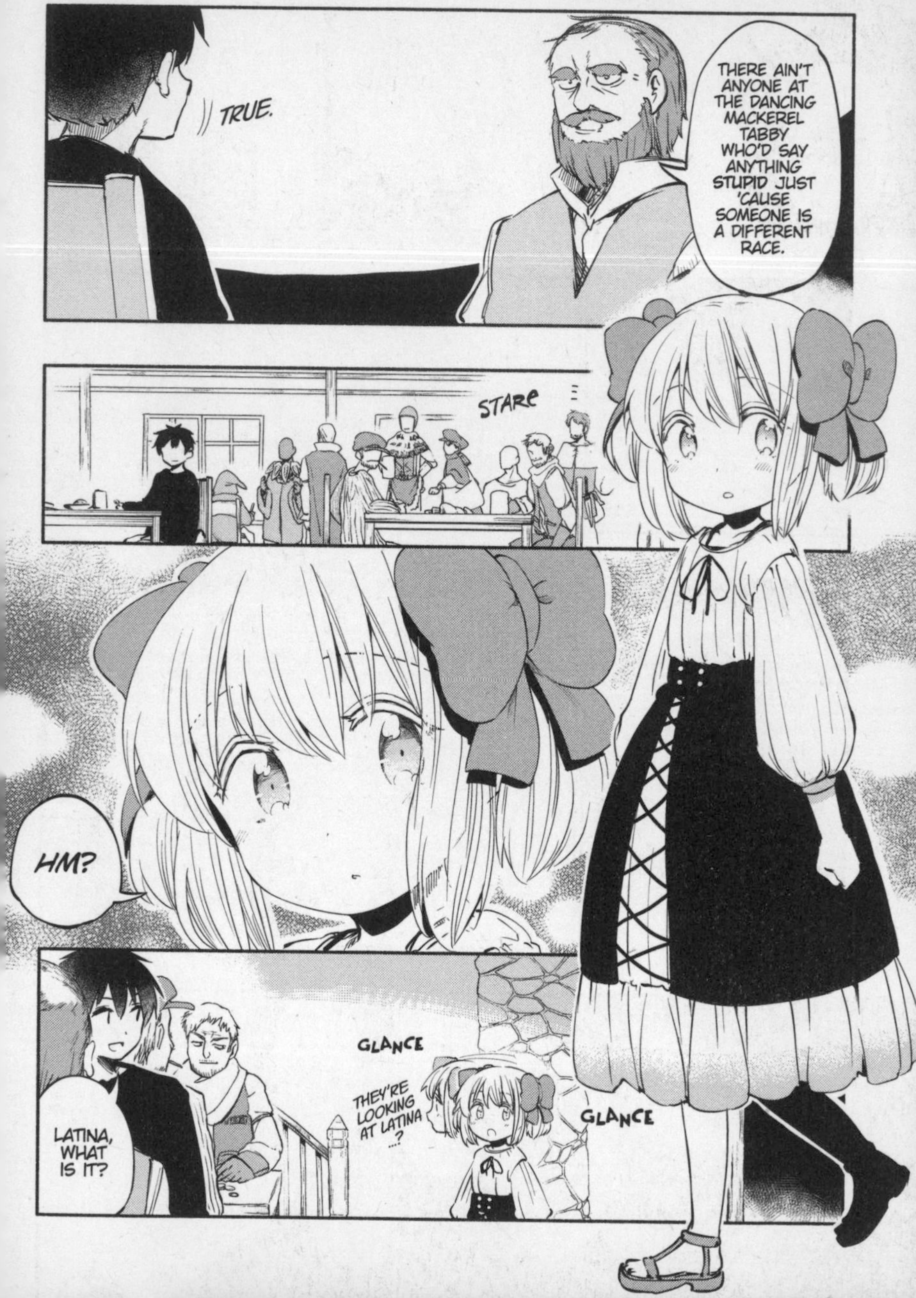
THERE AIN'T ANYONE AT THE DANCING MACKEREL TABBY WHO'D SAY ANYTHING STUPID JUST 'CAUSE SOMEONE IS A DIFFERENT RACE.
TRUE.
STARE
HM?
GLANCE
THEY'RE LOOKING AT LATINA ...?
GLANCE
LATINA, WHAT IS IT?

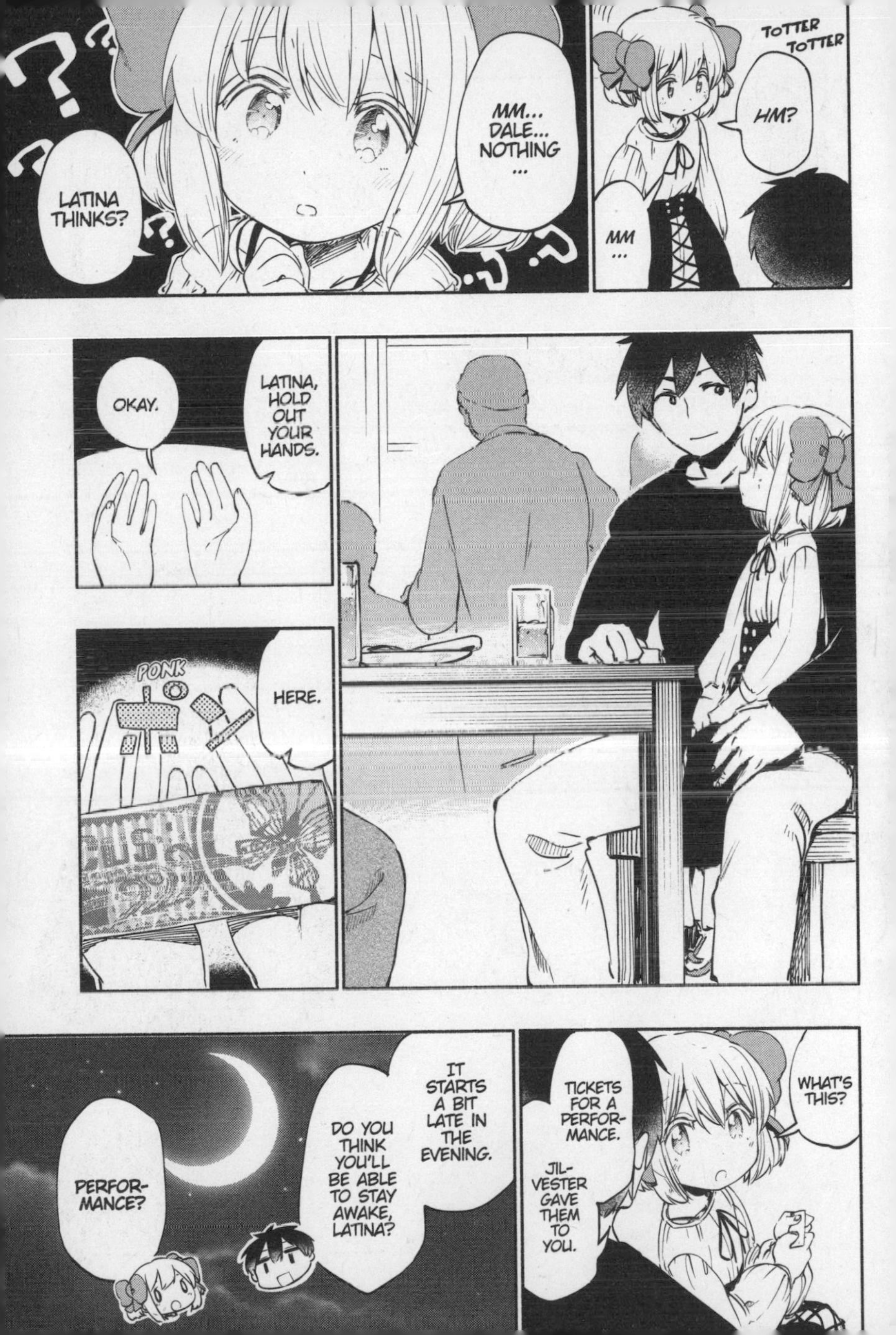
TOTTER TOTTER
HM?
MM ...
MM... DALE... NOTHING ...
LATINA THINKS?
LATINA, HOLD OUT YOUR HANDS.
OKAY.
HERE.
PONK
WHAT'S THIS?
TICKETS FOR A PERFOR-MANCE.
JIL-VESTER GAVE THEM TO YOU.
IT STARTS A BIT LATE IN THE EVENING.
DO YOU THINK YOU'LL BE ABLE TO STAY AWAKE, LATINA?
PERFOR-MANCE?

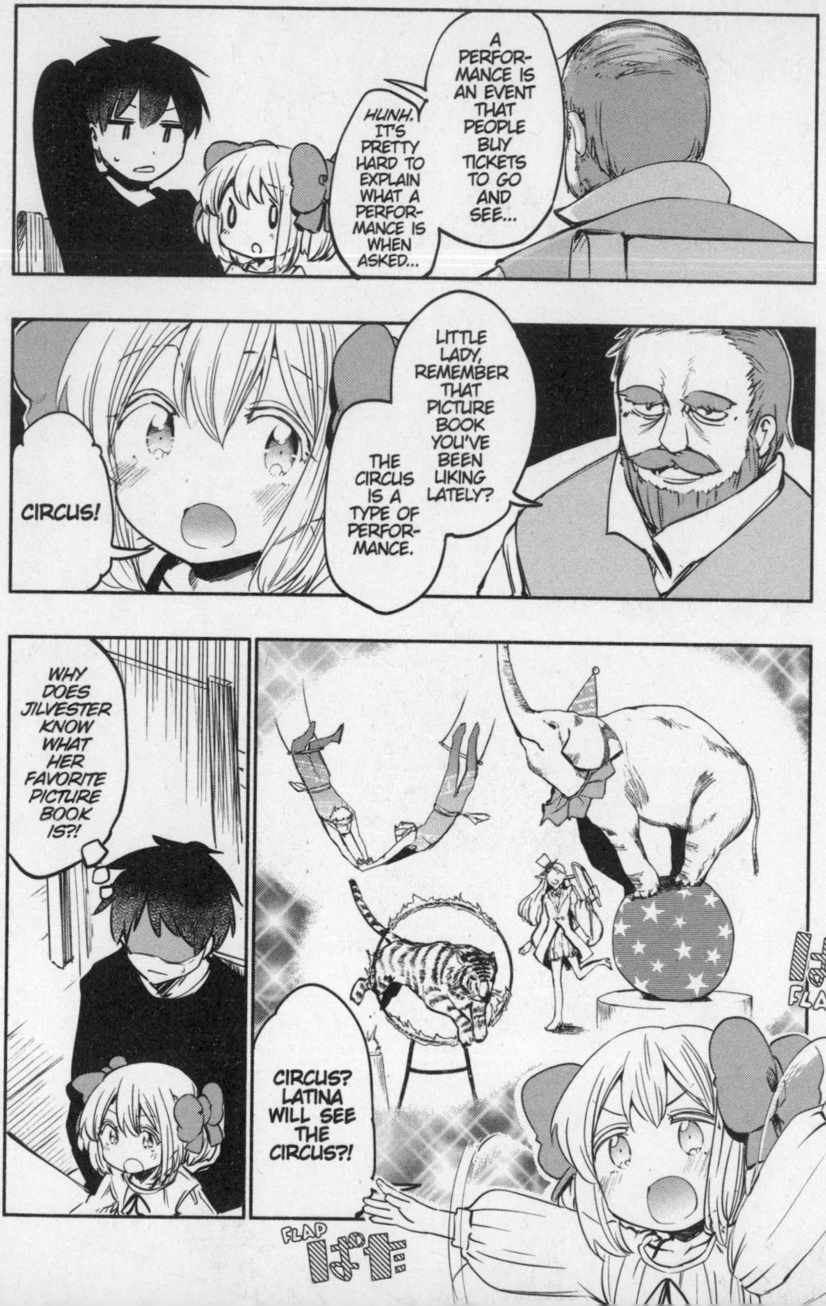
A PERFORMANCE IS AN EVENT THAT PEOPLE BUY TICKETS TO GO AND SEE...
HUNH. IT'S PRETTY HARD TO EXPLAIN WHAT A PERFORMANCE IS WHEN ASKED...
LITTLE LADY, REMEMBER THAT PICTURE BOOK YOU'VE BEEN LIKING LATELY?
THE CIRCUS IS A TYPE OF PERFORMANCE.
CIRCUS!
FLAP
CIRCUS? LATINA WILL SEE THE CIRCUS?!
FLAP
WHY DOES JILVESTER KNOW WHAT HER FAVORITE PICTURE BOOK IS?!

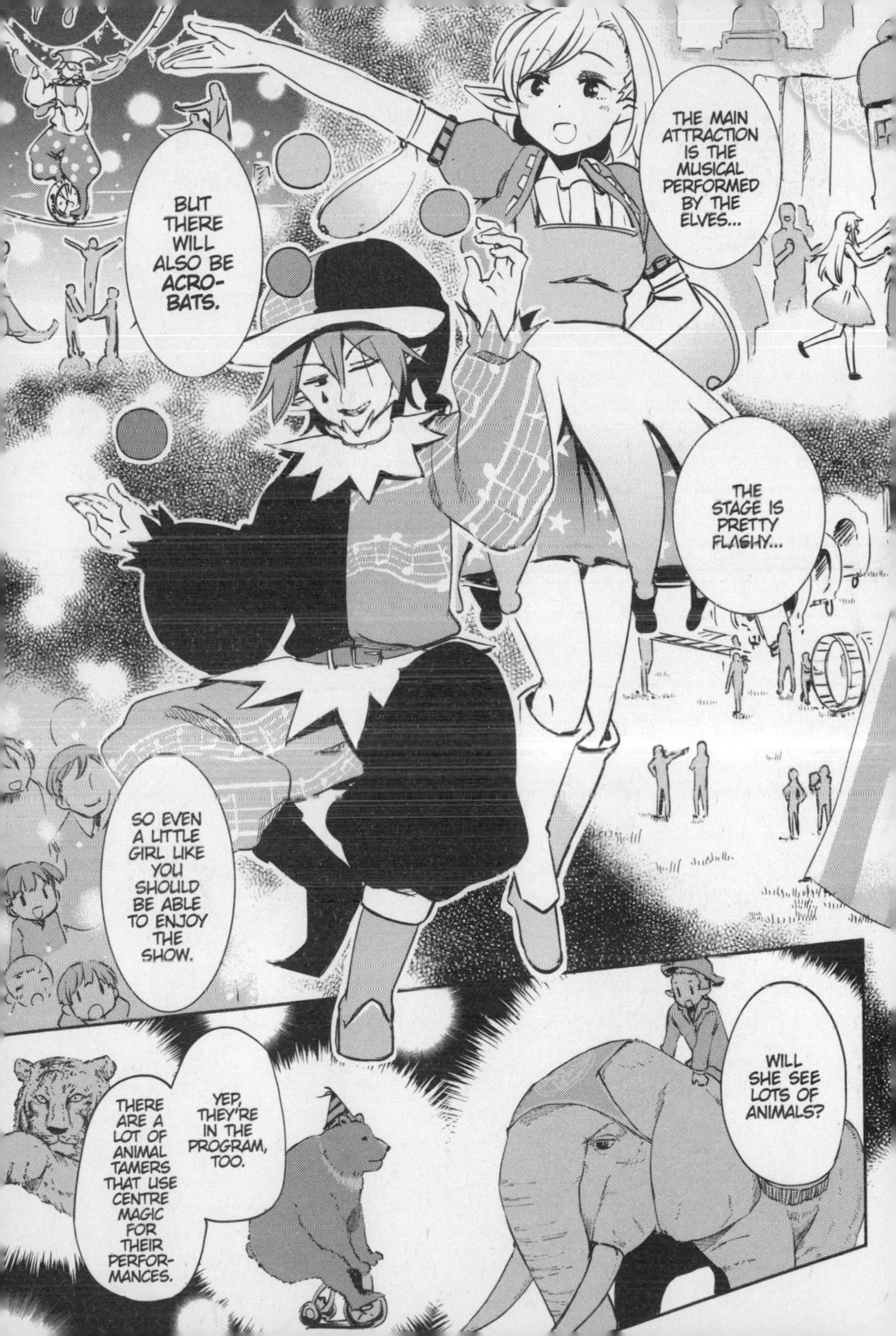
THE MAIN ATTRACTION IS THE MUSICAL PERFORMED BY THE ELVES...
BUT THERE WILL ALSO BE ACRO-BATS.
THE STAGE IS PRETTY FLASHY...
SO EVEN A LITTLE GIRL LIKE YOU SHOULD BE ABLE TO ENJOY THE SHOW.
WILL SHE SEE LOTS OF ANIMALS?
YEP, THEY'RE IN THE PROGRAM, TOO.
THERE ARE A LOT OF ANIMAL TAMERS THAT USE CENTRE MAGIC FOR THEIR PERFOR-MANCES.

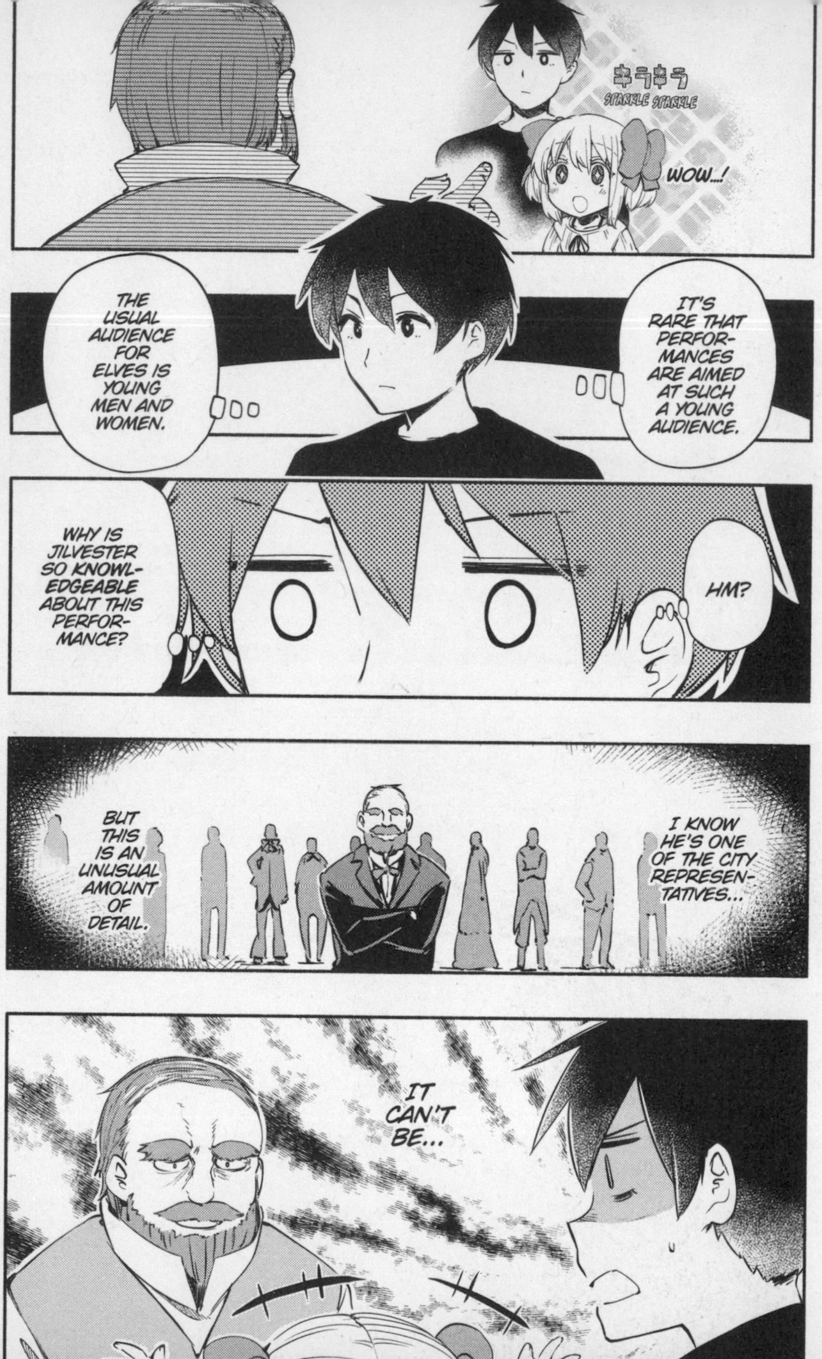
キラキラ
SPARKLE SPARKLE
WOW...!
IT'S RARE THAT PERFORMANCES ARE AIMED AT SUCH A YOUNG AUDIENCE.
THE USUAL AUDIENCE FOR ELVES IS YOUNG MEN AND WOMEN.
HM?
WHY IS JILVESTER SO KNOWLEDGEABLE ABOUT THIS PERFORMANCE?
I KNOW HE'S ONE OF THE CITY REPRESENTATIVES...
BUT THIS IS AN UNUSUAL AMOUNT OF DETAIL.
IT CAN'T BE...

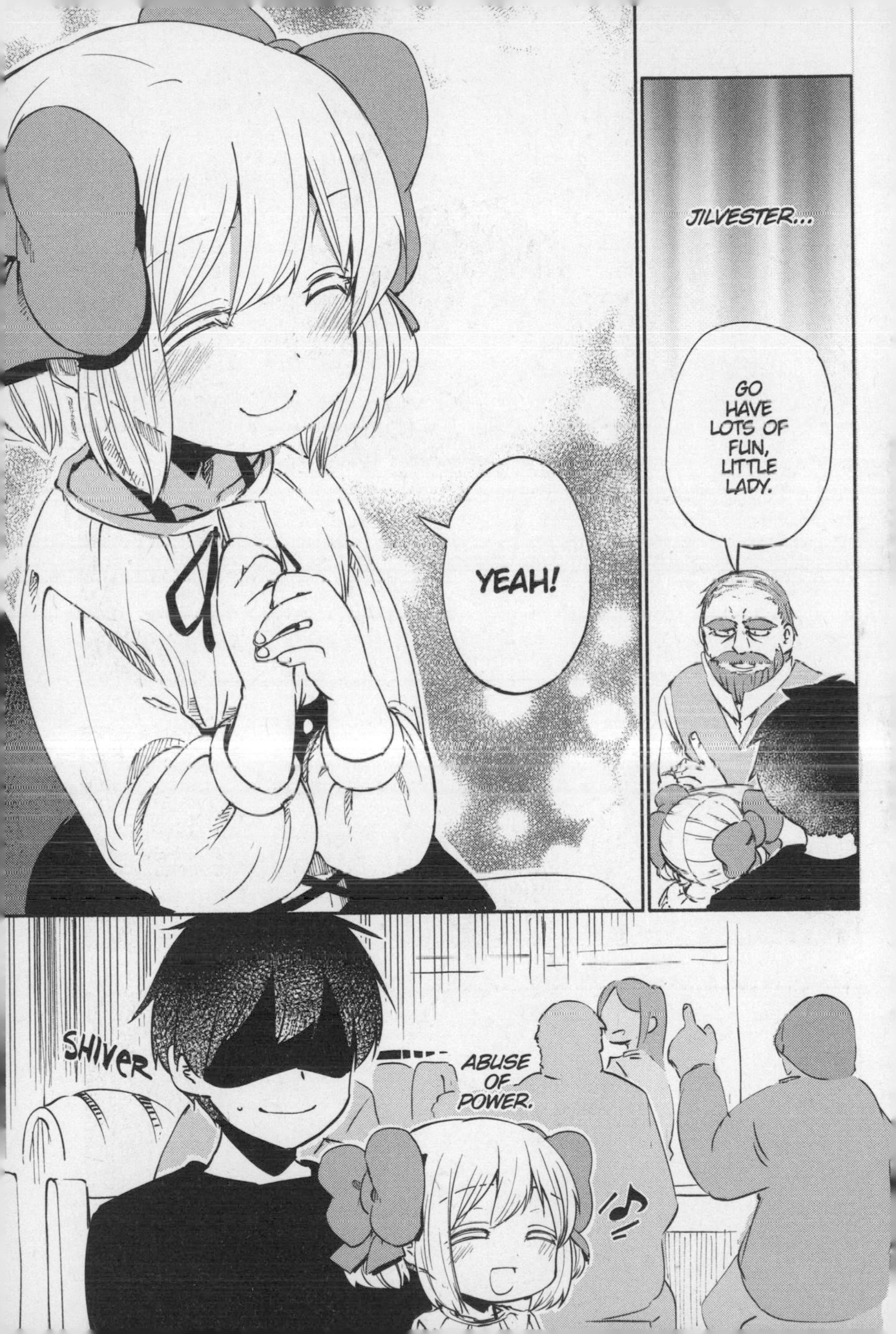
JILVESTER...
GO HAVE LOTS OF FUN, LITTLE LADY.
YEAH!
ABUSE OF POWER.
SHIVER

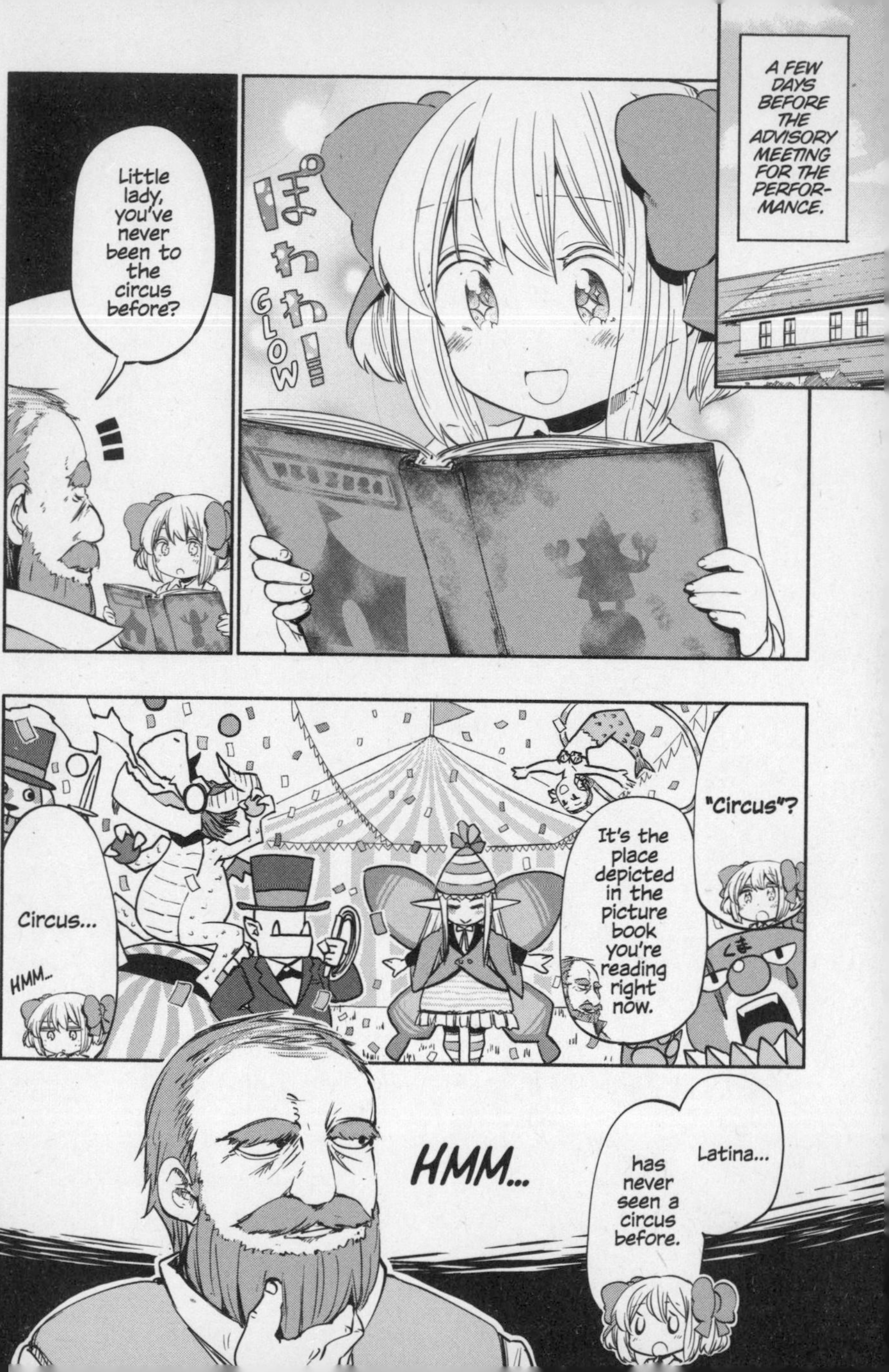
A FEW DAYS BEFORE THE ADVISORY MEETING FOR THE PERFORMANCE.
ぽわわ
GLOW!!
Little lady, you've never been to the circus before?
"Circus"?
It's the place depicted in the picture book you're reading right now.
Circus...
HMM...
Latina... has never seen a circus before.
HMM...

IF It's For My Daughter, I'd Even Defeat a Demon Lord

To be continued...!

If It's For My Daughter, I'd Even Defeat a Demon Lord.

If It's For My Daughter,
I'd Even Defeat a Demon Lord
SHORT STORY
CHIROLU

A Little Girl's Growing Sense of Modest Independence

One day, Dale noticed something was different.

"Hm?" he mumbled to himself as he took a second look. In front of him, Latina wore her "Dancing Mackerel Tabby" apron and was working hard like usual on her cleanup duties. The apron she was wearing was a seasonally-appropriate mint green. The ribbons that peeked out of the matching bandana she wore over her head were also the same as usual.

Latina wore navy ribbons today. Her white blouse and light blue skirt matched the apron and gave her an energetic appearance. She was perfectly coordinated for the season.

Yeah. Latina is as cute as ever today.

That was what Dale thought when he took a first quick glance at her. This time, he looked more closely, searching for what might be different. Latina scrubbed the tables with all her might to shine them. The dishcloths and rags used to wipe things down were usually made by cutting up old clothes. Latina was creating many such dishcloths while practicing her hand-sewing on the clothes Rita had been putting off cutting apart. Because of that, the new rags Latina was currently using were ones with clumsily-sewn edges.

But that shouldn't have been enough to make Dale feel that something was different.

As Dale tilted his head with curiosity, Latina twirled around to clean the soiled dishcloth. Her movements caused her twin ponytails to sway in a pretty circle.

"Hm?" Dale mumbled to himself once again.

He finally realized what felt off.

In order to hide her broken horn, Latina usually tied her twin tails high on her head, but today their symmetry was off. The right tail was up high like normal, but the left side was lower, creating a weird sense of imbalance. The bandana that covered her hair was also tilted a bit to one side.

"Hey, Rita...?"

Tying Latina's hair up was part of Rita's daily routine. Dale called out to Rita, who was doing paperwork.

"What is it?"

"Latina's--"

She looked over to where he was pointing and quickly put her finger to her lips.

"You can't. It's been bothering her a lot lately."

"Hm...? Oh...sorry."

He lowered his voice and apologized, waiting for Rita's explanation. Rita quickly understood Dale's intentions and began to explain in a hushed voice.

"Until now, I was the one who always tied up her hair. Lately though, she's been practicing tying it up herself."

"Is that so?"

"But it seems that she can't get it quite right... Her results today have been very upsetting for her."

Rita gave a wry smile as she spoke.

"It's actually pretty hard to split your hair up in two and tie it up yourself. So, Latina hasn't been able to do it to her own satisfaction."

"Is it really that hard?"

Dale had never tied up anyone else's hair, much less his own, and he tilted his head perplexedly at Rita's words. Rita looked at Dale incredulously and continued to explain.

"Matching the height of each tail, dividing your hair up evenly, and creating a clean line of division requires skill. It's a hair style that has lots of challenging points. You can't see the back of your own head, right? Even if you use a mirror, it's not the same as looking straight forward, so it requires getting used to."

"I see."

Dale was used to seeing Latina's twin tails. As a man who just combed through his cowlicks with his own fingers, he had never imagined that her hairstyle was the result of so many high-level techniques put together.

To be honest, Dale wasn't even sure if he could do a proper butterfly bow. He could tie a bow, but he felt it would be difficult to make both sides of the bow match each other and hang the same way.

Dale was greatly impressed by Rita's skill in creating such a cute hairstyle for Latina so easily on a daily basis.

Rita grabbed her own hair with one hand as she spoke.

"Tying your hair up in a single ponytail like me is pretty easy. But there's a reason she has to tie her hair up in those positions, so she can't do the same."

"I see."

As he spoke, Dale looked over at Latina again.

Now that he knew the reason, he felt that those unbalanced ponytails were the result of her hard work, and even that looked adorable to him.

Latina finished cleaning her dishcloth as Dale smiled dotingly at her, and she returned to cleaning the tables.

The reason Latina had taken up this little act of independence was because of something that happened one day at school.

As she did every day, Latina went to the school of the Yellow Deity, Asufaaru.

It was a normal day at school. Since she loved to learn, class was very enjoyable for her. But after class, Latina dropped one of her school supplies from her desk. Stooping to pick it up, she reached under her desk.

Though she was able to pick up the object, her hair got caught on one of the desk legs as she stood back up. There was no pain, but her ribbon came untied as she stood.

"Oh..." she said with a troubled expression.

She held her hair up as she thought. Latina always asked Rita to tie up her hair, so she didn't know what to do in a situation like this.

"What's wrong, Latina?" her friends called out to her.

"Oh. Your bow came untied."

"Here, I have a comb."

Looking at Latina's situation, Silvia and Chloe spoke as though it was nothing. While Latina stood still, silently surprised, Chloe brushed her hair with the comb she borrowed from Silvia and gathered it all up in one hand.

"Oh, Latina, your hair is *so silky*. I bet you have a hard time tying it up."

Latina responded to Chloe's words with a troubled smile. She didn't want to say that she didn't really know, since she always asked Rita to do it. Though she looked like an adorable child, she had quite a lot of pride in her ability to do things.

Her friends didn't notice her inner struggle.

For them, Latina was a talented girl who could pretty much do everything. Of course, there were many things Latina couldn't do, but to her friends, who were the same age as her, the bar of "things she couldn't do" was set unusually high.

As Chloe pulled Latina's hair up in a quick motion, she used the ribbon Silvia handed over in perfect timing to tie it up.

Chloe's skillful fingers created a tight butterfly bow. She released it and looked Latina over. Then, she adjusted the left and right side a bit before giving a satisfied smile.

"There. Done. As I thought, Latina's hair is silky and soft. My hair is really coarse, so once I get a cowlick it's really hard to fix it. I'm jealous."

"Your hair is pretty long, though, Chloe."

"Isn't it easier to deal with longer hair? You can just tie it back and not worry about fixing it up. Come to think of it, have you always kept your hair short, Sylvia?"

"It's easier to wash and dry short hair. And all I have to do is brush it."

From their conversation, Latina realized that her friends took care of their hair themselves. Her expression turned serious.

The fact that there was something she couldn't do that her friends could do was a big shock to the pride she had in her own abilities.

Of course, Latina knew that certain people were better at certain things than others. Even so, the fact that there was something they all could do on a daily basis that she could not fired up her competitive instinct.

Latina herself did not realize it, but demons were not accustomed to styling their hair. In fact, they even avoided getting hair wrapped around their horns, which were a proud feature of their race. Since demons' horns are on the sides of their head, demon hairstyles are limited, and the most they do is tie it back to keep it out of the way.

This is why Latina's hair was never tied up back home.

Since coming to Kreutz, Latina thought it was "normal" to have Rita tie her hair up every day. At this moment, Latina's values made a great shift.

That's what happened to Latina.

As soon as she returned home, she conveyed her conviction to Rita with a smile.

After that, Latina began to practice every day.

Brushing her hair every night before she slept became a new habit.

As Dale looked over her with new eyes, he watched her examine her own bangs in front of a vanity mirror he never remembered buying. The vanity had a white flower pattern painted on the mirror's frame and a small drawer where Latina put her comb carefully away.

"Latina."

"Hm?"

"Where did that vanity come from? Was it Rita?"

"Yeah. Rita bought it for me."

Regretfully, Dale realized that he had failed to anticipate things that a "girl" needed, even as Latina smiled up at him. On the inside, he was thankful they were in an place where a woman like Rita could be nearby.

"Your hair has grown out."

"Yeah."

"If you want to get it cut, we should go to a barber... *Hmm...*but it may be better to ask Rita about things like this..."

As he patted Latina's head, he noticed something: the hair that he combed with his fingers was much silkier than when they had first met.

"Your hair is so pretty and silky. You must be taking care of it every day..."

Latina's expression melted into a big smile as he complimented her. He felt a bit bad, remembering that pointing out the results of another's hard work makes them really happy.

Latina is cute.

There was no reason to say something so obvious. It was a truth that should be sung to the world.

That was why this wasn't enough.

The things she worked so hard on every day should be properly valued and complimented. If he, her "guardian," didn't properly compliment her, who would? Dale needed to understand, more than anyone else, her daily struggles and their results.

Latina was cute. But her cuteness wasn't something that

could be reduced to that one simple word.

Latina had no idea about the "doting parent" thoughts running through Dale's head as she smiled up at him.

"*Um,* Latina was thinking of growing her hair out. She has a lot of ribbons now and if she grows out her hair, her friends said she could tie it up in a lot of different ways."

"I see."

That was so very like a girl. Even when they were very young, they were already talking about ways to look nice. When he was about Latina's age, Dale's favorite thing to do was run around in the mountains, so he was quite impressed. She was so different from him.

As he thought about how impressive she was, he patted her head again.

"You do have such pretty hair. It would be a waste to cut it, after all."

Dale's honest words made Latina smile happily once again.

Today, Latina was working hard in the Dancing Mackerel Tabby, cleaning up.

She swept the floors with a broom in an experienced manner. The customers seemed to have developed better manners ever since it became common to see her cleaning like this. Dale couldn't help thinking there was much more trash and food on the floor back when Kenneth had been the one responsible for cleaning up.

As Dale considered this, Latina worked in front of him with her hair in properly matching twin tails. She had improved drastically in just a few days. This morning, she looked in the mirror, comb in one hand, with a satisfied expression.

The part was still a little jagged, but there was no need to point that out.

At this rate, she should be able to do it perfectly with a little more practice...

That meant he would only be able to see this slightly imperfect hairstyle a little longer.

Once she can do it well, I'll buy her a new set of ribbons to celebrate.

To match the coming season, the ribbons should be a light, airy color.

As those thoughts went through Dale's head, he couldn't help letting his face melt into a smile.

If It's For My Daughter I'd Even Defeat a Demon Lord

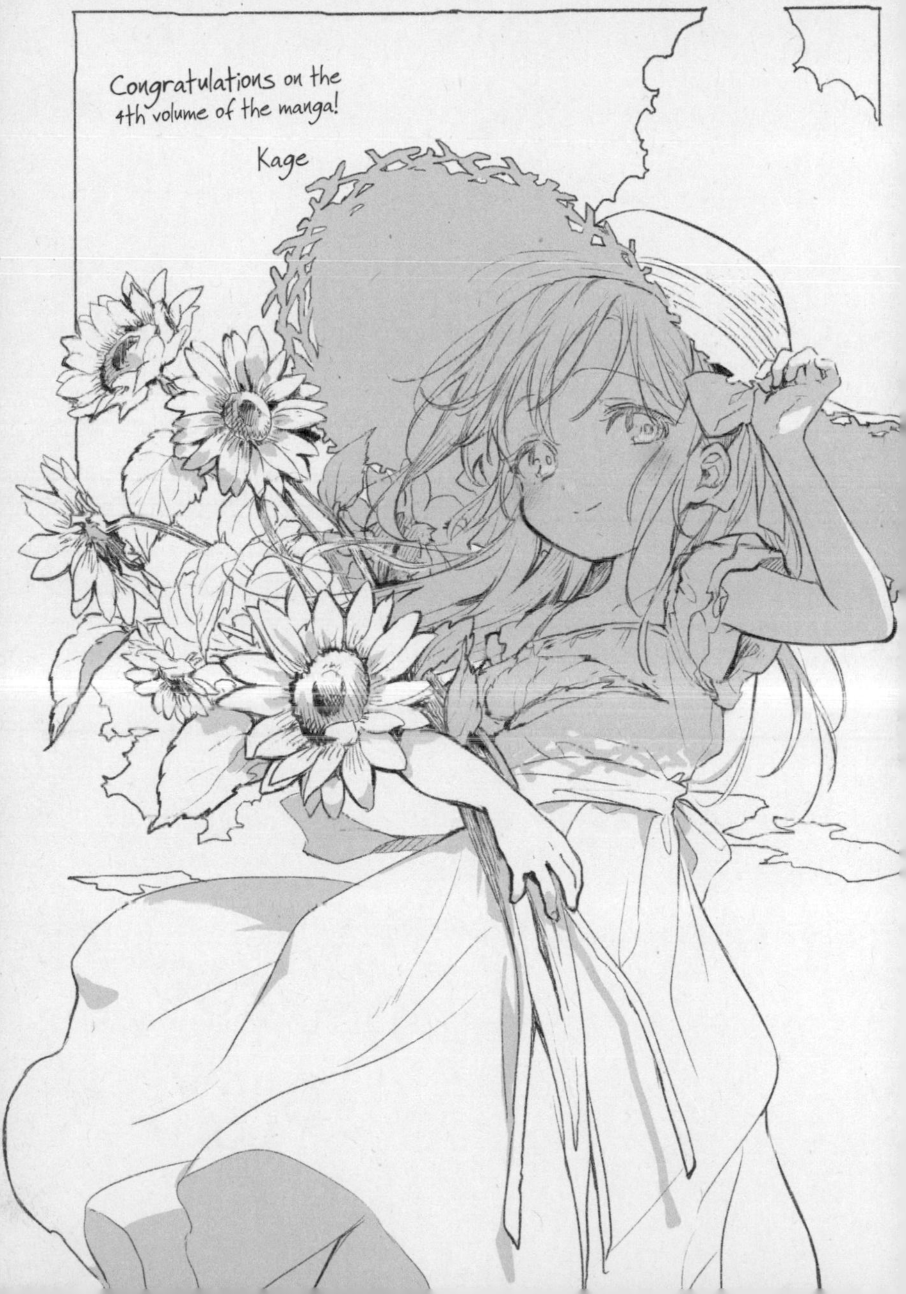
Congratulations on the
4th volume of the manga!
Kage

IF It's
For My
Daughter
I'd Even Defeat
a Demon
Lord

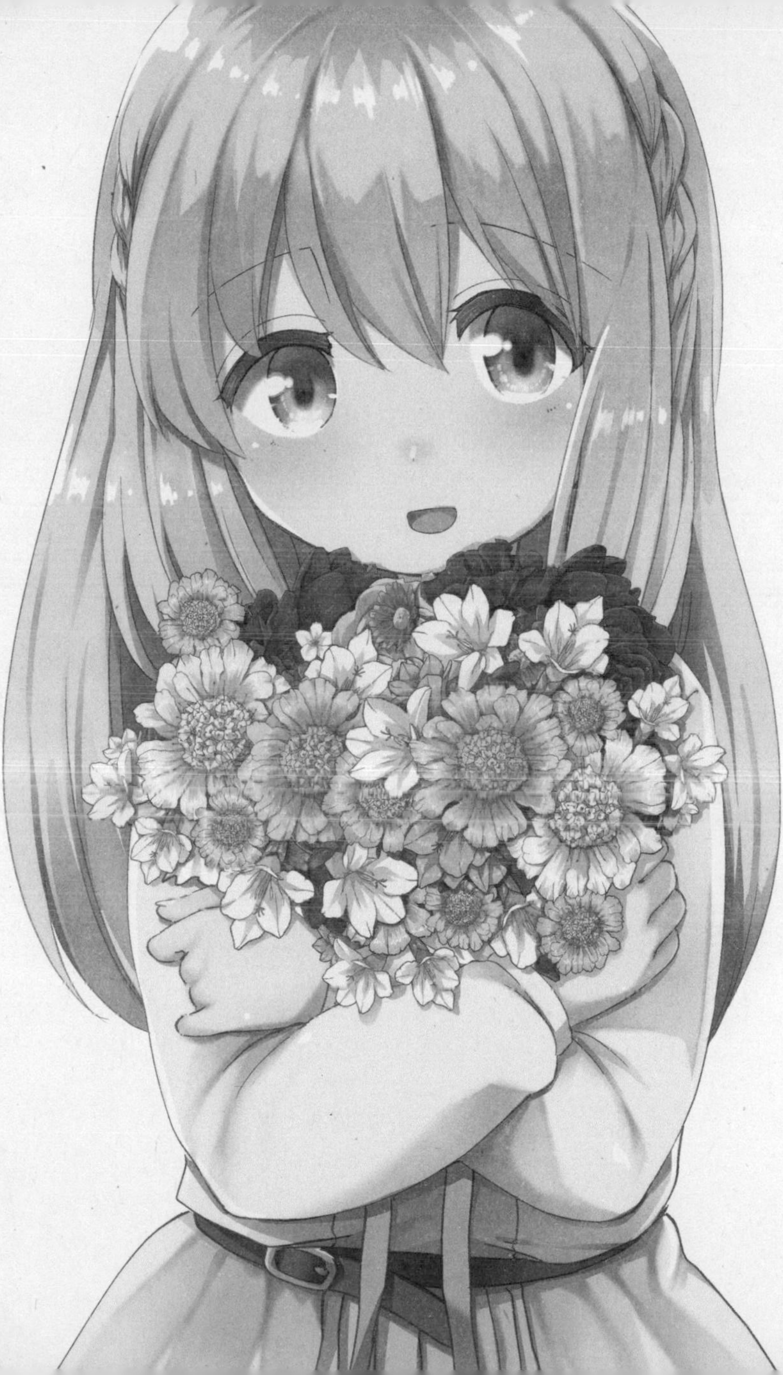

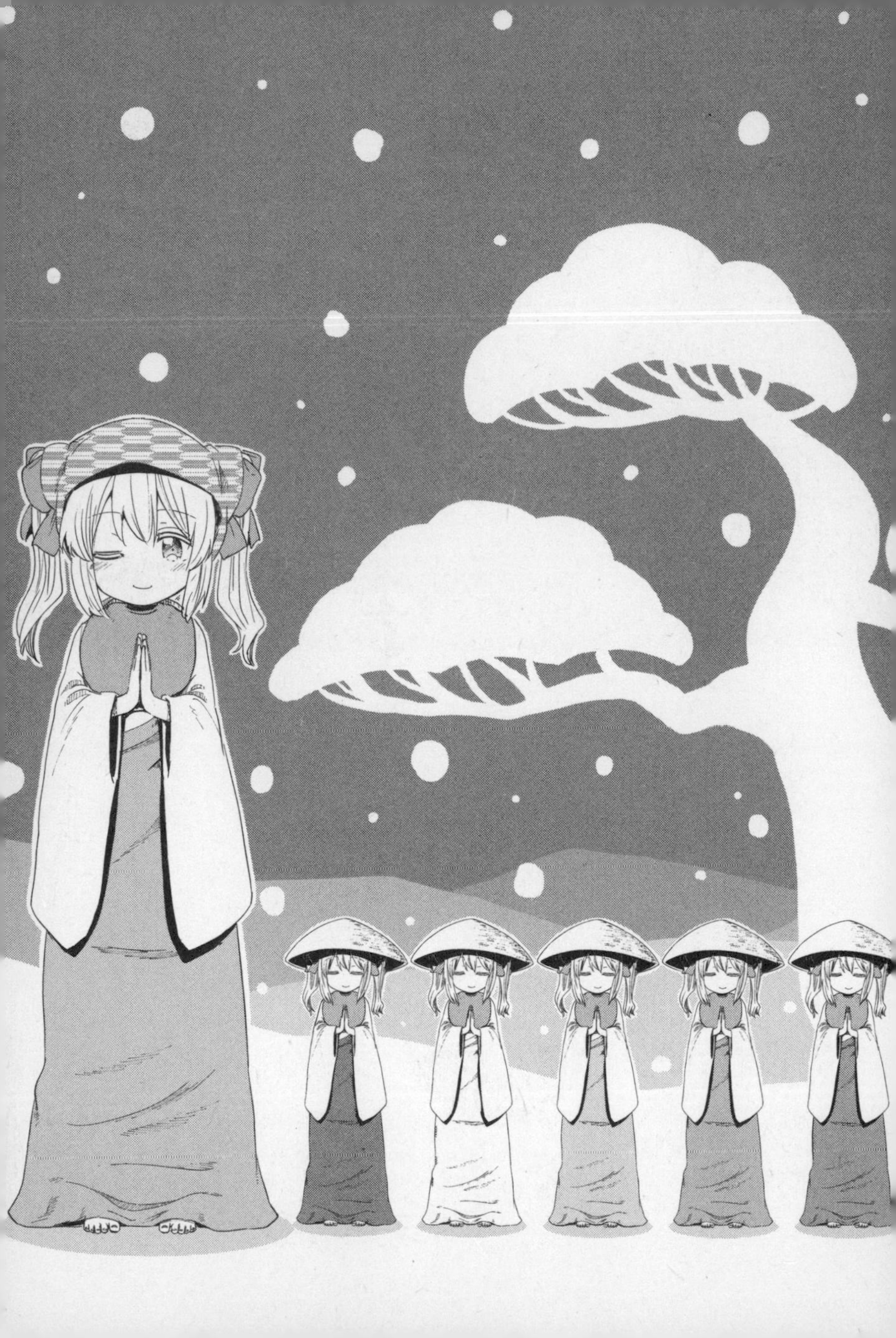

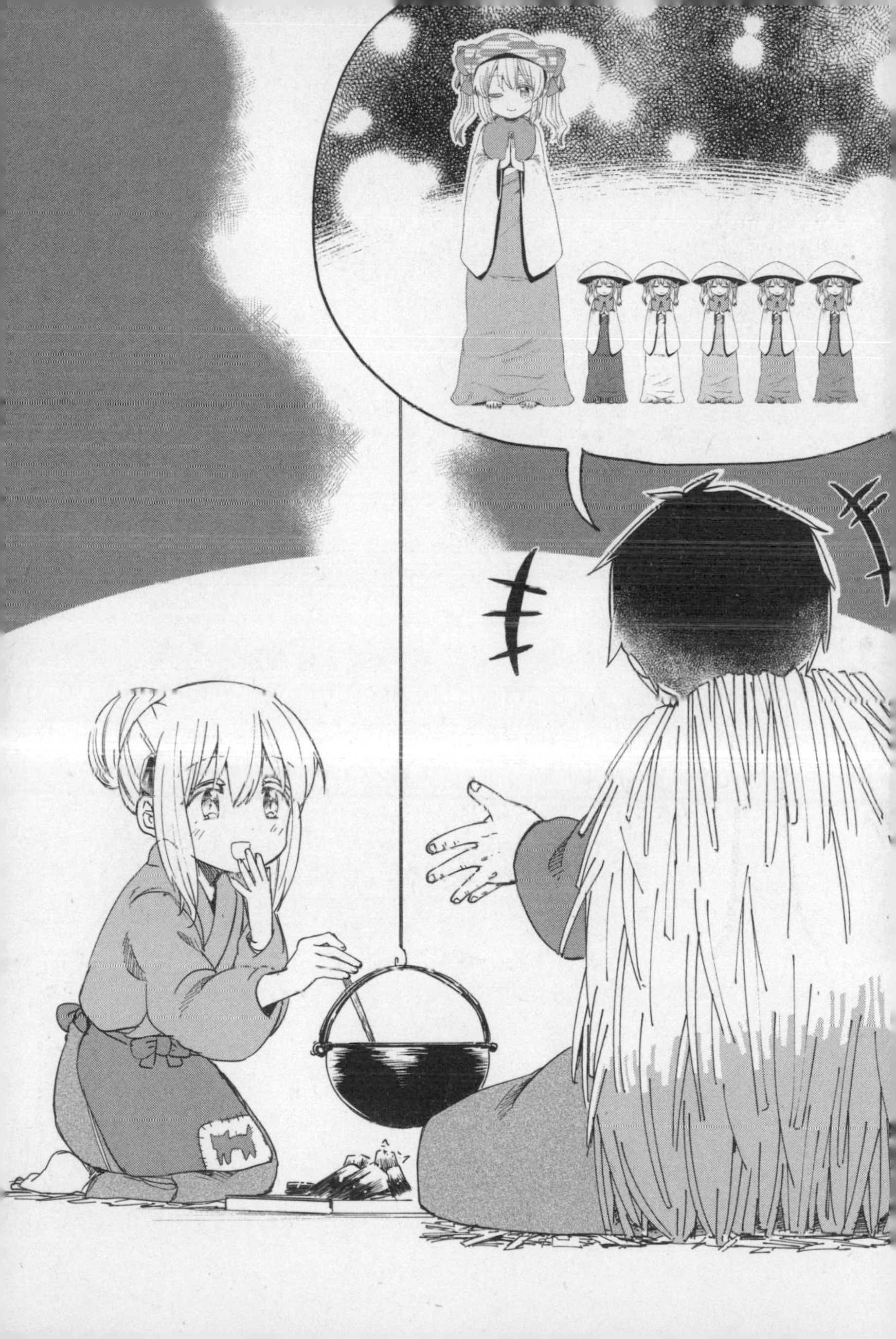

IF It's
For My
Daughter
I'd Even Defeat
a Demon
Lord